UNCHARTED JOURNEY

THE MEMOIRS
OF
DIMITRI D. DIMANCESCU
1896-1984

EDITED BY DAN DIMANCESCU

PUBLISHED BY

UNCHARTED JOURNEY
Second Edition

Front Cover:

DDD in 1946

Back Cover:
DDD's illustration from his boy scout diary

For details contact: tsgdd@mac.com

Typefaces:
Headers in Goudy Trajan
Text in Palatino
Copyright © 2016 by Dan Dimancescu
Concord, Massachusetts (USA)
All Rights Reserved

ISBN 978-0-9758915-1-3 (Paperback)

IN MEMORY OF

His brother
Ioan Dimancescu
1898-1951

His son
Dimitri D. Dimancescu, Jr.
1934-1994

His grandson
Nicholas D. Dimancescu
1985-2011

CONTENTS

FOREWORD

A life story that takes us back in time reminds us of the road traveled to bring us to where we are. We may learn from it. Then, too, we may see the same story told by others in a different light.

In just two lifetimes, my father's and my own spanning 120 years, one counts three-fourths of Romania's modern history from first becoming a nation in 1859. This is said only to suggest how young the country is both as a democracy and a modern economy. Those same 120 years, particularly the period of my father's life, brought the people of Romania both to new highs as much as it did to tragic lows. Much of its destiny was in the hands of others, imperial powers with conflicting ambitions of their own. The ensuing roller-coaster of events was his to experience: Carol I's legacy, World War I, the economically dynamic but eventually politically calamitous inter-war years, World War II, and then the sudden end to the democratic experiment when the dictatorial Communist regime took over in 1947 and led him to seek exile. That debilitating era ended in December of 1989 with the collapse of the regime and the killing of the dictator Nicolae Ceausescu and his wife.

By one set of measures my father lived a charmed life. Yet none of it was preordained or anticipated. His youth was stimulated by his parents' own intellectual grounding. His experiences came largely by force of personality and the luck that comes to those that take hold of the unforeseen and make something of it. He was a 'patriot' in the best sense of the word. He fought for his country in World War I. And as a diplomat did what he could, whenever and whenever, to improve its image and sovereignty. His life experiences brought him close to many of the headlining business, political, and cultural personalities of his time. With many, lifelong friendships were forged. The strongest of these survived from the best into the worst of times.

In retirement in Hartford, Connecticut, my father's memoirs were dictated during the 1970s to his wife, nicknamed Zézé, and to a visiting British friend. Both labored hard to record his words freehand and then to type them. Later, after his death in 1984, they were digitized by his oldest son, Dimitri, into a raw manuscript meant solely for family circulation. The memoirs as published herein were re-edited by me to include much more anecdotal dictated material. Contextual passages were added to each part of the book and footnotes were added where useful. Varied items from his extensive personal records (documented, photos, library, and correspondence) and from external sources have been inserted selectively to give greater breadth to his words.

He would have been proud to know that his grandson Nicholas, though born and raised in the United States found himself at home in Romania, inspired to travel all corners of the country and to meet all cross-sections of people.

For future readers, his life story brings to life both personalities and a period in history largely altered or erased from memory for Romanian citizens during the Communist regime's abusive rule between December 1947 and its demise at the end of 1989. For many of his peers lives would end tragically as prisoners of the regime as was indeed the case of his own brother.

Dan Dimancescu
Concord, Massachusetts and Bucharest, Romania

NOTE TO THE READER:
Country spellings may cause confusion due to changes over time and language differences:
Romania is the official name of the country. In English it was once spelled *Roumania* and *Rumania* until U.S. conventions changed it in the 1970s. In French it is spelled *Roumanie*.

PART I - YOUTH

At the end of the nineteenth-century Romania was a new nation not yet fifty-years-old. History and geography had never been the Nation's best friend. Russian, Ottoman, Austro-Hungarian imperial rulers persistently vied to gain control over its people, its wealth and its land.

Even French Emperor Napoleon III had been brought into the political gamesmanship for advice in choosing a King who might unify competing rulers from the country's two united principalities, Wallachia and Moldavia. In 1866, a member of the Hohenzollern-Sigmaringen family, Prince Carol was declared the country's 'Ruling Prince.' Fifteen years later, the Principality was declared a monarchy and the Prince became King Carol I of Romania.

Rapid development ensued as the Nation's assets in oil, wheat, and gold generated new wealth. Enlightened policies encouraged and supported by the King led to thousands of young Romanians traveling to Europe's best universities to get educated. During the same period many thousands immigrated to the United States to seek new wealth from work in steel mills, mines, and industrial factories. Bucharest, which was a dusty provincial town in the 1850s quickly turned into what became known as the "Little Paris" with tree-lined boulevards, lavish turn-of-century Beaux-Arts architecture, and a largely Francophone intellectual class. High culture had come to Romania.

All the while, these fast-moving changes were layered onto a deeply rooted peasant culture long dominated by land-owning Boyard families who would be violently challenged in the first years of the new century.

These were years of new aspirations and an awareness of a modern industrial world on the verge of a new era of motorized life: cars, airplanes, trains. Western ways were opening old and young to explore new opportunities.

CHAPTER ONE

GENIIS & DESTINY

I was a few months old in 1896 when an itinerant astrologer passed through our village. Mother consulted him and he left his findings on a card that was also preserved for me along with my father's skeptical comment: "Funny but not serious." The astrologer had made a rough sketch of my body inside a pentagon that was surrounded by a circle. There were some unintelligible computations followed by a note forecasting that at full maturity my overall dimensions would correspond to the "Golden Section," a term that I would only comprehend years later when I read the *Geometry of Life* by my good friend Matila Ghyka, a mathematician and diplomat. My life was to be dominated by the number seven. I was to travel far from my native land. Though I was born, according to the Gregorian calendar, under the sign of Cancer, my actions would be those of men under Leo. He predicted that I would live to be an old man and though I would not achieve any greatness myself, my life would be intertwined with the life of some great men.

The name of the place where I was born appears on my birth certificate as Titu, Dumboviţa County. It was a relatively small village, but being a district capital it had a courthouse, post-office, infirmary, church and grammar school. The village was on the main road between Bucharest and Craiova. There were houses on both sides of the roadway. There were two or three inns where travelers would stop to rest their cattle. There were no grocery stores but at one of the inns one could buy black olives, cheese and salted fish.

About two kilometers from the village on a road bordered by tall poplars was the Titu railway station. This was almost a separate administrative unit. The station itself was a complex of buildings dominated by the station building with offices, waiting rooms and a restaurant well-known for doughnuts made by 'Madame Marie.'

The station was an imposing red brick building with no particular architectural merit. Over the office on the second floor were our living quarters as my father was Station Master; a few rooms were used by Mme. Marie. Another group of buildings belonged to the two engineers in charge of maintenance. The senior engineer was a German who had stayed on. He spoke broken Romanian and half his conversations were in German. Nearby were housed the auxiliary services among which was the care of lamps. All along the station platform were kerosene lamps and every day a few hundred had to be filled, their wicks trimmed, and the smoky glass funnels cleaned.

Extensive wheat fields surrounded my native village. From my window I could see nothing but wheat as far as the horizon. In winter it was a flat table of snow and in spring the freshly plowed earth was almost black. In summer there was first green, then golden wheat until harvest time. The fields would then be pale gold until the winter snow came and remained until March. I delighted to watch this symphony of color. The love of wide horizons and the feeling of liberty has remained with me.

My parents lived for seven years at the Titu railroad station. This was father's empire where he governed as dictator. At home, he kept a neat register of his garden's productivity. Nobody was allowed to pick flowers or fruit without his permission. If plants did not grow according to his expectations, they were removed. Mother and grandmother had the duty of weeding. In this garden, I did part of my schooling.

GRANDFATHER

In my first six years at home, mother had very little to do with me. I have a vague recollection of father teaching me to write in some of his few spare moments. I can see myself in the house all the time by the side of my grandfather, Petre Petrescu, who became my self-appointed tutor. Moving

to our house, he brought his library with him, mostly of old books with fine bindings. He also brought a complete collection of *London Illustrated News* from 1842 to 1895 in large folio volumes to which, after his arrival, were added loose copies of his subscription.

I remember my maternal grandfather as a man of great distinction, with side-whiskers in the style of his time, and immaculately dressed. On the thumb of his right hand was a large gold signet ring, which he frequently used to seal his letters. His was a most unusual man with a very complicated past. He was in his late sixties, He was a distant descendant of Dimitrie

Cantemir, a former ruler of the principalities of Moldavia who lost his throne for taking the side of Peter the Great of Russia against the Turks. Cantemir became a trusted friend of Peter the Great, accompanying him on many of his travels.

"His whole sedentary life," Nicholas Tindal wrote of Cantemir in 1756, "was employed in cultivating his mind, the fruits if which appear in his works... His principal study was History, though he made good progress in Philosophy and Mathematics of which Architecture pleased him most. The Churches he built in three of his villages are of his design and manner. He was a member of the Academy of Berlin, and at the same time the news of his death reached Petersburg, the Emperor of Germany's Resident received for the deceased a patent creating him "Prince of the Holy Roman Empire."

When my family's records burned during World War II from American aerial bombings that destroyed our home in Bucharest,[1] it became impossible to unravel the mystery shrouding my grandfather's life. He wished to keep the secrets of his past from his contemporaries. We knew he was born in Bessarabia where his parents had a large property. This was lost when Russia took southern Bessarabia. Given the Christian name of Petre, in honor of his ancestor's friend and protector, he discarded the family name of Cantemir and assumed the family name of Petrescu. Though his parents had lived in Russia where he was educated, he remained at heart a Moldavian. He had studied at the University of Petrograd and he spoke Russian, French, and Romanian with a Moldavian accent. For reasons of his own, he developed a hatred of Russian Imperialism to the point that during the Crimean War of 1854-1885 he volunteered to fight as a soldier in a British regiment against the armies of the Czar.

In our home grandfather had a special throne-like chair. He would come to his chair in the morning and sit there until bedtime. At meal times he only needed to take a few steps. He adopted me as his sole companion and listener for his tales. They were mostly about the war in the Crimea.

Day-after-day he would come into my room with one of the heavy volumes, lay it on the table and turn the pages slowly. He carefully explained each picture with complete indifference for my age. He took me from one end of the world to the other through the large and detailed wood-engravings of the weekly *London Illustrated News*. There is no trace in my memory of ever having a book for children but I can see Queen Victoria and Prince Albert, Napoleon III, and Empress Eugenie, and pictures of sailing ships and of battles until I felt like a soldier fighting under the walls of Sebastopol in the Crimea.

---

[1] See page 231

The Crimean War had been grandfather's *own* war. He would pause in front of a sketch of the Malakoff Tower or the Balaclava camp, tell me a long story of what *he* did and how he was wounded by a shrapnel splinter. He would point to his left knee and show me where the deep scar was that made him limp and use a walking stick. He said that had been involved in the charge of the Light Brigade at Balaclava and spoke with some bitterness about a general who sent his men to an unnecessary slaughter.

PETRE

My maternal grandfather brought his old and trusted servant to our house, also named Petre. He was a tall Moldavian peasant with white curly hair and a bushy gray mustache, a widower with married children. He seemed a gigantic shadow to me. He wore the national costume of Romanian peasants, a homespun white linen shirt that hung over woolen trousers. Around his waist was a dark red woolen sash over which he wore a black leather belt. Tucked into this among other things was his one-bladed pocket knife. With this wonderful blade he carved all my toys.

Petre answered all my questions decisively and patiently. Even when I went through the obstinate stage of asking questions repeatedly, Petre had the gift of being able to come up with a satisfactory answer.

PIA

My mother worried about the kind of education that I had been receiving from grandfather. She wanted someone who could teach me the alphabet, how to write its letters and then how to read simple words. The village school had a new teacher - a young lady who had recently returned from Paris and the Sorbonne. She had to go through the misery of teaching peasant children the three "Rs." Her first name was Pia and I fell in love with her the first time I saw her. My mother secured her services. The irony of it was that I was not to learn to read or write in my native language, but in French. Her method was to have me memorize ten words a day. Later this was increased to twenty. Except for my illnesses it might have reached thirty or forty.

Every day Petre would take me after school to Mademoiselle Pia's. There, in the very modestly furnished parlor room, he would sit quietly in a corner while the rudiments of French were offered to me. My textbook was a small French "ABC" book with beautifully colored pictures of animals and objects illustrating each letter of the alphabet ending with a Zebra for Z. By the time I was six years old and ready to be sent to grammar school, I spoke fluent French, and so did my old faithful Petre, much to the amazement of everybody.

This happy period of my life ended with grandfather's death, which though expected by the family, came as a great shock to me. He had been ailing for some time and lay in bed. Twice a day I had to go to his room and listen to his stories, or to the poems he was writing with great facility. He had a message which he wished to convey to me and which obviously I as a child could not grasp. He told me again and again how much he loved my father, with whom he had much in common as both loved books and read a lot. He kept on saying that I should be a second Demetrius Cantemir, not a Prince in armor but a Prince of learning. At times he would just take my hand and pat it gently without saying anything.

On Easter Eve, close to midnight, mother came with tears in her eyes, took me out of bed and rushed me to grandfather's room. Everyone was there, including all the servants, and everyone was crying. There was only one light in the room and that came from a beeswax candle which was held by my grandfather in his left arm. He was sitting upright in bed with his head leaning against a pile of pillows. On seeing me, with his weak right hand grasped both of my hands.

"Please, please do not cry, as I want to talk."

When the room became quiet and one could hear only muffled sobs, grandfather began reciting his last Will and Testament, in verse. It went slowly and almost in a whisper, accentuated by painful efforts to breathe. There was advice for each of us. He wanted to be forgiven for whatever sins he may have committed. He had no material possessions nor money to leave us, as in life he had valued only the spiritual things. Then he asked my father to get nearer to him asking that he should remove from his finger the signet ring and give it to me. He watched while I took it in one of my hands. Then he pointed to two books on his bedside table, and even now I can hear ringing in my ears:

"Child, these are also yours, treasure them as your only tie with your forefathers of whom you should be proud... you should be proud... proud."

These were his last words. He died grasping my hand in which I was holding his signet ring. The last I saw of him, was his body resting in a coffin on a bier hastily put together in the parlor. The room was full of spring flowers Petre could find in the garden. Three tall candles burned at the head of the coffin. There were the candles used at the christenings of my sister, my brother and myself. Nothing had been changed in that Victorian interior with heavy plush curtains at the windows and four English engrav-ings on the wall.

Until he was taken away to be buried in the cemetery of the village church, Petre stood by his dead master. When he died too, only a month later, he was put in a grave alongside my grandfather.

Father bought a stone cross from Bucharest with my grandfather's name and birth date carved on it. Grandfather was buried to the right of the main entrance to the church. This was the only stone cross in the cemetery. According to the rites of the Greek Orthodox Church he was disinterred seven years after his death. The bones were washed in holy water and placed in a small coffin that was brought to Bucharest and buried in the family plot at the Bellu Cemetery to the right of the chapel.

Petre the Moldavian peasant, and Petre my grandfather had taken the first steps in shaping my character and mind. Pia, the Paris-educated teacher, had taught me to read and write in French and Romanian and also to love France, opening a new window through which I breathed a first whiff of invigorating air.

MOTHER AND FATHER

But with grandfather gone from our midst, mother and father came into their own. Suddenly they took an interest in everything I was doing. The entire interior of our house was redecorated, including my room. Its walls were whitewashed and on each of its four walls father had a painter write with large bold Gothic letters the slogans he wished me to learn by heart and adopt as my rules of conduct. These were beyond my under-standing.

"The only thing I own is what I give away,"

"To be happy one has to wish for less than he can have."

"A gentleman is one who thinks of others first."

And on a narrow space above the window:

"Rush Slowly."

Over my table there was added a shelf, on it were the two books left to me by my grandfather: *The history of the Growth and Decay of the Ottoman Empire*, written originally in Latin by Demetrius Cantemir late Prince of Moldavia, translated into English from the author's own manuscript by N. Tindal, M.A. Vicar of Great Waltham in Essex, London printed for A. Millar in the Strand MDCCLVI (1756), and *Satyres du Prince Cantemire avec l'Histoire de Sa Vie*, Londres Chez Jean Nourse, MDCCL (1750). I never parted with these two books which remained a fragile tie with a distant past, with nothing else to fill the gap between.

Mother in her turn, told me one day now dramatic my birth had been, I was born during a thunderstorm which scared her. Her fears were that something would happen to me. She was not frightened for herself but I must be protected from nature's fury. My grandmother who had been present told me:

"We were six women in the room. After tradition your father was not allowed to be present, but he kept inquiring from the door if there was much longer before my arrival in the world. In the room where your Mother was, there was a clock chiming the hours. You were born one minute after midnight. The midwife who replaced the doctor, who was supposed to be present, took care of your mother. The other women and myself washed you, combed you as you had a lot of long black hair, and wrapped you. When all these preparations were done, you were placed in your crib. I turned out the lights, leaving one small candle burning in a holder under Saint Demetrius' icon, because it was decided months before that if a son was born his name would be Dimitri. You were left alone in your room waiting the arrival of the *fairies spirits* who were to decide your future. None of us had thought what you may want to do in your life, although your father always had said that the first son must be an engineer.

Nobody ever knew what the *fairies* decided but my mother was convinced that I was born lucky. I cannot tell, up to now, how she interpreted luck, but often she told me. "Everybody has luck if they know how to recognize it and take advantage of what luck was offering. Luck passes us by very quickly and does not wait long. Those who have no luck are those who did not know how to take advantage of it."

My father, Dumitru Dimancescu,[2] wanted records of everything preserved in meticulous order for the grandchildren he would never see. Until the day he died my father collected all sorts of papers related to my life or papers that would help me understand my background. On every anniversary of my birth, he would make a neat bundle of documents recording the year's events, tie it with a red ribbon and seal the knot with sealing wax on which he would press his signet ring with the family coat of arms. He kept

---

[2] Dumitru D. - 1859-1916

these bundles in an old-fashioned coach trunk with a heavy, wrought iron lock. The key was kept hidden. This chest was to become mine on the day I would come of age.

He was no longer with us on my twenty-first birthday, having tragically passed away a year earlier in 1916. I opened his posthumous present with trembling hands and found a letter addressed to me:

> *"Dear son,*
>
> *Late one night at the end of last September - or was it the beginning of October? - I found your mother's message on the pillow of my bed. Today, the seventh of July, the Year of Grace, 1896, at five minutes past midnight you were born. We are so happy you have come, as together with your sister, you both will give an aim to our lives. Just a few minutes ago, when she recovered from the struggle to bring you into this world, she said to me that you, our first son, have been born under a lucky star, I pray and hope that this is true." She believes that the "ursitoare" - the genii of destiny, standing by your cradle - are at this very moment deciding what the course of your life should be. I do not share this belief of hers as I am not a fatalist and you too should not be one. God sparks our lives but the rest is up to us. With loving care your mother and I will give you until you will be able to look after yourself. From there on Fate will not fight your battles. You will have to do it yourself. The best we can do, from this very day of your birth until you will be able to fly on your own, is to shape your mind so that you can be strong of heart and wise in your steps."*

My father, was the son of Ion Dimancescu[3] who changed his name by adding the suffix "escu" at a time when many Romanians were doing so in a wave of nationalism.

My great-grandfather had been a cattle dealer in the Muntenia part of Romania. Once a year he took his cattle to Vienna where he sold them for gold. It was a long journey with many stops. By what my father related, my great-grandfather traveled behind the cattle herd in a small horse-drawn carriage. Tied to the back of the carriage was a trunk with iron latches and many locks. This trunk remained in our home and my mother kept her precious items in it. Often when looking at this trunk we remembered the past and the tragic way in which my grandfather had been killed with an axe because he refused to tell the robbers where the gold was hidden. Everyone in the family, including brothers and sisters, tried to find the treasure. They dug many holes around the village of Peretu in search of the gold.

---

[3] Ion D. - 1829-1886

Years later, the family suspected that the treasure had been found by my father's brother and priest, Barbu Dimancescu, who lived in the same village in grand style. Russian soldiers, who passed through the area at the time of the Romanian army's participation in the Russo-Turkish war, of 1877, destroyed the original family house. At the end of the war, Father Barbu built a beautiful house. He employed an Italian architect and Italian artists painted frescoes on the walls. But he never lived in this house, which he said he wanted to give to one of his nephews on condition that the nephew become a priest and live in Peretu.[4]

My father had wished to become a priest. At the age of seven, he was taken to Bucharest and left in the care of the church *Mitropolit*.[5] Until age eighteen, he lived a monastic life in the monastery adjoining the *Mitropolie*. Monks from Mt. Athos in Greece visited this monastery each year. They brought gifts for the Mitropolit and in exchange received money for the upkeep of the small Romanian church on Mt. Athos. From those monks my father learned to write and speak some Turkish, Greek and Latin. He could converse in these languages and read books that the monks brought from Mt. Athos. Most of the books were in the Slavonic and Cyrillic alphabets.

Nobody knew that during all the years that he was being prepared for the church, he was dreaming of "iron horses" for in those years an engine evoked the same visions in a child as a space ship might for modern children. As the date for him to be confirmed as a priest approached he disappeared from the Mitropolie. All investigations by the Mitropolit and public officials to find him were unsuccessful. Whenever he could escape from the monastery he went to the Filaret Railway Station to watch in awe the small engines that pulled the train between Bucharest and Giurgiu. He never told us who had advised him to go to Germany but he managed to enter the Polytechnic University at Charlottenburg.

His return to Romania a fully qualified engineer coincided with a political and economic crisis. Romania had agreed to give a German company exclusive rights to build, staff and operate the main railways. After construction of rails, bridges and stations were completed Romania, annulled the concession and took over management of the Romanian Railroad Company. Being a German-speaking Romanian with a German university degree, he was welcomed in the new company.

He started as the lowest level telegraph operator. But in a short time he was promoted and within a year he became assistant stationmaster in the town of Râmnicu Sărat in southern Moldavia.

---

[4] In Peretu was be found a superbly shaped silver 2,000 year-old Geto-Dacian helmet along with varied other artifacts

[5] *Mitropolit*: Priest; *Mitropolie*: church

In this small town he was well received and soon married the daughter - later to become my mother - of a landowner Petrescu, my maternal grandfather. As a wedding gift, father was promoted to stationmaster and moved back south to the small village station of Potcoava near Craiova where only two trains passed each day. I'm sure mother didn't realize how lonely the life of a stationmaster's wife would be.

Working to improve the railroad system, the railroad company decided to install a central switching system. Railroad accidents had occurred because of incorrect switching by untrained operators. The new system provided cabins with mechanical switches at the entry and exits of stations. The Titu station, 50 kilometers northwest of Bucharest, was chosen for the first installation. My father was chosen from hundreds of railway employ-

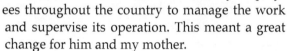

ees throughout the country to manage the work and supervise its operation. This meant a great change for him and my mother.

Mother was born at Râmnicu Sărat and was one of a large group of brothers, sisters and cousins. There was a rivalry among them and they often spied on each other to find out what they were doing. She was sent far away to attend an Orthodox school in Sibiu[6] across the Carpathian Mountains in Transylvania. Thus at the age of thirteen she found herself hundreds of kilometers away from home with no friends or acquaintances. The trip from Râmnicu Sărat to Sibiu was in a caravan of carriages that had to cross the mountains and wild forests. She only came home once a year during the short summer vacation. After three years of such hardship she refused to return to school. She was told that the only alternative to school was marriage.

Mother, who was only sixteen years-old, had the alternative of returning to school or marrying my father. She chose the latter. The wedding was a sensation among the locals. What interested them most was the dowry given to my mother. I never heard much said about the dowry, but I do know that it consisted of part of a wagon load of copper kitchen utensils

---

[6] Known then by its German name *Hermannstadt* dating back to the 1200s

and a fashionable *Biedermeier*[7] bedroom suite. As a child I used to admire the copper-ware hanging in the kitchen. Although seldom used, it was always polished and shiny. With the same pleasure, I used to admire the Biedermeier beds and cupboards that had such simple lines and seemed so beautiful to me.

When my father was transferred to Titu, our home became the apartment over the station building. There were many rooms arranged right and left of a long hall. It was decided to bring my mother's parents to live with us. As we were only 50 kilometers from Bucharest, my mother bought all the things for the house in the capital. She also ordered our clothes from catalogs that she received from Paris.

My mother lost nine babies before the first one survived. It was my sister, Octavi, two years older than myself. I also had a brother, Ion, two years younger. As both my father and mother had a special way of bringing us up, I hardly remember seeing my brother and sister. Until I was six I barely knew they existed! Each one of us was put under the care of other people.

MY ROOM

In my room I had a large pine wood table and chair. Here I spent hours making paper houses and furniture, an art taught to me by my father. My greatest achievement was a three-story house carefully assembled room by room. The third floor was supposed to be for my grandmother. When she said that she was old and overweight and that it would be inconvenient for her, I answered that I had already thought of that and there would be a basket with pulleys to pull her up.

Religion was never discussed at home and yet it was an integral part of life. When I was six father taught me *The Creed*, which was hard for me to understand, and the *Our Father*, which was simpler and more explicit. I learned it by heart and repeated it mechanically without thinking about the words. At Easter everyone except the children went to *Resurrection Mass* at midnight. They came home at dawn with their candles lit. When I was six I was taken to this service, but I fainted because of the crowds. I was taken onto the porch and sprinkled with water. We didn't leave the Church until the priest chanted: "Come and take light." This meant lighting the first per-

---

[7] *Biedermeier* was an influential style of furniture design from Germany and Austria during the years 1815–1848, based on utilitarian principles. Emphasis was kept upon clean lines and minimal ornamentation.
Source: wikipedia

son's candle from his, and the next person from him, until the whole gathered crowd inside and outside the Church now held lit candles.

When we arrived home, I had the first symptoms of pneumonia. Our family doctor, Dr. Crutescu, who lived in 40 km away in Târgovişte, was brought by my father who had gone on a fast shunting engine to get him. The doctor's treatment consisted of mustard plasters to draw the inflammation from my lungs. Then hardly was the pneumonia cured than I developed jaundice *(an aggravated form of hepatitis)*. This meant a very strict diet - boiled carrots and baked potatoes. A dislike for these was added to my other idiosyncrasies.

During these first seven years of life, two important events had taken place place. At the time little did I realize their importance. The end of the century was referred to at home as the "Fin du Siècle." There were predictions that it would end with a world catastrophe. But the Twentieth Century started with a new vitality and with it a change of homes because father had been promoted and transferred to Bucharest.

BUCHAREST

For mother the change was an upheaval. From a large well-ordered home in a small community, she now had to move to the capital city and find a house or apartment near schools. At first, I was enrolled at the Moteanu girls' school with my sister on Calea Victoriei. Aurel Jiquidi, who would become famous artists and one of my best friends, and I were the only boys. Of course our presence caused conflicts and we were obliged to

13

leave. I was then sent to the "Cuibul cu Barza" (*The Nest with a Stork*) much further away on Stirbei Voda Street. This school was a complete change from the one-room school in Titu. From the first day I was under strict discipline.

Our teacher was a real witch. She did not talk to us but yelled. In her right hand she grasped a ruler. At any act of misbehavior, she would order the pupil to stretch out his hand and would hit him one to five times. I did not suffer much punishment, but while in the classroom I hardly had the courage to breathe. In the evening on the way home, I would sigh with relief. For homework I would read my ABC book and practice my letters on a small slate on which we wrote with chalk. It was a great relief when the school year ended, although there was a disastrous outcome for me. Instead of being first or second, I received the third prize, a bronze medal. I came home crying and declared that I would not return to school.

My father finally found a suitable house for the family on Strada Frumoasa. This obliged me to change schools again. I was registered at Elementary School No. 30, also known as Saint Voievozi. It was a happy choice. My second grade teacher was Mrs. Lenuțe Grol. She was kindness itself. The ruler disappeared and the worst punishment for misbehavior was to be sent to the corner of the classroom, either facing the wall or the class. The second grade ended with a small improvement for me. I received second prize, a silver medal. I remained in this school until the end of my grammar grades. At the end of the third grade I tied for first prize.

In the third and fourth grades we had as our teacher Mr. Teodor Iliescu, principal of the school. He was an enthusiastic bicyclist and had become well-known as a result of a Bucharest-Paris cycling journey he completed. He paid little attention to his students and during every recess he polished his bicycle.

For some reason, the school was chosen for an experiment. An army captain, Justin Marinescu, had the idea of giving elementary school students a pre-military education. The third and fourth year boys were chosen as small *dorobanți* (cadets) and were provided uniforms consisting of a white shirt with a large belt and a sheepskin hat with a large goose feather pinned on it. We were also given toy wooden guns. To train, we used a large gym that was seldom used for sports. In those times the small "dorobanți" were a sensation though our few influential political-liberals were against any military-type education. When I finished elementary school I left the "dorobanți." Captain Marinescu eventually went off to Sweden to learn "Swedish military drills."

In my three years at the St. Voievozi School, we were obliged to go to a church of the same name every Sunday. It was a modern building with modern paintings. Even the priest had a small beard and short hair and no longer wore braids. We had to carry a clean handkerchief in the left hand and a few coins in the right hand to buy a candle and leave some coins on a tray for the priest after we had said our prayers and kissed the icons.

During the month of August in the year that I graduated from four years in primary school, father told me that I had to be ready and seriously prepared for the next four years gymnasium school entry examination. We were competing for only 80 vacancies. But on the day of this examination, 800 candidates from all over the country gathered in the schoolyard. Among them was a boy wearing a Panama hat who had traveled by private carriage whose driver wore a silk top hat. These hats were symbols of wealth. All sorts of things were tried to reduce the number of candidates, even a medical exam was conducted. I do not remember how we were grouped or how we were rated. After three days we received the results. On top of the list with the best marks was the boy with the Panama hat. Then by a miracle the third on the list was me!

But in the evening that same day father confronted me with a surprise. He had registered me for another exam for a scholarship as a boarder at the St. Sava School. He explained that though we lived in Bucharest and there was no need to be a boarder, to earn a scholarship was an added title of achievement. Most of the great men, he told me, had scholarships at St. Sava. He wanted me to understand, though I did not appreciate it at the time, that his wish was for me to become a great man.

Three days later I had to take the scholarship exam that was much harder than the gymnasium admission test. I remember there was a hard arithmetic problem the answer to which I knew by heart because my father had once asked me the same problem. The question was: if two trains left from opposite directions, with different speeds, when would they meet. I knew the solution perfectly. Out of 200 candidates at this exam, 40 passed and of the 40, ten were eliminated later on. Then we were all brought into the school amphitheater and brought before a blackboard in groups of ten. Each one had to recite *The Creed* individually. None of the other boys in my group knew it. When my turn came, I recited it so mechanically and fast that the examiner told me to slow down. The next day we received the results of the exam. I was at the head of the list.

The year that I took the scholarship exam was the last year that students were obliged to wear uniforms. I went with father to a special officers' uniform tailor, near the Hotel de France. For the first time I was treated like as big as a man being measured in every detail. A week later I wore the uniform and a "kepi" (a cap similar to French army style) with a wide white band.

The uniform was only one of the problems of getting ready for high school. Mother also had to provide me with a 'kit': six shirts, six pairs of socks, six sheets, six pillow cases as well as two blankets and a mattress. All of these had to have my name and number assigned by the school embroidered on them. All this made ready, father took me to school in a carriage to Stirbei Voda Street and a former mansion that had belonged to General Ion Florescu, who had been Minister of Defense during the War of 1877 against the Ottomans. A large iron gate opened to let us in and after the luggage was discharged father said good-bye and left me alone. With tears in my eyes, I faced the school where I was to be a student for eight years.

The boarding school was not an "institution" it was just a large dormitory where the scholarship students slept. The real value was in the association with the other two-hundred scholarship students, each one with his own personality and characteristics of his particular region. The dormitory had been a rich man's residence with large rooms and an architectural conception that emphasized the military glory of its former owner. The main entrance had three doors, each fifteen feet high. In the center of the building was a hall 10 meters high with frescoes representing military subjects. Next to one of the walls there was a huge cupboard reaching to the ceiling in which was the writer Heliade Rădulescu's book collection. One cold winter, because of the supervisor's neglect and some of the boarders' stupidity, all these valuable books were burned due to a shortage of fuel for the stoves where we would sit to prepare our lessons for the next day.

There were four smaller rooms, each reserved for the students of the first, second, third and fourth year grades. And adjoining the large ballroom there was another large room, almost as large as the ballroom, reserved for the students of the superior grades, fifth, sixth, seventh and eighth. In each classroom there was a pulpit in which sat a monitor to supervise us. He did nothing but watch to see that we prepared our work and did not talk. That we were really working is another story. Anyone could hold a pencil and scribble on a sheet of paper, or even read a novel. Around that time a banned novel in school was Maupassant's *Une Vie*. In spite of the ban, the risqué novel was smuggled into school and passed around until all the 200 students had read it. I read it too, trying unsuccessfully to find the page or paragraphs considered pornographic.

Our day started at 5 a.m. when we were awakened by a loud bell. The supervisor on duty went from dormitory to dormitory ringing the bell and shook the heavy sleepers who claimed not to have heard it. Each dormitory had a washroom with about fifty washstands. We were obliged to wash down to the waist This was painful in winter time as the room was cold and the water icy. Most of the students pretended to wash making a loud sound with their mouths as if pouring pails of water on themselves. After this we had to run quickly to the big hall where our names were called at 5:30 a.m. Then we went to the dining room one floor below where we were given a slice of bread and a glass of hot tea.

All meals had to start with a prayer. The supervisor would point to a boy who immediately had to say the prayer: "The poor will eat and will extol the Lord. In the name of the Father, the Son and the Holy Ghost, Amen " Once Oianescu, the rich one, was told to say the prayer which he adapted it to his own situation: "The rich will eat and extol the Lord." This led to a discussion between the superior and Oianescu who won his point by arguing that "The rich remain in the prayer because the Lord made them rich."

Our entire small group of scholarship students was supervised by university students. They received free room and board in exchange for their duties. One was on duty every day of the week. One of the supervisors escorted us from the boarding house to the school. We were lined up by the gate two-by-two with the smaller boys in front. Before leaving there was an inspection to see if shoes were polished - many boys only polished the toes while leaving the heels muddy. This delayed the departure while we waited for the insubordinates to go and clean their shoes properly. Just as severe was the inspection of brass buttons. In the days of uniforms there were many buttons that had to be polished with a special cream called 'Amour'.

There were two columns of boys. The longer one crossed Stirbey Voda Street to where the high school was located. Once the boys were safely inside, the supervisor returned to the boarding house for the smaller column of scholarship boys. These were registered in a special section of the Gheorghe Lăzar High School. As they were older boys they were allowed to go on their own under the supervision of an eighth-year student. They went down Stirbey Voda street and crossed the Cişmigiu gardens. This shortened the walk and the crossing of the gardens was a pleasure. The first column had its compensation also. At noon, when everyone returned for lunch, on Diaconese Street they met a column of girl boarders from the Catholic school. Though the girls were guarded by four nuns, two in front and two at the rear, no one could prevent an exchange of more or less amorous notes according to age. I exchanged notes for three years with the tallest and ugliest of the girls. By the time she grew up her looks improved. She was Magda Lupescu, a redhead who was later to be at the center of a scandal as King Carol II's mistress.

Lunch was one dish and a slice of bread. After lunch we had half an hour of free time to get ready for the afternoon session. In the evening we were escorted back to have two free hours from 4:30 to 6:30. What could we do during this time? Behind the boarding house was a garden with tall trees which made the garden impossible for any sports. Some of us played marbles. Another game was *Turac*, an ancient folk game usually forbidden because it resulted in broken windows. It seems strange to me now, that no one was made to pay for them. There was another popular game, *Poarca* (leapfrog), in which some players injured their legs and had to receive medical attention. We *philosophers* did not lower ourselves to play these games. On a nice day we would sit on a bare mound reserved for the savants. There was a school tradition that the first-year and second-year boys should call the older boys "mister." All the "misters" had privileges. They could call a younger boy to polish their shoes or to fill their fountain pens. In the basement there was a room in which each student had a small box to keep shoe cleaning materials. They also served to store private food. At 4:30 free-time, the room filled up with rich boys visiting their boxes and permanent 'beggars' of the rich. We scholarship boys received a plain slice of bread from the linen keeper. The evening meal was at 6:30 when we received a bowl of tasteless soup before the main course.

Once a year on the day of Saint Sava, patron saint of the boarding school, we were treated to a culinary orgy: turkey with apricots and as much fruit and nuts as we wanted. Usually this resulted in a fight around the fruit basket. Later, the same day we had a show where those with talent would perform acrobatics, recite poetry, act a scene from a play, or play the violin or flute. One year I had the misfortune of being chosen to recite a poem that ended with the words "Toc, Toc" and so, with my hands behind my back, knocked Toc, Toc, Toc three times. On this occasion, the writer Teodor Rosetti was in the audience. He liked the way I recited the poem and invited me to his home to repeat it in front of his guests. I was to be taken there by the school Principal. To my relief both the Principal and Rosetti forgot about this invitation.

Though we were not allowed to wander around town, I was allowed as an exception to go to the theater and concerts on condition that I was back by 11 p.m. When I grew older I had an understanding with the gatekeeper who gave me an extra key to open the gate when I returned late. He lived in one room near the gate with his wife and two children. I always brought something for the children that also gained me his wife's protection.

The school was separated from the beautiful Cişmigiu Park by a solid, high wall. In spite of this, some of the boys had learned how to climb and jump over it for nocturnal escapades. No one was caught as there was no one guarding it. On Sundays a military band played on *Monte Carlo*, an islet on the park's lake. On weekdays there would be a band of gypsy musicians. All these interludes helped us to endure the hard life of scholarship students.

Growing older I started to reflect on my own circumstances. I thought that it was unfair to have to live in such a sterile environment. After all, all that was expected of us was homework and study all the time. Under these conditions, I was able to learn my lessons very quickly as I had, and still have, a photographic memory. I could read a page from a history book and then recite it almost by heart. During my free time, I thought that my school could have been a much better place. Eventually, as one of the favored ones I was allowed to go home every weekend.

There was not only music, art and literature. We became good customers of the two best bookstores in Bucharest. We bought French books one at time. I first read English literature in French translations. The same was true for German and Italian literature. Looking back, I wonder how we found time to do so much but I know I read all that I could possibly find that was worthwhile reading, even if it had little to do with my school courses.

When I transferred from St. Sava School to the Gh. Lazăr High School, I found a totally different atmosphere. The principal Marin Dumitrescu had one preoccupation: discipline. We were not allowed to run in the hallways, not allowed to talk loudly, and we had to be neatly dressed. He had found a way to choose his students from the richest circle of society. Naturally he had to accept scholarship students who were selected on the basis of year-end marks.

Unlike St. Sava, I liked none of the teachers at Lazăr. Had it not been for what I was taught at home, I probably would have lost my scholarship. What I liked best was the outside activities that were unrelated to school work. I had a passion for aviation. At home father received a monthly French magazine L'Aerofil that I read avidly without understanding most of the technical articles. What intrigued me most were pictures of airplanes invented in the West by the Wright Brothers, Blériot, Santon, DuMont and others. This prompted the idea of building my own airplane. I made models that I launched from a mound in the school yard. None flew successfully. They immediately turned upside down and fell to the ground. Bit by bit I realized that I had to find the center of gravity and added small weights in the wings. I succeeded and soon my models could fly straight for up to 15 meters. My enthusiasm soon waned and my interest turned to real airplanes I read about. But they were still inaccessible until Blériot, the Frenchman, came to Bucharest and gave a demonstration. Those who wanted to see him fly had to pay. I remember well that it was eight lei. My father bought tickets in the racetrack stands without realizing that once the plane was in the air it could be seen from beyond the demonstration.

An engineer went to France to buy a "Wright" type of plane and in

Wright biplanes imported in Bucharest-Chitila for school, 1910.

1910 installed it at Chitila on an airfield five miles from Bucharest. The plane was launched by a system that propelled it forward as he started the engine and fly forward for two or three minutes. He planned to start a pilot school and also charged money for flights. I don't know how much he charged but father made a sacrifice to pay for the short flight or several hundred meters. I would have liked him to pay for me but I only watched.

In school the only authorized 'sport' was "oina," something akin to baseball in which you hit a ball with a stick. Some of others found ways of joining more active sports clubs. One of them was "Columbia," a football club sponsored by an oil company. In exchange for my helping out, I was admitted without paying member dues. When balls went beyond the field, I would run and retrieve it. For me only it felt like an honor just to hold the ball. But soon I changed from football when I heard that some young men returned from France had formed two rugby clubs. I was chosen to join the "Sport Club" team which played a match every week. Pretty soon high schools in Bucharest had teams and I was one of the founders of a Lazăr team in 1913.

The family would go to Sinai for summers and even at age eleven I was allowed to go with my brother on the Piatra Arsa. It was there that I learned to love the mountains. Gradually we learned to climb as far as Omul and Caraimanul and to return by way of the Ialomiciora grotto. With Sandy Bogdan, son of Nicolae Bogdan who was secretary of the National

Assembly, we eventually managed the narrow and dangerous pathway called the Briul Caraimanul below high cliffs. Knowing that two high school brothers had slipped on the same route and fell to their deaths made it even more fearful. I did not want my brother to accompany the few of us who set out. With our backs glued to the mountain wall, we took three painful hours to make our way. We were tied together with ropes but knew that if anyone fell we would all go down 1,000 meters. I was miracle that we arrived safely. Since then my mountain 'alpinism' has been limited to excursions that entail no risks.

In winter, I was also one of the first to buy skis and in winter went to practice in Sinai. But some boys or richer parents had discovered bobsledding, a costly sport. The sled had steering wheels and came from abroad. Two brothers from my rugby team had one and they included me. Some time later when I had come to know Prince Carol I told him about my dream to one day own a 'bob'. He told me that he had four of them. But his sister Princess Elisabeth having broken a leg on one, their father King Ferdinand forbade any more bobsledding. He then told me that I could go to the Pelişor Palace garage and chose one for myself. Nobody believed me when I appeared with my own huge bobsled. My team trained to compete and received a second prize in one of the races. When this became known at Lazăr, I became a small 'sports hero' and the principal put my silver cup prize in the teachers' meeting room.

CHAPTER TWO

BOY-SCOUTS

Oh ne day while I was in algebra class at Gheorghe Lazăr College, the school secretary came and told the teacher that "the student Dimancescu is asked to come to the Principal's office."

My heart became smaller than that of a flea. To be called to the principal's office one had to be guilty of a serious offense. The secretary told me to bring my cap. I could see myself expelled not only from Lazăr but from all the high schools. The only thing I could think of that I could be reproached for was that I had chalked an announcement on the blackboard inviting students to form a boy-scout troop. I had asked permission to do this and about thirty boys had responded. We had met in the amphitheater and we constituted the first boy-scout troop in Romania in 1913. We had been functioning for two or three months, going out on Sundays and attracting attention with our London-ordered uniforms. The press had published a few articles explaining what we were doing and how I read an article in a French magazine, *Lectures Pour Tous*,[8] about the Les Éclaireurs (Boy Scout) movement that had been founded by England's Lieutenant-General Baden-Powell. An article explained that I had written directly to Baden-Powell who replied and encouraged me to form a troop. He had personally sent me several books, including his most famous book, *Scouting for Boys*.

All these thoughts vanished from my nervous mind when I entered the principal's office. Without telling me anything Mr. Marin Dumitrescu took me outside where a horse and carriage were waiting for us. We drove to the Ministry of Education, which was normally closed to visitors. Admitted immediately, we went up the main stairs directly to the Minister's office where his secretary, Gabriel Giurgea, received us amiably and said to me: "The Minister is waiting for you." The principal was told to wait in the secretary's office!

At this point my mind was at a stand still. The Minister, L. G. Duca, took me in his arms and embraced me. There was a moment of silence and then he asked me: "How did it occur to you to form a boy-scout movement? Giurgea and I were thinking about starting it for some time, but you did it! Continue and do not let any one stop you!"

He embraced me again, took my hand and went back to the secretary's office where he told Mr. Dumitrescu in a curt tone, "Sir, make it possible in every way for Dimancescu to succeed with his movement. Give him all the free time to go anywhere, any time with his boys." While I breathed a huge sigh-of-relief, I was immediately fearful of the honor and privileges that were being bestowed on me. The principal took me back in the carriage and gave me the afternoon off.

I never abused the privileges given to me. I was embarrassed by the situation that this created for me at Lazăr High School. When Mr. Dumitrescu met me in school, he was the first to say "Good day"! It was evident that Minister Duca's order had been discussed with the teachers' committee. Everyone was good to me.[9] At one time an attempt was made to re-write the history of the Boy Scout movement, attributing the role of founder to Prince Carol. In the first printed history of the movement neither my

---

[8] *Lecture pour tous*, 15 Septembre, Hachette et Cie., 1915, p132.

[9] The details of the founding of the Romanian boy-scouts were explained in detail in a history of the school: *1865-1935 Liceul Gh. Lazăr Bucuresti*, Chapter "Cercetasia la Liceul Lazăr,' pages 282-287.

name nor the name of Lazăr High School were mentioned. For me these omissions did not mean much, but for the first time the notion of dishonesty crossed my mind.

A week after my meeting with the Minister I had a multitude of requests from boys wishing to join the scouts. I set a limit of one hundred members. My classmate, Mitilineu, suggested that we change the name from *Boy Scouts* to *Cercetaşii* (seekers).[10] For the whole following year, I led my team of "cercetaşii."

During the prior summer months of 1913, I was in Sinaia with my brother Ioan "Nell," and Alexandru "Sandy" Bogdan, when we formed our first patrol of "cercetaşii." The three of us translated the Boy Scout laws into Romanian and recomposed the text of promises for the "cercetaşii" creed. We were joined by the two sons of Colonel Grigore Berindei and the two sons of the owner of a chocolate factory. All summer long we took short mountain trips, and with our parents' permission we would camp at night in the woods, making our shelter of pine branches.

I was anxiously awaiting the start of the school year in-order-to recruit more members. Suddenly there were a hundred and I realized what a responsibility I had assumed. To go on a trip with a hundred boys of all ages created a big problem of discipline. I had to impose order even though I was the same age as the older members. I made one rule from the start: *No one was allowed to participate in an excursion unless they had a permission statement signed by their father.*

The most rebellious and undisciplined member was Ionel Taranu, the son of the codirector of the magazine *Furnica*. He did not know how to obey an order and I could not place him anywhere. He would always be 20 feet ahead of us or 20 feet behind. During marches he would make fun of everyone. I did not have the heart to expel him because he was clever and he was amusing.

The school year passed quickly. Then came complications with my youthful leadership. Colonel Berindei, who commanded the Royal Peleş Palace Guards in Sinai, saw an opportunity and tried to take over the leadership. Others like Professor Murgoci and Captain Marinescu also wanted to take over the leadership. Another ambitious person, though well-intentioned, also appeared on the cercetaşii horizon. This was Professor Mugur from the rural grammar school of Sinaia. He organized his own troop and had the uniforms made locally. His school was occasionally visited by Prince Nicholas. By enrolling the Prince in his troop Mr. Mugur suddenly became very visible.

---

[10] The 100th anniversary was celebrated in 2013. See:
www.scout.ro/2013/05/17/expozitie-100-de-ani-de-cercetasie/

During the summer following our inaugural year at Lazăr High School, twenty of us were brought to Sinaia at Colonel Berindei's request. On a Sunday, we were to be presented to the Royal Family members who were now very interested in our activities. Prince Ferdinand, Princess Marie and Prince Carol were to review a parade.

Sinaia, September 1914: DDD Presented to Prince Carol by Col. Berindei

I arrived with a group of my Boy Scouts all correctly dressed in their uniforms. We were assigned a place in the square next to the Palace Guards. An officer came to review us before the arrival of the Royal Family. When he saw me with bare and hairy knees, he rushed me to one of the barracks where a soldier shaved my legs! The prudish officer told me that I could not be presented to Princess Marie with what he called "indecent, hairy legs." After the parade, I was introduced to Prince Ferdinand and his wife Marie, who congratulated me and introduced me to Prince Carol, the presumptive heir to the throne.

A few days later I was called to the Pelişor Palace in Sinaia by Prince Carol who told me that he wanted to join the "cercetaşii." Even though he was only three years older than me, I answered that it was not up to me - a mere high school student - to accept his entry. I notified Colonel Berindei about his request. He quickly proposed the creation of a "Committee of Leadership of the Cercetaşii" in which all the honorary members became founding members. Prince Carol would be nominated as the Supreme Chief of the "Cercetașii."

At the time, the only troop was the one at Lazăr High School. Professor Mugur, Professor Murgoci and Col. Berindei constituted themselves into a cercetași founding group in contradiction to all of Baden-Powell's precepts. They saw the movement as an extension of school education and the military regimentation of future cercetașii units. They conceived the idea of creating new units of cercetașii by ordering all high school students to join. They ordered fifty uniforms per week and these were sent to other high schools where those who fit into the uniforms would be required to swear allegiance in front of Prince Carol, the Supreme Commander.

At this stage of the cercetașii movement, the Ministry of Education, the War Ministry and other institutions provided substantial funds to the Executive Committee. The founders had a "big cake" to cut from as there was no administrative control. They rented a large house and created a bureaucracy full of employees. These were "sinecures" that contributed nothing to the "cercetașii" movement. They only slowed the progress down. I protested, but I was ignored.

One result was that Prince Carol summoned me to the Palace and gave me an honorary title of the "Chief of the Royal Troop" along with serving as his private secretary. From this position I could have easily undermined the Executive Committee, but I thought it would be wiser not to interfere with a movement with which I no longer had anything in common. Prince Carol was easily influenced. He believed everything he was told and never properly investigated the accusations that were brought against those who served him. He would easily part with friends and assistants without telling them why.

The enrollment of "cercetașii" started taking place county by county. Ion Nistor, who was in the good graces of Professor Murgoci and Mugur, was sent ahead with the uniforms, staffs, and hats with which to create an instant troop of "cercetașii." After they were sworn in, the uniforms were recovered and brought back to Bucharest. Occasionally, a few high school boys and an officer or two would continue the troop after its sudden birth. But there was nothing sincere about the official movement. Yet, in the course of a year, the committee was proud to announce the enrollment of thousands of "cercetașii."

All the activity was of great value to Prince Carol. My own troop traveled with him from Bucharest until his return. He visited county districts and became acquainted with local people. At each enrollment, they came from far and wide to see the Prince. A routine was established. In each county town, he was received by the local county prefect, the town's mayor, the relevant army commander, the chief of police and lesser officials. After the pledge, the Prince made a speech to which the Prefect replied. Then all the officials would accompany the Prince to the county capital where an enormous lunch was served.

The cercetașii were forgotten and left alone in a field to feed themselves or perhaps the mayor would arrange for a restaurant to provide a meal. If the distance was too far to return in the same day, we the honor guard had a special sleeping car attached to the Royal car which was attached to an express train. During the trip Carol would come into our car and ask us to sing folk songs and he would join in. Sometimes he would remain late into the night, talking to me and asking many questions about things he never had an occasion to know about. Part of his schooling was through our "cercetașii." Thus was established a friendship between us that lasted until his death in exile in Portugal. There were periods when he would ignore me completely, but he never forgot to send me telegrams at Christmas and New Year.

During his trips into the country he was treated with the highest respect, as was his due. Thus he became more comfortable with the idea that he was different from other people. The talks that he had with his guests were about administration, something he knew little about, and yet he had to give answers. Sometimes on the way to a new enrollment he would come to my car and ask me what he should do. I had no better knowledge or experience than he about talking to mayors and local officials.

He had grown up within the walls of the Royal Palace at Cotroceni. His experience was extremely limited. Everybody's concern was to conceal from him things that were "not fit for a Prince." When he was of high school age, teachers from various high schools in Bucharest would go to the palace to tutor him privately. One teacher he became fond of was the historian Nicolae Iorga, whose knowledge was not just limited to history. Iorga made long digressions telling him about current social and political events. Iorga changed Prince Carol into an informed nationalist, impatient to see unification of the Romanian people. None other of his teachers influenced him as much.

At a time when it was inconceivable that the Austro-Hungarian Empire or the Russian Empire would ever be dismantled, some of our politicians thought that they could resolve the disputes with Russia by arranging a marriage between Prince Carol and one of the Tsar's daughters. This project moved almost to realization when the Tsar accepted an invitation to meet the Romanian Royal family in Constanta. The Tsar's daughters hated the idea of such a marriage and while traveling on their yacht between the Crimea and Constanza they decided to get sunburned and arrived with peeling faces! The meeting between the two families was a fiasco. Our national problems were not destined to be resolved by a royal wedding.

His other 'school' was our cercetaşii. He looked forward to the pledging ceremonies and was eager to go. I tried to instill in him the idea that in his speech he should mention a historic event relating to the region he was visiting. As a good student, he scoured the best history book which was, of course, by Iorga; it is very confusing to read and easy to get lost in the relentless detail. So I brought him Agulletti's very simple history.

On one occasion late in the Summer of 1915, Carol went to the small town of Vaslui in a remote part of central Moldavia. My troop accompanied him as usual. The troop leader, chosen by me, was Vintilă Mortun. The pledge took place in a meadow outside the town and followed the ritual established by the Committee of Leadership. At the end of the ceremony the Mayor took the Prince to the town hall and we the honor guard, went to a small restaurant. Someone representing the mayor told us that there was no set meal but that we could eat and drink whatever we desired. I was not happy when I heard the word "drink" because our normal beverage was fountain water. We were not all seated at one table but were divided by small tables of four or six "cercetaşii." We were also joined by the new Vaslui "cercetaşii" who were our hosts. But then I noticed the waiters serving beer to some tables and orders were even being doubled. I immediately realized that this would create a scandal. So I went to the restaurant owner and asked for separate bills for each table to be signed by Mortun and me.

A few days after our return to Bucharest, I discovered that the Vaslui Town Hall had sent a very high bill for our luncheon asking to be reimbursed. Since I did not participate in the Committee's meetings, and I did not know how the payment was handled. Then a short time later, I happened to go by the headquarters to see what news had been published. What I saw I could hardly believe. There was a notice on the bulletin board stating:

"By order of the Leadership Committee of the Cercetaşi Vintilă Mortun and Dimitrie Dimăncescu are permanently expelled from the 'cercetaşii' movement."

The signature was illegible. It is difficult to explain my emotions at that instant. I felt as if I had died a thousand deaths. I did not go into the building and left without trying to ask for an explanation. What crime had I committed? I could not find an answer. Soon I would learn from a friend that Mortun and I had been accused of drinking numerous beers and getting drunk at the luncheon in Vaslui.

My uncle Petre Antonescu had a property near Vaslui and I went there to think things over. A good night's sleep would help. The next day, a horse-cart and its driver took me to Vaslui where I settled in a coffee shop across the street from the restaurant where I had "committed my crime." I ended up spending more time at my uncle's wrestling with what to do. Surely there was someone who could prove my innocence.

When I heard that the next cercetaşii "pledge ceremony" in Bucharest would take place in the Roman Arena.[11] Prince Carol, Supreme Chief, would be present along with the Minister of Education and the entire staff of the Leadership Committee. I immediately set out. The train was overcrowded and while I stood in the corridor, I could see myself going to the Roman Arena and giving a speech for everyone to hear. I was inspired by a speech by Mihai Kogalniceafu, one of Romania's early Prime Ministers in the 1860s. We learned it in school. To the rhythm of the train's wheels, I spent hours rehearsing silently until I arrived at just as good an approach as Kogalniceanu's - or so I thought.

On the day of the ceremony, I went to the Roman Arena which was full of spectators and cercetaşii. Dressed in civilian clothes, a sport jacket and no hat, I took a seat in the stands. The event started with the arrival of the members of the Leadership Committee who took their seats on the stage where Prince Carol, dressed in the uniform of the Commander of the Cercetaşii, was received royally.

Roman Arena in Carol Park, Bucharest

The introduction of religion into the movement was Prince Carol's idea. And so first came a recital of the Lord's prayer with a Greek Orthodox priest, a Roman Catholic priest and a Jewish rabbi present. (When performed in the eastern Dobrogea region, there would also be a Muslim mullah). After the actual pledge ceremony, Colonel Berindei was supposed to

---

[11] The Roman Arena still stands in what is now known as Carol Park.

make a speech, but there was a brief delay as he fumbled with his papers. I took the moment, to stand up from my place in the stands and shouted:

"Your Highness, a cercetași not dressed in a uniform speaks from his heart."

Everybody turned their heads toward me. Right away, Prince Carol, Minister Duca and the Committee members recognized me. Colonel Berindei, standing behind the Prince, made desperate signs for me to sit down but nobody could stop me. I recited my speech dramatically. When I finished, the cercetașii and the audience stood up and applauded me at length. Before the end of the applause the Prince's aide came to tell me that the Prince had invited me up to his stand. When I arrived he embraced me, shook my hand and congratulated me. Duca did the same. The Committee members were stunned and even Berindei gave up his speech. Prince Carol spoke briefly and took me with him when he left. To the surprise of the Committee he took me in his car and we went to the Cotroceni Palace.

On the way he asked me where I had been hiding and he told me that he had been looking for me. He asked what had happened and was surprised that the "Gentlemen of the Committee" had accepted Professor Murgoci's version. He then asked me to return to the "cercetașii." I thanked him for the honor but said that I did not want to return as the cercetașii no longer corresponded to my original ideas. Under Col. Berindei's influence, I recounted, many troop leaders had been appointed, though serious and well-intentioned, who had no training for the responsibilities. My refusal surprised him and I had the impression that he did not like it too much.

When he asked what my future intentions were, I answered: "We are on the verge of war, which whether we wish it or not, we shall be dragged into it by pressure from the Allies." At my age, I saw it as my duty to join the army to be ready to fight for my country. Satisfied with my answer, he responded with another offer.

"If you enlist as a volunteer, come to my Regiment of Vânători de Munte (Mountain Hunters) of which I am the Commander."

The next day I was dressed in the Hunters uniform of No. 2 Regiment "Queen Elisabeta."

This was Thursday, October 8, 1915.

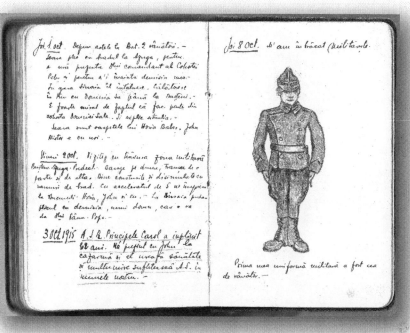

Last page of DDD's Boy Scout Diary.
The illustration at the opening of the chapter is also from his diary.

PART II - WAR

Since Napoleonic times, as Europe's Empires grew in strength, animosities between them intensified. Russia sought access to the Mediterranean. Germany and Austria sought to consolidate their territorial boundaries and military power. France and England expanded their colonial tentacles worldwide. As the continent witnessed the lighting of a fuse that exploded into World War I, smaller countries such a Romania could only watch and even delayed committing on which side to enter the War. In 1914, Carol I died to be succeeded by his nephew King Ferdinand. The latter favored the German side by virtue of his own heritage and a belief that it would win. However, his Council of Ministers, and his wife Queen Marie grand-daughter of England's Queen Victoria, favored the Allies and on August 27, 1916,* declared War against the Central Powers of Bismarck's Germany and the Habsburg's Austro-Hungary.

Though counting 23 divisions and almost 700,000 troops, Romania's army was ill-equipped for what had turned into a 'modern-era' war. Attacked from the South by German-led forces counting nearly 300,000 troops, and from the north by another 350,000, Romanian divisions and supporting Tsarist Russian armies fell into rapid eastward retreat. By December of 1916, Bucharest was evacuated and the government and Royal family moved north to the Moldavian capital of Iași. One of Europe's harshest winters on record followed and helped stall any enemy advances northward into Moldavia. The army having suffered more than 400,000 casualties counted only 50,000 remaining combatants,

French military strategists, fearing that a full defeat on the Eastern Front would allow German forces to be strengthened on the vulnerable French Western Front, sent 1,700 military advisors, supplies, and logistical support to Romania. All this was under the leadership of the French General Henri Mathias Berthelot. Successfully and rapidly, they rebuilt and modernized Romania's armed forces. During summer heat-waves of July and August 1917, Romanian divisions stopped Germany's invasion at Mărășești in central Moldavia and held the lines in an ultimate battle on Carpathian Mountain hilltops near Oituz known on military maps as Hill 789. An armistice ensued into 1918 allowing the capital, Bucharest, most of Wallachia and part of Moldavia to remain occupied by the Central Powers. Important to them were the country's abundant oil riches around Ploiești. Late in 1918, as the tide turned against Germany, French armies moved northward from Greece and across Bulgaria and Romania re-entered the War.

With the post-War break-up of the Austro-Hungarian Empire, the reward for Romania's War efforts and huge losses in human life was the transfer of Transylvania and its heavily-majority Romanian ethnic population into what became known as United Romania. This doubled the Nation in size and population.

* NOTE: August 27 was based on the Gregorian calendar used in Western Europe for several hundred years. Romanian still used the Julian calendar with a 13 days difference until 1919. This meant that for Romanians the War started on August 14. These dating differences cause substantial confusion when comparing dates of events recorded by German or Hungarians armies during their invasions and those of Romanian forces.

CHAPTER THREE

SOLDIER[12]

"Queen Elisabeta" No. 2 Regiment, Company No. 1

Without losing any time, Prince Carol ordered Sergeant Chiriţă to train me in everything that he had already trained recruits of the prior year. Chiriţă treated me as any other soldier. He taught me to stand straight, head up, chin pulled in, to draw in the stomach and keep my heels together and toes apart to form a "V". I learned the parade step, how to turn to the right and left. For some reason what was most difficult for me was to turn around from the left. His greatest contribution was to teach me how to execute an order. I had to start by saying: "Yes Sir, Sergeant, I understood. I have to go to the store and bring you a packet of cigarettes."

The first time I came back empty handed as he had not given me any money. He repeated the order. I went back to the store (not too far) and came back with a packet of cigarettes that I paid for out of my own allowance. This order was repeated twice a day and after two weeks Sgt. Chiriţă brought me in front of Prince Carol praising me as a good soldier.

At lunchtime while I was in my barracks Prince Carol sent me an invitation to go and have lunch with him in the officers mess hall. In the middle of the table there was a bowl where anyone who spoke of work would drop a fixed sum of money. With this they bought one or two bottles of champagne! The meals were very good and Prince Carol often held a lively conversation with his officers. He was greatly amused by stories or indecent jokes recounted by Captain Nicolceanu who later became Prefect of Police of Bucharest. I kept silent. I was the smallest in my class and did not know any indecent stories, nor did I enjoy them.

I had an advantage over the others in my company. I was a "teterist" (a young man with a reduced term of service). This title was given to all high school graduates and I received this title with honors for being ranked first

---

[12] "It is not my intention in these reminiscences to give a history of the war of Greater Romania. A better source of details is a book by Constantin Kiritescu, *Istoria Razboiului Pentru Intregirea Romaniei*, published in three volumes in 1921, by Casa Scoalelor."

in my graduation examination. What had helped me was the thirty-minute speech I delivered on the "History of Aviation," a topic I selected from a list of ten. I had read almost everything I could about the progress of aviation and I spoke without any notes in a declaratory tone. What produced a sensation was my prophetic peroration. In rhetoric class I had learned that a good speech should end with a dramatic closing message. I said that in a far away future, mankind will become poor as the soil would lose its natural resources and our salvation would be to board a large aircraft and fly to another planet. The president of the review panel, Professor Titeica, came up to the podium and congratulated me. He asked where I got the idea of my closing line and laughed when I said I found it in my head.

I did not stay long in the Hunters Regiment because the Commander asked Prince Carol to transfer me to the reserve officers Military School of Infantry for specialized training. I packed all my military belongings and was driven in a horse carriage to the Military School in Dealul Spirei with an *Order of Service* signed by Prince Carol.

My arrival at the school in the uniform of a "Hunters" soldier produced a sensation and hilarity. There were over 800 students in the school. The reserve officers, many well educated, wore the uniform of the Infantry Regiment. As France and Germany were already at war in 1915, all the Romanian students who were at Universities in those countries, were obliged to return to Romania. As they arrived home they were all drafted as their exemptions were invalidated. We others, who were only high school graduates, were considered "insects." One of my "insect" colleagues, Ghița Harsu, whose mother was a well known writer, had assumed the role of making fun of all the "doctors" from Paris and Heidelberg whom he nicknamed "intellectual lice!" My presence among the insects and the lice made me realize how inferior I was. These colleagues had a Western culture and were better prepared than I was to get a job or practice a career. But the officers who were our instructors saw no difference. They treated us all alike as equally unprepared for military duty. We did military exercises independent of the weather. Sunshine, rain, or snow, we were on a plateau. We were divided by companies and platoons; Ghița Harsu and I were at the tail of the first Platoon of the First Company. We were commanded by Lt. Dumitrache, who later became a famous general.

One day, we were all gathered in the school amphitheater where the Commander, Colonel Sturdza, gave us a problem to consider: "A soldier has five bullets in his rifle. If he shoots four, how many are left?" We were ordered to answer immediately on a piece of paper. There was a general murmuring in the room. We all felt insulted about a problem of arithmetic at the level of a child in the first grade. But, we did it and a week later we were again gathered in the amphitheater, where Colonel Sturdza read the results. Out of 800 students, no two gave the same answer. The majority turned this simple problem into stories, some two or three pages long! In Colonel Sturdza's opinion we would be taught to give the same answer in short, precise words: 5 minus 4 = 1. Every morning for one year, we repeated: "5 minus 4 = 1".

I cannot say we were abused but we were disciplined into achieving a unity of thought. During the year I went through all of a soldier's emotions and received promotions to corporal, then sergeant and before the end of the year to sergeant major. This last title gave me the right to wear a huge saber. Here too, I competed with one of my colleagues, D. Vechiu, later a well-known newspaperman. To our satisfaction we both graduated at the end of the year as head of our units.

Towards the end of our training, we practiced for marching in the May 10th parade. In my platoon, I was placed on the right so my duty was to look straight ahead while the others did "eyes right" to honor the King who would be reviewing the troops along Kisseleff Avenue.

The day before was Sunday, and my father insisted we should all attend family lunch, as he liked this. He took great pleasure in presiding over these family gatherings. Usually he was very entertaining with his stories, for he was a good speaker. On that Sunday he told us about his morning walk to the Botanical Gardens which was one of his favorite walks. This Garden was actually a park on Cotroceni Avenue and was very well kept, but there were very few visitors. The fact that it was called Botanical Gardens discouraged people from visiting it.

Father told us that while he sat on a bench, he heard a cuckoo bird sing nine times, which meant he would live nine more years. This is an old saying and we told him jokingly that he would live for another ninety years! After lunch, he asked me about the parade and said he would watch me from the street. The next day, before leaving for the parade, my younger brother came running to the Military School to tell me to return home at once as my father had been taken ill suddenly and had not much longer to live. I thought this was another of the Family's false alarms, so I told him I would come immediately after the parade. I was too late. He died just before I got there. Apparently, he had gone shopping in the morning. Someone pushed him and he fell, striking his head against the curbstone. He was able to get up and take a carriage and to give the driver his address. Once home, he walked upstairs called the maid and gave her money to pay the driver. He went to bed without muttering a word and a few minutes later he was dead.

He did not leave a will as he had no material possessions to leave us. His small property in Dobrogea had been confiscated by the State as he had not lived there for the last thirty years as required by law. He had refused to get his share of inheritance from his father. He said he did not feel right to possess houses and land for which he had no sentimental ties. Money never interested him which is something I inherited from him. Certainly in my life I was paid with higher and higher salaries but I never gave a thought to seeking promotions to have a higher salary,

I refused to look at my father dead. Because I much preferred to remember his image as a living man. I was against any kind of funeral which would call for relations and friends to see him. The first night I arranged to have him placed in a coffin and taken after midnight to the Chapel of Bellu Cemetery. Just my brother and me followed him all the way to the cemetery. Day and night until the funeral, I stayed at the cemetery. The day of the funeral I did not go near the grave and was surprised at the crowds of people who had come to be present at his internment.

With his departure, the most important chapter of my life closed. For me, he was like a majestic oak tree in whose shade I was able to grow up. We children did not lack anything we needed. Mother, with tears in her eyes, came to me and said: "Now you are the head of the family. You have the responsibility to take care of all of us"

There wasn't a penny left in the house. But quite unexpectedly a stranger appeared and gave us 10,000 lei, a very large amount for those days. It was an amount that father had lent him. As we found out, this explained to my mother what father had done with part of his money. He had lent money without asking for receipts to those who needed it. In his desk, I found a notebook. There he had written sums of money with initials to

37

them for those to whom he had been given the loans. None of us could decipher these initials and the sums came to a considerable total. There was also found a large stack of shares from the "Albina Insurance Company." This was divided into small piles, each one marked for my mother and us children. We soon discovered that "Albina" had gone bankrupt. All that my father had accumulated for our own good was now lost.

By now my sister and I were independent. She, a student in the last year of medical school, had been offered a post as an intern at Dr. Antoniu's sanatorium with a very good salary. Myself, as a soldier, could count on my upkeep plus my sergeant-major's wages. My brother, still in high school, was inspired by the general spirit overcoming the whole country that we would probably soon be at war. He entered the Military School of Infantry as a volunteer student. All the normal formalities for such an admission were ignored.

When I finished at the Military School, I returned to the "Vanatori" Hunters Regiment where Prince Carol welcomed me openly. One ritual was the company's morning report. A soldier could speak up if he had a complaint to make or a favor to ask. The first to come forward on my first day was Sergeant Chiriţă asking permission to go home for a week. Carol asked him why he wanted to go in the middle of the year. Did he want to get married? "No," answered Chiriţă, "I want to start building a house for my mother who is a widow." Prince Carol told him he would think about it. Soon after I was requested to go the Chancellery, he told me confidentially that I must go to Chiriţă's village and buy a house for his mother. He gave me a stack of money and said if I needed more he would give me more, but under no condition should anyone know that it came from him. I fulfilled my mission and bought a small house for Chiriţă's mother. I begged her not to mention anything to her son until he came home. About three weeks later, I called Chiriţă forward during the morning report and Carol told him he was given a month's leave with no explanation. I never found out about the meeting of Chiriţă and his mother in the new house. Soon after the Romania's entry into the War, he was one of the first to be killed sadly before my eyes. Prince Carol's secret remained until mentioned here.

❧

AUGUST 27, 1916
ROMANIA DECLARES WAR
(August 14th on the Julian calendar still used in Romania)

We had managed to remain neutral in the War. At my family's social and economic level, we only knew what was in the newspapers. However, there was a rumor that our turn would soon come. I reported daily to my regiment where the only work I had was in an office. At the same time, all of us were being instructed in the use of rifles. This was so monotonous that it was boring for even the simplest man. The order was: "Put in the bayonet. Take out the bayonet." And then we attacked an imaginary enemy with it. This was repeated day-after-day.

I wanted to get my mother used to the idea that very soon I would leave for the front and that the probability was that I would not return. It was a heartless story which she refused to acknowledge.

One day I was having lunch at home when a soldier from my company called me urgently to return to my regiment and to take my military trunk with me. This was made of wood to the regulation measurements but there were no instructions of what to put in it. My mother had sewn with her own hands three sets of underclothes of silk because, once folded, they would take less room. There were also heavy boots, toilet articles such as three cakes of soap, razor blades and a great luxury, a bottle of toilet water called "Ambre d'Orsay".

This small trunk was put on the military "wagon train" which consisted of five carts each pulled by two strong horses. This train was supposed to follow us at a distance of a few hours marching, so it would not be caught by the enemy. In the first cart rode Sergeant Major Grigoriu who carried a metal box containing our wages and the soldiers wages plus a reserve of money for emergencies. Grigoriu had always been considered an important person. He was settled into his cart ready to travel like an Arab "pasha" on a woolen mattress.

Mother came to the top of the stairs of our apartment. She embraced me, kissed me and told me she would only live for my return. With a spontaneous movement she took off one earring and gave it to me saying she would keep one ear bare until I returned with the other one. I quickly ran down the stairs so that she would not see that I had started to cry.

We were a company of bicyclists, a novel means of mobility already used on the Western Front. We were to be attached to the 1st Cavalry Division. At the barracks, our regiment was organized by companies and platoons. Two soldiers, cooks by trade, were going from one man to another cutting any brass or gold rings off their fingers and throwing them away. It was done by order of the regimental commander in case a bullet might strike the hand and cause an infection. This was a brutal doing and impressed us very much.

Prince Carol was not present as we prepared to depart. The command of his company was taken over by Captain Nicu Tătăranu. There were three other officers in the company, Captain Bădulescu, Lt. Mavriki and Sub Lt. in reserve Aslan, and myself. Though I had not been promoted yet, I was considered as a future Sub-Lieutenant.

That day, after a short speech telling us that Romania had entered the war, we left in a southwesterly direction where we were told we would find our division. This is the way the war started rarely knowing exactly where we were going. The general direction was the headquarters of the 1st Cavalry Division whose troops on horseback could travel 30-40km km per day. We on our bicycles on muddy roads full of holes and bumps could hardly travel 30 km and thus had to travel at night just to keep up. The moment we would join our division, at daybreak, they would leave for the next stop.

Map from National Geographic Magazine *article showing DDD.'s 1200 mile war journey starting and ending in Bucharest. Grey line shows lengthy frontier in 1916. Dotted line shows country frontier in 1916 (before Transylvania was added at the end of the War).*

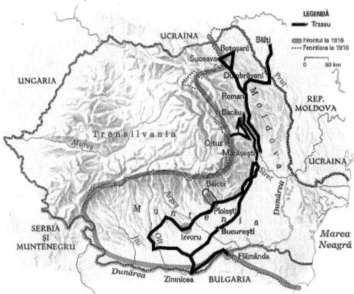

DDD a participat la câteva lupte şi evenimente importante parcurgând un traseu to 2.200 de km, dintre care 525 pe bicicletă.
Sursă: *National Geographic Magazine* / Decembrie 2008

The first days we became used to this pitiless treatment and there was nobody to protest to. The Company Commander and the other two officers each had a motorcycle and were going on the beaten track on the side of the road. I had no motorcycle so I had to share with the soldiers the misery of hard pedaling. The short time I had been with the cyclist company I had not had the time to train. Worse than this we experienced many punctures and blown tires. No one had taught us how to repair the small valves on the tires of which we should have had a large supply. It was our rule that if one of the "machines" broke down, the whole company would come to a stop and everyone would wait until it was repaired. If the bicycle could not be repaired, the soldier would remain behind and wait for the wagon train and be brought in a cart to the next stop. Some sly soldiers had learned about that and by the evening they would arrive in comfort with the "regimental train."

Our first major stop was at Alexandria in Teleorman County. In the evening we were lodged in different homes. I was sent to the house of a Greek family who told me they had no room. They showed that in the large front room slept the master of the house and his wife and in adjoining room slept the fifteen-year-old daughter. Without much argument I suggested they take the girl in their room and I slept in the girl's bed. It was the last time I was to sleep in a comfortable bed with two pillows for a long time.

The next day at dawn we continued cycling and marching until we came to Zimnicea on the Danube River facing Bulgaria. The townspeople people had been evacuated the prior night as ordered by the commandant. The Bulgarians were expected to bomb it and the town was emptied of inhabitants. On the streets were cats, dogs, chickens and animals looking for food and for their owners. The people had been ordered to leave the doors of their houses open and we went in any house that we wanted. I chose the house of a lawyer. He had left with his family and their bed-linen. In the living room there was a large sofa with a blanket lined with black Persian lamb wool. When I left Zimnicea I took the blanket with me. Later I had a coat made of it which I carried with me throughout the war.

During the night we were awoken and sent to the north of the town where there was a small hill. We were ordered to dig a trench across the road which led to Alexandria. Our mission was to stop the enemy's advance northward. This effort was just an illusion because a cyclist company could not oppose a well equipped army. As encouragement, two 75 mm guns were installed 300 meters behind us from horse artillery attached to our division. The commander of these two guns, which were placed in an open field, was one of the Costa-Foru boys, friends of mine from boy scout days.

The Bulgarian front was along the hilly right bank of the Danube from where the enemy could see every move we made. Unknown to us an armored Austrian "Monitor" gunboat lay in hiding behind an island on the river. We had not even finished digging the trench when it started to bomb us. The shells exploded around us with great precision. One of the shells landed between the guns beheading young Costa-Foru. We buried him beside his gun which was also damaged. His soldiers, who were without a leader now, withdrew I do not know where. We expected to be hit again at any moment, but evidently the enemy calculated that it was not worthwhile to spend ammunition on a handful of Romanian peasants digging a ditch.

Costa-Foru's death reminded me of his father, who had been extremely good to me and had encouraged me to collaborate in writing for his magazine, *The Opinions of a Spectator*. C. G. Costa-Foru was fanatically anti-monarchist, and though a great admirer of the "Cercetașii," he refused Carol's help because he disliked him. I was friendly with Costa-Foru even if he was an anti-royalist. From the very beginning, his three sons joined my first cercetașii team and they did not share their father's anti-Carol sentiments. Two years before, in the summer of 1914, Costa-Foru had organized an excursion in the Carpathian Mountains to show how to build up the "Cercetașii." It would leave Buzău, climb up the Penteleu and from there along mountain ridges all the way to the Danube's River's Iron Gates, a 300 km adventure. He published his plans for the trip in the newspapers announcing that those who wished to participate had to pay 100 lei fee and to have adequate but expensive camping equipment.

I told him I would have liked to accompany him but I did not have 100 lei. Costa-Foru told me he would take me without paying. There were only three participants who had paid: Volanski, the son of a pharmacist from Bucharest; Ornstein, the son of a rich merchant from Brăila; and Goldberg, a very fat young man who was sent by his parents, hoping he might lose some weight. We left Buzău and climbed the Penteleu, obliged to stop many times because Goldberg could not follow us and had to be hoisted onto one of the five mountain horses carrying our luggage. Otherwise all was very pleasant. In the evening we prepared our meals over a campfire with old Costa-Foru telling us stories. He not only had his sons with him but also his daughter who was very intelligent and better than any of us at walking. We walked along the ridges to Sinaia where we lodged in the villa of the Volanski family. Here we not only had good meals but took the opportunity for baths too. The next day after this welcome stop we climbed-up the Omul and Caraimanul descending on the Valea Alba toward Brașov.

We were all very excited now that we had crossed the boundary into Austro-Hungarian Transylvania and were now "abroad." Our pleasure did not last long. Hardly had we reached Brașov when the news came that Austria and Hungary had declared war on Serbia starting the First World War. We took the first train back home thus ending the Costa-Foru adventure. [13]

But now positioned at the battle front near the edge of Zimnicea town, we were quicky told to retire and were sent on a forced march to Flamanda 100 kilometers eastward along the Danube. General Alexandru Averescu had conceived a large attack against the Bulgarian-German armies west of Turtucaia on the River's south bank. He had been given a great number of divisions in-order-to execute this operation, including the 1st Cavalry Division which included our cyclists company.

On the way to Flamanda we met a number of troops with the same destination. A side road had been quickly built over a mound of mud dredged out from the Danube marshes. This side road connected the main road from Giurgiu to Flamanda and to a new narrow pontoon bridge crossing the Danube which was very wide at this point. The pontoon bridge was constructed by our engineers after the first troops had crossed by rowboat to create a bridgehead on the southern Bulgarian side. The rough road surface made it impossible for us cyclists to ride our "machines." On foot we pushed them as far as a small inlet where there were five infantry divisions crowded together waiting to cross into Bulgaria. The Averescu action was almost sure to succeed for the Bulgarian and German enemy troops were taken by surprise. In Bucharest they already spoke of a great victory at Flamanda. In spite of all our hardships, the rumor of a victory influenced us too and we anxiously waited for orders to cross the Danube.

Meanwhile we took shelter under a large acacia tree which had a hollow in the trunk the size of a man. All the officers except myself, had been called to a meeting at headquarters. Overhead were German planes that I knew were there to try and bomb us. I got into the tree trunk and told my soldiers to lie down on the ground. At one moment I saw a German plane diving in our direction. I felt ashamed to remain hidden in the hollow tree so I came out and lay on the ground with the soldiers, face up in-order-to

---

[13] NOTE: Almost 60 years later, through a strange coincidence my youngest son, a US citizen, took the same route and fulfilled Costa-Foru's dream by coming down 900 km from Bucovina following Carpathian Mountain ridges as far as the Iron Gates on the Danube River. This was published in the *National Geographic Magazine*, June 1969.

follow the plane's movements. Three soldiers hurried to take my place in the hollow tree, pushing each other to see who would get in. The one who got in was my former instructor, Sergeant Chiriță.

Suddenly, I heard a whistling noise and saw a white bomb coming up our direction. I shouted again, "Lie down!" The same instant the bomb fell in our midst killing about ten men. One fragment hit Sgt. Chiriță in the forehead killing him. All around one could hear moans and yells from the wounded soldiers. We buried Sgt. Chiriță under the tree. Then we sat there waiting for another air attack. We had no antiaircraft defense and our group of fighting planes had not arrived to defend us. Then a sudden gathering of clouds and an outburst of rain was our salvation, but at the same time the storm damaged the bridge. Soon, from behind the clouds came three German "Monitor" aircraft which bombed the rest of the bridge into small pieces and killed soldiers along the river bank. Our artillery could not reach them as the guns had too short a range.

Faced with all these setbacks, General Averescu counseled with headquarters and decided to cancel all operations at Flamanda. Each division received an order to withdraw back across the Danube from Bulgaria and the Flamanda zone. This was done with small losses. We left, taking a northwestward direction of the Olt River Valley. We did not know then that the Germans under General Erich von Falkenhayn, descending across the Carpathian Mountains with more than 350,000 men from the north, had broken the front to the west at Târgu Jiu and that another German army, several hundred thousand strong led by Field Marshal August von Mackensen, had now crossed the Danube at Zimnicea.

Under heavy rain, carrying our bicycles on our backs, we struggled against knee-deep mud all day. Our morale was low and we were walking like automatons. For two nights we slept in ditches along the roadside. Our clothes were soaked and the ditches were like small rivers. We were all so exhausted that we fell asleep as-soon-as we sat down without thinking of our state. We were ordered to reach Caracal in Oltenia. The unit on horse back bypassed us and arrived ahead of us.

Another great plan was conceived by the General Commanding Officer. The 1st Cavalry Division would stop the advancing German troops that had crossed the mountains at Târgu Jiu. This would be done with a rapid push overnight up the Olt and over hills to fall behind the German advanced guard somewhere on the road between Târgu Jiu and Craiova. When we arrived during the night at Caracal, I received the order to immediately place patrols across the road from Craiova to Caracal in-order-to stop the German troops who had crossed the mountains southward.

As one of our patrols entered a village, it was shot at by a peasant with a simple rifle. With all the worries confronting us, we had to be stopped by a Romanian peasant! An officer colleague of mine made a brief report and arrested an old man who was taken to Company Headquarters. It was decided by Captain Tătăranu that the peasant should be executed by my group. At dawn when I went to the execution site, the old man was already tied to the pole. I then had a shock of seeing my father's image in the old man's face. I went to the commanding officer, Tătăranu, and told him I could not execute his order. He warned me that I could be shot for refusing an order in the face of the enemy. In turn, I explained that beside the resemblance, I was convinced the old man was not guilty. Although any minute we were expecting to meet the enemy, I went to the old man's home with the soldier who had arrested him. There another family member admitted he had fired the rifle and was afraid he would be punished, so he accused the old man. That man was then shot. Such incidents, odd ones, affected me very much. No one could read my mind but if the old man had not strongly resembled my father, he would have been executed.

During the day we received a new order to leave without any delay towards Piatra Olt. On the way we received discouraging news. The 9th Rosiori Regiment charged the enemy at Robaneşti where a German column was advancing towards Caracal. It was a slaughter. The Regiment was almost totally decimated. The enemy allowed the regiment to attack and then machine-gunned them almost to the last man.

Our company arrived at Piatra Olt where we were supposed to find other units, with which to execute the action on the Jiu Valley. We were now told that these orders were canceled and we were to cross the Olt River to Slatina. In Piatra we found a small unit which was ready to blow up the bridge between Piatra Olt and Slatina. We would have liked to leave Oltenia but the engineers did not succeed in blowing up the bridge, so we expected at any moment to be attacked by the Germans.

Then again a new order reached us at Izvorul de Sus on the Teleorman River where our Divisional headquarters were now located. Here I took part in an action which was probably the most important experienced by the Company so far. The Commander of the Division personally gave me the order to take my soldiers and settle on the edge of the Perticari forest. Then I was to take a platoon over the Teleorman Bridge, where the Germans were expected to come. But by the time we were supposed to reach the bridge, the Germans had already crossed it with armored cars, taking the bridge intact into their hands. On my own initiative, I decided to make a barricade in the nearby hamlet "Vai de Ei," thus delaying the German advance towards Izvorul de Sus and the Divisional Headquarters. I still have some of my notebooks and reports of this event.

To make the barricade, I sacrificed all our bicycles and some peasant carts which we put across the road. The German column approached led by two armored cars. As it became dark, I settled with my soldiers in the ditch and waited for the armored cars to arrive at our level. I figured that if we were to fire our rifles from about 50 meters the bullets might penetrate the armor plating or at least blow the tires on our side. The German convoy was stopped. I know from a book written by a German officer after the war, that this skirmish created a long delay. The rest of the cyclists company had shot at the Germans and during this exchange Captain Tătăranu was wounded and evacuated. Bădulescu took over the command. My small group lost contact with the company and the division.

In my report three days after the action, I wrote: "The, Germans started machine gunning us from their armored cars. In the dark they could not tell where we were. Their bullets passed over our heads. I took advantage of the dark and with my soldiers, we crouched around the village houses. In silence we came to open fields and took a northeast direction."[14]

---

[14] In 2009, his grandson Nicholas would reenact these events for a film documentary in the exact locations mentioned in his diary.

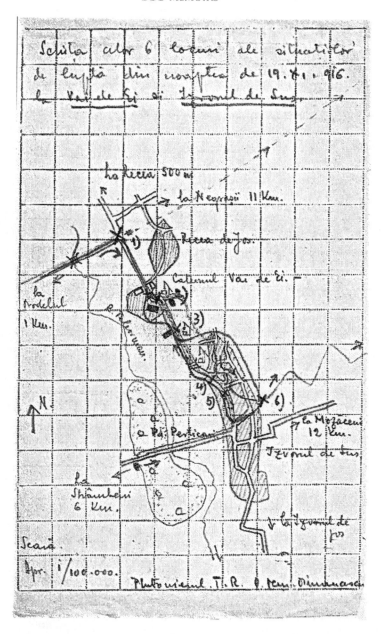

Page from DD's war diary showing skirmishes against Germans at Izvorul de Sus (Teleorman River valley)

RETREAT

All night we walked in hiding, once-in-a-while we found a Romanian military unit to which I asked to join. No one wanted to accept my offer. In the village of Stefan cel Mare, we came to the Headquarters of the 2nd Division, commanded by General Alexandru Socec and I presented myself to him. He had his office in a small peasant house and he worked at a table which was dimly lit by a kerosene lamp. I related to him all that had happened and put myself at his disposal. He thanked me, but told me to go and find my own division. He did not know its whereabouts either.

Around his small headquarters was a mass of troops in great disorder. If the Germans had advanced a little faster they would have caught them. One, thing that impressed me in those days was the presence of so many scattered soldiers or groups of soldiers lost from their units. All were anxious not to be captured, and all were looking for their units. Everyone, like myself, kept asking the whereabouts of their divisions. I asked about the 1st Cavalry Division or the cyclists but no one knew.

Among these lost groups the rumor had spread that preparations were being made for a great battle along the banks of the Argeş and Neajlov rivers in-order-to defend Bucharest. On the lower end of this front was the Russian army which had arrived from Dobrogea but which no one could count on. I figured that if our division would fight for the defense of our Capital, it would do so on the northern flank. All during my march eastward through the fields, I tried to find the flank. At the same time, I told myself, if the German advanced guard caught me from behind, I would not have a chance. Therefore I traced a straight line across the wide open, flat plains towards an imaginary line between Ploieşti and Cămpina,

My group's most immediate problem was food. The peasants we met in the small hamlets would not even speak to us. All their chickens and small stock had been stolen from their yards. So, we were fighting hunger as well as exhaustion. As we marched, we were in continuous visual contact with the mounted German soldiers. The Germans advancing towards Bucharest had sent out patrols out to capture all small Romanian groups that had become separated from their units. When we lay on the ground we were afraid to sleep for fear we might sleep so soundly that the enemy troops which we could see might capture us. None attacked us as they were more vulnerable than we. An infantryman against a man on horseback has an easier target.

At one point, I crossed the railroad tracks on the Bucharest-Piteşti line near Titu, my birthplace. I noticed with a heavy-heart a large number of German troops already on the station platform. I was now maybe 40 km from Bucharest where I knew that my Mother, sister and her wounded fiancé, Dr. Teodor Weber, lived. He had been wounded in the mountain village of Dragoslavele and brought to the military hospital in Bucharest. I was tempted to enter the capital to see my family but I resisted my personal impulse and continued to withdraw with my soldiers.

As we got nearer the Ploieşti-Campina line I could see in daytime a long black cloud rising from the oil fields on a shallow hill where the wells had been set on fire so that they would not be captured by the enemy. At night it was a frightening spectacle with huge flames rising skyward. We were now between this wall of fire and the German wave of troops pushing up from behind. Suddenly to my surprise we encountered a car with an English officer whose name I recall well as Colonel John Norton-Griffiths. Behind him were several trucks with Romanian soldiers. Norton-Griffiths' had a blown out tire. In perfect French he informed me that he was the leader of a group setting fire to the oil wells and other installations. He was sent, I found out much later, by British Intelligence to prevent the German army from getting those vital fuel and food materials. When we spoke, I mentioned that I had been told that the best method to destroy an oil well to take large industrial sized screwdrivers and to wedge them upside down deep into the well's pipe. Dropped in the right place, the screwdriver completely de-joints the gears and makes them unworkable. This made it almost impossible for the well to be repaired easily.

Taking me and my group with him to demonstrate to his team how to execute this method, we worked fast. But neither then nor now do I know how many oil wells were destroyed by this method. The large heavy-duty screwdrivers successfully sealed off each oil-well. At the end of the war I found out it took the Germans two years to repair the damage we did and get them back in working condition. More than 640,000,000 gallons of oil were set afire. During this time Norton-Griffiths gave us food. He then asked me to take my group to defend the railway between Ploieşti and Campina so that they had freer communication and movement.

We were taken there by truck. There we found another infantry unit executing the mission given to me by Norton-Griffiths. Meanwhile, the advance guard of the German army were nearing Ploieşti and I could hear rifle shots exchanged between them and our own troops. After some time I realized that my presence at the railway station would not be any use so I left with my group. We went towards the center of the town stopping at each house to ask for food to take with us. One house had a sign on the wall with the name "Attorney Nazopol." We went in the yard and rang the bell. A lady opened the door and said she was Mrs. Nazopol. She said her husband was an officer and away at the war somewhere. When I begged her to give me a set of his underwear to change, she said he had taken all his clothes with him. At my insistence, she offered to give me some of her lingerie, which she did. With her permission, I went quickly to take a shower. I left my dirty clothes on the floor and put on the ones she gave and then my military uniform. During this interlude, my soldiers had collected food and coats. It was already December and we were all still wearing our summer uniforms and everyone was dreaming of heavy coats which were soon "obtained" at Ploieşti. We left town and took the road to Buzău. This road was overcrowded with withdrawing convoys.

We made our way through open fields and narrow dirt roads, taking a northerly direction to Buzău. We walked and walked, by-passing the town and going towards Râmnicu Sărat. In the distance I could now see Russian cavalry patrols moving southward. Soon a rumor spread that our Russian Tsarist allies would arrive in mass and stop the advancing Germans. Greatly encouraged, we arrived at Rămnicu Sărat and found the town full of mounted Cossacks. They were going from house to house looking for alcoholic drinks. We moved swiftly among them until we found the house of my Uncle Anton Antonescu, my grandmother's brother. His yard was full of horses left by the Russian soldiers. They were still saddled and also had saddlebags attached.

I was received with great joy by Aunt Aurelie. I suggested that for her safety she leave and come with me to Moldavia. But she said she wanted to stay and take care of Uncle Anton unaware of the tragic fate that awaited. Their devoted Transylvanian maid cooked a good hot meal for me and my soldiers from a hidden supply of food. We ate in the attic so the Russians would not see us. She also prepared a hot bath for me and a set of under clothes belonging to a cousin who was about my size. I felt like a new man and my morale and that of my soldiers was lifted. After twenty-four hours rest we continued our march in the direction of Focşani. We walked along pathways parallel to the main road and railway both of which were overcrowded with troops.

In this area the traffic was even more jammed by Russian Cossacks going to Rămnicul Sărat where there was more rumoring about a big battle in preparation at Buzău. This great battle never materialized. As the Romanians troops arrived at Rămnicul Sărat, some received the order to remain there and for others to go far north towards Siret.

Arriving at Focşani, I went directly to my aunt's house which was near the railway station. To my great surprise I found my Mother there! Also my sister, Dr. Weber and my brother still a student at the Military School which was being evacuated to Botoşani. By luck they were making a stop at Focşani. We held a family council. Each one had thought the others lost. Because, we were all pessimistic and could not see how Moldavia could be saved from German occupation, we took a decision. They would try by any means to get to Russia and from there to Paris.

None of us wanted to live under German occupation nor to live as refugees in Russia. We then parted keeping the vague hope of seeing Paris. My aunt fed me and my soldiers just as we had been fed at Râmnicul Sărat. She gave us a supply of food and some of the clothes belonging to her sons who were at the front. Just before taking leave of her, she received the news that her middle son had been killed. My Mother, my sister and Dr. Weber who was on a stretcher managed to get to the railway station at Focșani and to board a military train to Iași. With a heavy heart I parted from them all and took back to "wandering" the road northward with my soldiers. Winter hit us hard. No one remembered one so cold. The only benefit was it stopped the Germans from advancing.

In retrospect the first phase of the war had ended. Looking at it now, after so many years and in spite of our defeats, the best of news was that it had not ended with a fatal disaster.

؇؇؇

DIFFICULT TIMES

We were all going towards Moldavia with the hope that we might be able to stop the Germans somewhere north of Focșani. In a small railway station I met an officer who told me that he had seen our Division heading north. He advised me to wait for an opportunity to get on a train. This I did but cannot remember the details of how we traveled. The train was very slow and stopped at every small station. But eventually we arrived at Botoșani where we were ordered to get off. I immediately went to report to the commander of the garrison who told me the good news that our Division and the Cyclists Regiment were located at Dumbrăveni 30 km to the west. I obtained right away a telephone connection to the 1st Cavalry Division where I had many friends among the officers. They said they would send trucks to fetch us.

As we arrived, a soldier from our company was waiting at the edge of the village. We got out of the trucks and lined up as if ready for a march. With him leading the way we entered the village. He led us to a house where the rest of the company was waiting with our Commander Captain Bădulescu. He honored us by ordering the soldiers to present arms and we marched in front of them in a parade step. It was more than a dream. After he counted us and updated his reports, we were lodged in the remaining houses of Dumbrăveni village. Most houses were occupied by a cavalry regiment. In the center of the village there was a two story house which belonged to the administrative staff of Prince Ion Ghica's estates. This was taken for Cavalry Divisional Headquarters.

After we settled down and had exchanged our stories since we were parted at Izvorul de Sus. Captain Bădulescu took me to Headquarters where I was received with effusion. They all believed I was lost, dead or a prisoner. "Jamborel," as the Division's officers had nicknamed me, had returned.

The company was left with only two officers, Captain Bădulescu and Lieutenant Aslan. Then after a new reorganization we were left with only three companies. The third one was assigned to me though I was still an N.C.O. with reduced term. My documents with my promotion were buried somewhere at the Ministry of War on somebody's desk. The reorganization of the army and of our units, called now the Detachment of Cyclists (without bicycles), was done in very orderly manner in our area. After an anxious life during the withdrawal it seemed now as if we were living in a summer resort. We were sleeping well and eating well.

The peasant houses in Dumbrăveni (Moldavia) seemed to me of a lower standard than the peasant houses in Muntenia (Wallachia). In one house, Cpt. Bădulescu and Lt. Aslan arranged a corner in their room where the officers could play poker. Luckily I was lodged with a French veterinary surgeon who had been attached to our division. We each had a very clean room decorated on the walls with embroidered mats in red. We spent the evenings together which was a special opportunity to practice speaking French. He had piles of magazines but not one book.

The officers from the cyclist detachment ate at the Division's mess hall. Given my holding the lowest rank, my daily menu was fried chicken necks and wings. The chicken breasts and legs went to the senior officers. In addition I had to sit at the end of the table.

It was a pastime of mine to make a daily menu with colored illustrations and once-in-a-while my complaints were among the jokes. One of these jokes was that I expected, from day to day, the chicken wings to grow and the necks to multiply. The Commanding General understood my "complaint" and ordered that I should be served first. I was so embarrassed at this honor that I continued helping myself to necks and wings! My menus were in great demand and never got to keep one for myself.

Across from the Divisional Headquarters was the old home of the land-wealthy Boyard and highly cultured Leon Ghica. It was furnished beautifully and in good taste. He had a billiard room and a living room where bridge was played after supper. Though he continued to live his patriarchal life in this beautiful home, it also lodged the Commander of the Division who allowed no one else to enter the house.

What was special was that the French government had sent a large contingent of officers and engineers to retrain the Romanian forces. They were under the command of General Henri Mathias Berthelot. New equipment and arms had arrived, too.

The best part of the day was when we were taught the handling of modern machine-guns which were given to us and the handling of the dangerous French-designed hand grenades. To shoot with a machine-gun gives a wild feeling of destroying something. We collected empty bottles, set them up and then tried to hit them with one burst on the trigger. The use of the hand grenades was only taught to the officers by a French officer who had learned a little Romanian. At the edge of the village we dug a trench and from there, in a standing position, we threw them towards an imaginary enemy,

The skill in handling the grenade was to throw it in a three step movement immediately after it was activated. First, take the grenade in the right hand with the arm stretched; second, hand towards the back and count one, two, three; and then throw at four. It would then explode. At the first step, one hit the activating button with the left palm. By repeating these instructions many times, I had raw blisters on the left palm. To alleviate the pain, I tied a small board to my left hand with which to hit the button. But when we started the exercises with live grenades, the grenade caught in the board and I had just enough time to pull it off and throw it in front of me. It was a miracle that the grenade exploded on the edge of the trench! I was so frightened I fell to the ground. The French officer thought I was dead but in-fact I lived to throw many more.

When we were sent back to the battlefront, I carried two sacks of grenades and they became my favorite weapon. Besides grenades and machine-guns we were given gas masks and French metal helmets. The gas masks were a problem for the soldiers and myself for we could not breathe with them on. Having them was a precaution against rumors that the Germans might have used gas as they had in France. We carried these masks hanging around our necks and fortunately never had to use them.

Occasionally I was given leave and I went to Botoşani which was a small Jewish town. It had nothing special, but in those times when so many things were lacking if one knew where to go one could find everything. The townspeople were extremely polite and respectful among themselves and with us. For me, it was a big godsend again to find there my mother, sister and brother. Because Moldavia was small it increased the possibility of meeting but I was still amazed that it happened. My mother, sister and brother-in-law had left Focşani but were obliged to get off at Botoşani. My brother had already been relocated there with his Military School. Though the town was overcrowded with refugees, my sister being a doctor in the army, was lodged immediately in the home of a Jewish family who had a pharmacy on the first floor. The second floor had been requisitioned by the army for important people. My sister was counted among them from the first day she arrived as she started working at the Military Hospital installed in the Town Hall. I did not take advantage of my family's position but when possible I would go to see them and have a good meal. It didn't matter that we had all decided not long before to meet in Paris, here we were settled in northern Moldavia.

News from the front was not too good regarding the temporary calm we experienced. More Russian armies were still planning to enter through Moldavia. But already, there was speculation about what would happen with a Spring and Summer offensive if the Germans might conquer this last half of our country. There was talk of a "Death Triangle" in which what would have been left of our army was completely annihilated in a final battle. The Royal Family and the Government, caught in the middle of this triangle, would wait to be captured or killed. Another variation was that what was left of the army would take the Royal Family and the Government across the Prut and Nistru rivers to take refuge in Russia.

However, the King and the Government were convinced we should resist on the crests of the Moldavian Carpathian Mountains and along the Siret River. Fortunately morale in the fast revitalized army was high. Besides the older ones who had experienced the fateful withdrawal from Wallachia, the army had grown with many new recruits. Many of the young men from Wallachia had taken refuge in Moldavia knowing well that they would be drafted eventually and sent to fight. A component of the recruits were the "cercetașii" (Boy Scouts) who were children not obliged to do military duty but had joined one regiment or another that came to Moldavia. Others came organized in small groups. All the country heard stories of the bravery of the 23 year-old teacher, Ecaterina Teodoriu, who with thirty "cercetașii" helped defend a bridge the summer before on the Jiu River north of Craiova thus delaying the German advance. They did not withdraw and were killed to the last one. Ecaterina Teodoriu became a national symbol of courage among Romanians.

In the village of Sculeni, near Iași, the "cercetașii" were given a grammar school building where they could gather. The majority of the boy scout recruits found Professor Mugur as he had taken refuge as well as Professor Nedelcu who taught Latin at the Gheorghe Lazăr High School in Bucharest. The latter had taken charge at my first meetings of "cercetașii." He had a heart of gold and was adored by the scouts. Now at Sculeni, he organized and gave life to the "cercetasii" center which thanks to him had become independent of any outside help. He was strictly against any public begging and had the scouts plant vegetables on empty lots around the school. They had a yard with chickens and even a few cows so they quickly became self supporting.

Unbeknownst to me and at the suggestion of the Commander of the Division, Captain Bădulescu proposed me for a decoration. I do not know how it was done but the "Military Virtue Medal" came very quickly. This honor was intended to recognize the fact that I had delayed the advance of the Germans army at Izvorul de Sus and Val de Ei thus allowing the regiment time to be retreat. I considered that this merit was due to the whole platoon and I refused to take it except on behalf of the whole cyclist unit. I kept it in my pocket for the remainder of the war.

The Dumbrăveni interlude eventually ended. The 1st Cavalry Division was dismounted and became an infantry division. We left as "cyclists" in name only no longer encumbered with actual bicycles. The French veterinarian was recalled to France. Before he left he sold me his French uniform complete with kepi. A military tailor altered it to my size but the jacket remained short as required for the French. The Romanian army had adopted the blue color for its uniforms but the one I had bought was a lighter blue. People who did not know me thought I was a French officer. I hadn't much choice as some of my belongings had long been lost with the regiments train during the withdrawal from Izvorul de Sus. Thus equipped I left Dumbrăveni with the entire Division which was headed to the front on the foothills of the Carpathians at Oituz where there was already a climatic battle fully engaged.

The German army had been held not far away in Mărășești and now they were attempting to break through from the west in Transylvania and across the Carpathian Mountains into Moldavia at Oituz and Târgu Ocna. It was August. A heat-wave was bearing down on all of us. We were taken by train to Onești and from there we were sent over a low barren hill to the hamlet of Poiana-lui-Boboc. This time we had one more officer, my brother, who had finished his Military School and had been promoted Sub-Lieutenant. Meanwhile, the rank of 1st Lieutenant had been given to me. So we arrived at Poiana-lui-Boboc with two Dimancescu Lieutenants: Dimitri and Ioan. The company commander also bestowed on my brother the nickname "Jamborel." Soon I became "Jamborel the Elder" and he "Jamborel the Younger." Mother had given him her other ear ring with the same loving plea to bring it back. My great worry was that my brother might be wounded or killed before me. I constantly kept an eye on him following all his actions. He had been given the reserve platoon, so that when ordered into the fight, I was ahead of him and he would be a few steps behind.

At Poiana-lui-Boboc, a wonderful piece of news reached us. Our former commander, Captain Nicu Tătăranu, wounded in Izvorul de Sus and taken prisoner from a hospital in Bucharest, managed to escape. He crossed the German lines and rejoined our side. He had made the crossing in the area of Oituz Valley not far from where we were. Nothing was said at that time about his courageous act. Instead, some said that the only explanation was that the Germans helped him to escape in-order to bring us a proposal. This supposition was quite false. When I met him later at Iaşi, he told me the Romanian volunteer ladies at the hospital where he was prisoner helped him to escape and hid him in Bucharest. He let his hair and beard grow and dressed in peasant costume traveled from village to village until he arrived behind the front. After many long and weary miles he found there was not longer a continuous front line. Gaps existed through which it was possible to pass. Peasants and shepherds from the mountainous Oituz Valley helped him. He had no contact with the Germans since his escape from the hospital. There were days and nights when he had no food at all but he was careful to be near a stream of water. Eventually, his bravery was recognized and he received a medal and a promotion. Many years later, in 1930, he was sent to Paris as the Military Attaché.

Poiana-lui-Boboc, a small cluster of farmhouses was located at the foot of a hill called Coşna or in topographical terms "Hill 789," the number corresponding to its height in meters. Over a several week period in July and August, the high ground had been captured by troops of the élite Würt-temburg Regiment. They expected this to be the breakthrough place for German armies finally to sweep into northern Moldavia. When we arrived the treeless crest-line laced with trenches was on the verge of being lost by the 9th Rosiori Regiment. The order was given me to join the counter attack and with extraordinary energy we struggled up on top of the steep dusty hill forcing the Germans back. This was only temporary as the Germans prepared to counter attack by launching an artillery attack against our lines

In our turn we were obliged to retreat to the village with the Germans in pursuit. An infantry unit arrived to help us and we started counter-attacking before the enemy reached the village. At least six times we were fighting up the steep dusty hillside to the crest-line, then retreat back down, then up. The heat was terrible. Again our soldiers conquered Coşna Hill 789 not knowing how this back and forth "game" would end. Another "Hunters" regiment was dispatched north of Coşna and with a surge of bravery fought the Germans at Cireşoaia Hill and pushed them back.

Ziua 8-a a bătăliei dela Oituz.
Lupte pe frontul Div. 7, 1 Cav., 6, 8, 12 şi 3.
Detaş. col. Alexiu intervine şi opreşte înaintarea stângei C. 18 Arm. Rez. pe liziera S. Muncelul—D. Podişu.

Ziua 9-a a bătăliei dela Oituz.
Div. 71 atacă Div. 6-a şi o dă înapoi, contra-atacă fără reuşită. Div. 218 I, atacă D. 12-a, care respinge atacul.
Detaşam. col. Alexiu luptă contra stângei C. 18 Arm. Rez. germ.

Ziua 10-a a bătăliei dela Oituz.
Lupte pe frontul Div. 7, 1 Cav. 6, 12 şi 3. Gl. Averescu vrea să ia ofensiva în direcţia Muncelui cu Div. 1-a, dar g-lul Grigorescu se opune.

Bombardament reciproc de artilerie.

C. 8 Arm. A. U. (Div. 70, 71, 117), atacă D. 7, 1 Cav. şi 6-a.
Div. 117 I. cucereşte D. Coşna (789)—703

General Averescu's Report of the Coşna Battle

What enraged our commandant was that we had no communication with the left flank Romanian troops along the front. The problem he confronted was an empty space along the front dominated by German machine guns. It was only years later that I found out that the officer commanding the Germans was Lieutenant Erwin Rommel[15] famed later as commander of the Afrika Korps in North Africa during World War II. As young as he was, only 22, he was given charge of 1200 men to make a breakthrough on Hill

[15] Erwin Rommel published his World War One experiences in book entitled *Attacks* in 1937. It was used as a basic training manual by the German military. That book remains in print in Europe and the United States. More than 125 pages were devoted to his war experiences as a member of the famed Württemberg Regiment in the first invasion of Romania in 1916 and its return to lead the attack at Mount Coşna, "Hill 789." In 2010, Dimitri's grandson, Nicholas, would direct the making of a documentary on these WW-I events under the title "Hill 789: The Last Stronghold" (Kogainon Films, Boston, Massachusetts); the *National Geographic Magazine* (Romanian Edition) published in 2010 a companion article based on Dimitri's memoirs.

789. A year earlier he had been charged with a mountain top breakthrough above the Vulcan Pass during the initial invasion from the North. He had become famous already on the Italian front and invented ways of using machine guns as offensive weapons. During these fierce days of battle on Mt. Coşna, he was wounded but stayed in command of his troops. It was him that my men and I confronted. During those few days and the next few to come, our Romanian forces held the line. The Germans never broke through.

While we were waiting in the hamlet for our next orders, a messenger brought an envelope addressed to Lt. Dimancescu. I took the envelope and opened it and saw that it was an order for my brother to take a patrol to that open gap in the front line and find out exactly where the Germans were located. This order seemed a death sentence. Knowing that another patrol which had left with the same mission had not returned, I did not give my brother the order but instead I left with a soldier. Telling him I was going on a reconnoitering mission, I left him the command of my soldiers.

Dimitri and his brother Ioan

Waiting until it was quite dark, we crawled up to a corner of the crest-line where there was a clump of thistles bushes. We lay facing the enemy without moving or talking. When dawn broke, a hundred yards in front of me was a German soldier lying on the ground face forward. Simultaneously, both of us took our rifles, eyed each other and fired. I saw him drop his head and realized he was dead. Simultaneously, I felt a burning in my left foot, A bullet from his rifle had pierced my leg and hit my soldier's head killing him on the spot. After a few quiet moments the Germans started an artillery bombardment all over the flat crest-line which had a length of about 500 meters and a width of about 300-400 meters. Wounded, I remained all day not making a move while the Germans continued firing until dark. Only then did I manage to crawl through a thicket behind me where there was a path linking us "cyclists" and an infantry regiment to our left.

The pain and loss of blood made me incapable of moving any further and I waited for a chance that a patrol would find me. Two infantrymen found me lying down and they dragged me to a medical post beyond Poiana-lui-Boboc. I told the two soldiers quickly what had happened and they rushed to my company to tell them where I was. Then they went back to recover my soldier, who had been killed, and brought back the dead German's helmet.

At the first aid post they cut my boot and pants which had hardened with blood on my left leg. They gave me some medicine to numb the pain and called for an ambulance to carry me to the town of Oneşti five or ten kilometers away. My orderly came from the company and remained with me, traveling in the ambulance to the hospital.

≪୬୨≫

WOUNDED

In spite of the pain, it hurt to see my special boots cut with scissors at the first aid station. When my orderly arrived and saw the state I was in, his first consoling words were that he would make me another pair of boots.

Weeks earlier, while I was in Dumbrăveni, I had been given leave to go to Iaşi and with great difficulty managed to be received by Vintilă Bratianu who was Secretary of War at the time and years later Prime Minister. He had known me in the "cercetaşii" and had been very polite in his reactions to me. I explained to him that against military orders I went over my superior's head to request of him my rights to be promoted 1st Lieutenant. While I was in his office, he ordered the decree retroactive and the payment of my salary payable from October 1916. When I returned to Dumbrăveni, I now had the right to have an orderly. I chose amongst the soldiers of my platoon the one who seemed the weakest. His name was Ghiţa Banescu, small and thin I had the impression he was not capable of holding a rifle.

59

Later on I found him to be the best cobbler and tailor. During the remainder of the campaign he kept me well shod with new boots. While we were in Rămnicul Sărat, he had managed to buy from the Russians a supply of leather bags which proved excellent for any kind of boot.

The ambulance in which I was taken to the hospital was a Ford, one of forty sent by the American Red Cross. Unfortunately it was a car made for better roads in the United States. The road we traveled was full of holes from the shelling. There wasn't the smallest bone in my body that was not shaken. Banescu held my hands telling me it was not much further to the hospital. Eventually we arrived to find that the hospital was a long tent covered with large red crosses to indicate to the enemy that it should not be bombed. I do not know if the Germans were color blind given that they targeted the hospital daily. The tent had been partly destroyed and all around it there were hundreds of men on stretchers awaiting their turn inside. In my whole life I have never heard so many sorrowful cries and never will I forget those at Onești. Most were calling for their mothers who were not there to help them.

My turn came to enter. A doctor came to examine my leg and marked in chalk on my stretcher: "Amputation." This meant cutting off either my foot or my leg. I called my orderly, Banescu, and told him to find a stretcher-bearer and take me out of the tent. Behind the hospital was a freight train by which the wounded were sent to the interior. There was a total lack of supervision and no one asked me what I was doing. This made it possible for Banescu and a fellow soldier to take me to the train and place me inside. I do not know how many doctors and interns were on the train. At each station they inspected the wagons to see if any of the wounded were in need of immediate help or to be let off at the first town which had a hospital. As for me, they decided I should get off at Bacău, a larger town 40 kilometers north.

With three other wounded men, I was sent in an ambulance to the town's hospital. By an extraordinary coincidence, the first doctor to meet us was my brother-in-law, Dr. Weber. He had recovered from his own wound and was now the chief of this first-aid post. He had been notified from the station that an ambulance was on the way and waited at the door to receive only those in need of urgent medical attention. The surprise was reciprocated when he saw me and immediately took care of me. Though not having a free bed, he put me in his own bed in a very small room. The other wounded men for whom there were no available beds were left on their stretchers along the corridors.

His first worry was to stop the onset of gangrene which required changed dressings frequently night and day. My left leg was already discolored and swollen as large as a log. I was in pain only if I moved. Any body movement gave me reflex pain in the nerves of the foot. Weber also discovered that above the left knee I had a metal splinter which penetrated the muscle but only superficially.

I have always been convinced of the phenomenon of telepathy but I have not had the opportunity to read a book on this subject. The day that I was wounded my mother felt restless all day and said to my sister she was sure that something happened to me on the front. My sister had been transferred to St. Spiridon Hospital and my mother was at Iași to be with her. Though my sister attributed my mother's restlessness to pure imagination, this did not discourage my mother. She quickly dressed and went to the War Ministry to find someone who could tell her if I were safe, wounded or dead.

In fact, there was no one at the War Ministry with records or reports about the state of the wounded. From there she went to the Army Headquarters where she was almost kicked out approaching General Brezeanu's door. Without abandoning her decision to find out if anything had happened to me, she went next to the temporary "Royal Palace" in Iași asking to be received by Prince Carol. Hearing my name, which was well known to the Palace staff, she was immediately received by his aide. In her presence, he telephoned the 1st Cavalry Division where they told him I had been wounded but no one knew where I was located. When Prince Carol came into the aide's office and was told the news, he assured my mother there was nothing to worry about. He guessed I could be in a train carrying wounded towards north Moldavia. How had my mother sensed that something had happened to me? I remember that the instant I was hit I thought of the earring mother had given to me and of my promise to bring it back.

Thanks to Dr. Weber's good care my leg was saved. He told me that the bullet had fragmented the tarsal bones and smashed the big toe of the left root, With infinite patience he managed to take out all the bits of bone and by frequently changing the dressings my leg was back to normal size. I looked with delight at the return of a healthy pink color of the skin. I could not walk yet except with the aid of crutches. Dr. Weber decided to send me to a larger hospital also in Bacău that was next to the High School.

Eventually, Captain Bădulescu, found my whereabouts and every two or three days he sent me news from the front. I cannot explain even now, after all my many travels and moves, how I succeeded in keeping one of his letters to me written from the front on 19 August 1917 to me. Here is the text:

Dear Dimancescu,

In great haste I am writing to you a few lines. Million thanks to you and your "dears" for the good wishes that you sent me for victory. After we stayed a few more days at Poiana-lui-Boboc. Because of the many losses that we suffered, we withdrew for two days in-order-to reorganize my unit after which we were attached to the 2nd Cavalry Brigade and together with a battalion from the 7th Hunters we attacked Zone 383. After four bloody attacks I was left with only four fighters from the company.

After much insistence we withdrew again to the Reserve of Marginea and tomorrow I believe that they will withdraw us again to Oneşti to keep us away from the fighting. The total losses up to now are 121 dead and wounded and 14 lightly wounded and not evacuated - a grand total of 135.

As you see the sacrifices are very large. The company has been very brave. Poor Parva has been seriously wounded on his arm while he was leading his platoon to attack. Christofor Istrate, Vasiliu, Emil and many other good men have been killed.

I am deeply saddened by the loss of our men whom shall revenge. Also Poor Vulturascu Nini and Captain Stoenescu from the 12th Roşiori Regiment are dead.

The Division will give me all the help to reorganize my unit. "Young Jamborel" is well, in good health and I will take care of him. I also received a letter from Aslan from Iaşi. He is at the St. Spiridon Hospital. With love and impatience to see you again. Please convey my regards to your dear ones and quick recovery.

As your brother, Capt. Bădulescu

Something else saddened me very much. When the soldiers recovered the body of the German I killed, they searched through his pockets and found a letter from his daughter saying she was knitting him a pair of socks and would give them to him when he came home at Christmas. The thought tormented me that I had killed a man who had a family expecting him to return home. The fact that he was an enemy and the roles could have been reversed did not comfort me for years. Not even now am I reconciled to the idea of the unfairness with which men kill each other in wartime.

The new hospital to which I was sent in Bacău was in the largest high school,[16] which was an inspiring building with large rooms, high ceilings and windows of large dimensions. It was extremely clean and everything was working fine. Rather, it was not a hospital for serious cases or emergency surgery but lighter and intermediary wounds.

The hospital was administered by a group of "high society" women. They were all very competent and all dressed in spotless white uniforms. They were doing a good job but were very authoritative. The majority were the wives of superior officers from the 2nd Army Headquarters whose chief was General Averescu who had led the ill-fated cross-Danube invasion of Bulgaria a year before. This tie with the general command meant that any request from the hospital was immediately fulfilled.

I was settled in an extra bed in a large room with thirty other wounded men. I was the only officer in that room. My share of misery was the change of bandage dressings done every morning. It was done by a nurse who was a nun. The worst part was pulling the bandages which were stuck to the skin because of the clotting blood. This was torture and I would have run away from the hospital but I could not walk. In this hospital my orderly was not allowed to stay. Fortunately, the nurse made a discovery. If she poured gasoline on the bandage the blood clots dissolved and I did not feel pain when she pulled it.

Daily a tall strong nurse brought me a pair of crutches. She helped me up out of bed and fitted the crutches under my arms. I went up and down the corridor on one leg and crutches. I could not manage this very long so I was brought back to bed. I was propped up on two large pillows where I spent my time drawing caricatures. I created a series of heads on military bodies, of old men, young men, nurses and the volunteer ladies. This pastime attracted the attention of one of the volunteer ladies who adopted me in the French custom of being a "godmother." Now I was no longer a lonely man. But while all my family had fled luckily to Moldavia, my new god-

---

[16] Known today as "The National Ferdinand-I College" it stands unchanged in Bacău as does a house next to it where he was moved to recuperate.

mother was jealous of any affection shown to me and poured countless attentions on me.

She knew very well General Averescu so that through her the commander of the 2nd Army was informed of the health of a young officer and she repeated to him the tales she heard of the front. I disliked all this attention and would have liked to move back to the hospital where my brother-in-law served but there was no room for me there. I was not a serious medical case.

In the middle of this treeless square near the school was an anti-craft gun. Every day at exactly 11 a.m. a German plane would fly over the town on reconnaissance flights and the anti-craft gun would fire at it, determined to bring it down. The noise of the gun was deafening and all the wounded panicked before and after 11 a.m. The windows and the walls shook and for some, as in my case, too, the shaking of the whole building was enough to induce terrible pains in my leg.

One day there was a great commotion in the hospital. Queen Marie had come to visit. She went from room to room, ours being the last one she entered. She started with the bed from the other end of the ward so that I was the last one she visited. She went from bed to bed talking separately to every wounded man. By a system of her own, she held in her left hand a paper the size of a postcard on which she had the name of each wounded man in each room with a few details such as if he were married or not, if his wife was in Moldavia or Wallachia, or if he had children. They were all flabbergasted that she knew their names and, in some cases she had news to share about their families.

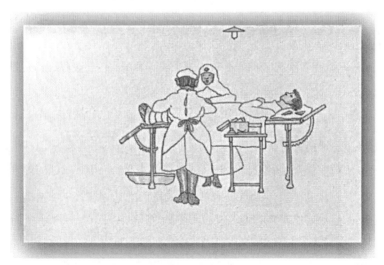

Visiting-card-sized self-portrait by DDD in Bacău hospital

When she came to my bed, she recognized me immediately as the former "cercetaşi." I told her that my mother had had news about me through Prince Carol. She answered that now she would personally give mother news about me and tell her I was perfectly well. I had in my hand about a dozen visiting cards on the back of which I had made some drawings depicting "The Story of a Wounded Soldier" who, once healed, returned to the front. I told her I would give them to her to give to Prince Carol. Not only did she take the cards but all the portraits I had made of various people.

In her own memoirs, Queen Marie described her visit to a remote treatment center for wounded and dying.

"I wandered about amongst the miserable, dark little huts in which the sick were huddled together, giving them sweets and cigarettes, and brandy and tea to the most ill! The misery of those improvised hospitals defies description. I tried to bring them as much consolation and encouragement as I could, giving each man a little cross to wear round his neck. Many grateful eyes looked up at me and I felt recompensed. But what suffering hidden away in those huts! At one place there was a low mound at the top of which stood a wee church, and the bell was tinkling like a cracked voice. On the bank beneath the church all those who were not actually dying had been brought and laid out in the sunshine, a parade of skeletons. It was very hot and there were hundreds of them; they all wanted me at once and kept crying for me from all corners at the same time, stretching out bony hands as though to grasp me and hold me fast.

"I spent a long time in the hospital, which is quite full. There were terrible wounds. I must say it was an awful moment, and the place was full of screams and groans. Seeing all the suffering, the immense folly of all this war struck me again why, why, why? And such young creatures, and so mutilated; arms and legs missing perforated lungs and bowels, paralyzed spines, trepanned skulls, etc.; oh, what cruel folly."[17]

After a while, I do not remember how long and why, I received an order to go to St. Spiridon Hospital in the Moldavian Capital of Iaşi. When I arrived, I was sent to a section of the hospital for nearly recovered wounded. Imagine my joy to find there my sister and my mother! My sister had been transferred there when I left Dumbrăveni and of course mother had gone with her. Nowhere in the town could she find a room so they settled me in the attic of the hospital. With empty boxes they made a sort of screen in a corner of the attic with two stretchers for beds. Between the

---

[17] Marie Queen of Roumania, *The Story of My Life*, Cassell, London, 1935.

stretchers they put a wooden crate as a table and my sister paid an electrician to bring up a wire for a lamp placed on the table. During the daily round mother was a voluntary nurse. I do not remember how long I was there but my stay was extended as I had jaundice. There were many cases of this particularly infectious jaundice said to have been brought into Moldavia by Russian soldiers. I was given a medicine in liquid form which was very unpleasant and hard to swallow. Fortunately, the wounds of the left leg started to heal very quickly. My sister sprayed them with sulphur powder which apparently helped the healing.

When I was almost recovered from jaundice and the wounds were closed I was evacuated from Iași and sent to a small mountain village somewhere in Moldavia. I did not know its name nor its location on a map. At the railroad station, I was met by the village priest, a young man, in whose care I was left. He arranged through official channels to correspond with the 1st Division to send me my orderly, Ghiţa Banescu. Lodged in a peasant's house, I had one room with two beds, one for me and one for him. The priest came regularly from one o'clock until six o'clock. I could not get rid of him! He brought, a backgammon set but not once to the end of my convalescence did he manage to beat me.

My life was much simplified from the fact that at Iași I had been given a strict diet of baked potatoes. Day after day there were baked potatoes and again baked potatoes. I was not allowed to drink milk but Banescu had found some grapes in the village. Finally when I thought I was well, I obtained through the village priest the authorization to rejoin my unit at the front. I could walk with the help of a cane but I was still very weak. The Cyclist Detachment, which had been almost annihilated in my absence, had been retired to a hamlet near the railroad at Tecuci-Iași. There I found my brother lodged in a grammar school with two large rooms and one smaller room which had been the chancery.

In the larger room were housed the soldiers of his platoon as well as mine and he and I shared the chancellery. There were no mattresses, pillows or blankets. The village had been evacuated by its inhabitants with the exception of a few old men and women who refused to leave. The company had been brought here to rehabilitate new recruits with our old soldiers, too few of whom remained alive. The newcomers had to be instructed in the way of "elite troops" as we presumed ourselves to be. Field instruction was given by my brother and I gave the moral education of the Company.

I still walked with difficulty and I did not like to be seen with crutches or the cane, both lent to me by the hospital. When I went out of the school I just walked around the building. I do not remember going into the deserted village.

RUSSIAN WITHDRAWAL

But there was another and bigger danger. It was Fall of 1917 and the Russian Revolution loomed. The Russian troops who shared the front with us warned us all the time that they would withdraw. They were encouraged by their re-educated 'comrades' to lay down their arms, throw away their equipment and return to their homes in Russia. They were no longer executing their officers' orders. Some of their superior officers promised our Commander that they would participate in certain battles but that they were unable to force their soldiers to be active on the front.

My own efforts at raising military morale with my soldiers were hard due to the complete disorder in the Russian sectors. It was very difficult to talk about political philosophy with young soldiers who had no more education than grammar school. My primary goal was to explain that it was "your duty to chase the Germans from Wallachia and return to your homes." The majority were the sons of peasants from the Dumbovița county north of Bucharest. News from the Division and other neighboring units were not at all encouraging. On Hill 789 near Oituz daily butchery was continuing.

But instead of being sent there, one day we received an order to go not to Oituz but 100 kilometers east along the Siret River in-order-to make a liaison between our 1st Division and the 30th Russian Division which was at the point of open fraternization with the German troops facing them along the stalled front to the south. Some of the Russian Soldiers were getting out of their trenches and taking bags of bread to the Germans in exchange for bottles of brandy and cigarettes. We had no way to stop them.

It was said that General Constantin Cristescu had given a secret order to Romanian troops to shoot any Russian soldier that fraternized with German soldiers -- and of course to shoot any German who met them. In my duty as liaison officer I had another task to perform with the Russians. Almost every hour I sent a report to the Division. These reports were acknowledged by formal notes or personal letters. Here is one I received from Major Pleniceanu.

December 8, 1917

Sublieut. Dimancescu,

The general has seen your report and has sent it to the Cavalry Corps. Seeing the difficulty of the situation of the officers' Russian comrades, the General says for you to discreetly tell them that they shall be received

by us when they wish to come. Please be very careful as not to start any discussions with the Russian soldiers in which they could be angered.
Be as reserved as possible. This should be recommended to the Romanian soldiers who are with you. It might be good, for your own sake, to take one sergeant and one soldier under the form of secretaries etc. so that nothing should be guessed.
Let me know if you need anything, cigarettes, etc.

Major S. Pleniceanul

This letter, sent to me in an envelope marked "strictly secret, confidential, personal," is still in my possession. My principal preoccupation was to watch over the growing fraternization between Germans and Russians and the risk of contaminating our soldiers.

A soldier, who was from Bessarabia and spoke perfect Russian, served as my interpreter. As a plain soldier dressed in a Russian uniform, he was accepted in the midst of the Russian soldiers. This is how one day he happened to overhear that a group of Russian soldiers had decided to kill me. In fact, they had already shot some Russian officers who had refused to execute orders given by the soldiers to their officers! Of course I reported this plot to the Division and immediately I received the order to return to the Division Command quarters. I was replaced as liaison officer by my brother who was now in the same dangerous situation. Nothing happened to either of us as we had made a number of friendships among the Russian officers, friends that we bought with țuica (plum brandy) and cigarettes. We both kept detailed official diaries of those days.

During our stay in this area on the left bank of the Siret River, which dominated the region, my brother and I found a half demolished brick house. One room and half the roof was intact. We settled in the one room. The German front was far enough away not to be able to reach us with their field artillery. Thus we lived in peace in the small house having the feeling that we had a home. From up the hill we could see through binoculars the German sector facing us, and behind them a road with peasant carts. Neither the German nor we wished to stir up the quietness of this area. The Germans, at least, were sure that we would not attack them due to the situation of the Russian troops on our left.

To improve my reports, I invented a type of map with circles which became smaller in perspective at a certain scale. Every day I made such a map which I sent to the Divisional Headquarters in-order-to flag the changes that I noticed in the German sector. At first I did this as an amusement but at the Division my maps were so much appreciated that they were requested as an order.

From the half-house in which I stayed with my brother, I moved to a hut. The troops who had occupied this territory before us had dug a chain of trenches that was very well planned. At certain intervals from the trenches was a hut where at night the respective unit could sleep. Each one, by imagination and improvisation, had transformed these into pleasant homes. Mine was small, just large enough for two men. It had a heating stove with a hotplate to cook on. Between the two beds was a table and a chair. My first thought was to include my brother but he decided to remain with his troop. I had no difficulty in finding a 'tenant': Colonel Bubi Ghica who was part of a team from the Commander of the Division of Cavalry. He was a real "character." When he went to bed he undressed completely and put on a nightgown long enough to reach the floor. On the yoke was embroidered the coat of arms of the Ghica family. The nightgown was almost in rags as were the others he had with him. I went to bed dressed, merely removing my boots. In case of an alarm, I wanted to be ready.

Such an occurrence happened one night when I received the order to leave at once with my platoon back towards Mărășești in-order-to keep cover for a battery hidden under some trees. At about three hundred feet from us was a large hut which could have sheltered the entire platoon. The battery was firing continuously day and night. The enemy had guessed the direction but not its place exactly. They were returning our fire but not really aiming well. They were trying to lengthen or shorten their aim. I was afraid they would soon hit the hut where I remained with my men during these exchanges. Behind us, almost 200 meters from the battery were some empty trenches. We moved our "domicile" but just when I thought we'd reached a safer shelter, I received an order to return to the trenches on the banks of the Siret River from where we had come.

Ghica suffered from insomnia and to amuse himself he would talk to me even when I was dead tired and fell asleep. He had a thick stick with which he would bang the edge of the bed to keep me awake and also to scare the rats which ran freely around us. Actually, Ghica was very interesting to talk to. He was well educated, well read and he knew many Romanian and French personalities. Although I lost a lot of sleep, sometimes I listened attentively in his tales. The subject that interested him greatly was the sadness and the calamity of the Romanian people who were fated to be at the junction of three great powers: Russia, Turkey and Austro-Hungary.

Not only Ghica but all of Romania was astonished at the way the Russian colossus fell apart. The Russian army had been the most powerful in Europe but nobody realized that this army was a vast conglomerate of simple men who had no notion of patriotism nor of a national ideal. In their simplicity they considered themselves only as the Tsar's soldiers. This belief constituted the sole cohesive element of the Russian army. When the Tsar disappeared in the midst of the October Revolution of 1917, the army became a headless amorphous mass with no sense of where to turn. When Lenin came into power, the soldiers referred to him as the Tsar "Vladimir."

Similarly, though the Austro-Hungarian troops were showing signs of weakness, we could not imagine that their Empire would collapse quite so soon. One thing certain for us was that up to the end of 1917, the Russian army was no help to us. They had withdrawn in 1916 from the southern Dobrogea region. Then they then refused to take the offensive in defending Bucharest. Now, completely disorganized, they were ready to return home. Some had already gone. They went to railroad stations behind the lines and asked for trains home. If this demand was not satisfied they would break the windows. In the end they were obliged to walk, stealing whatever they could on the way. Village people ran away from them as of barbarians who had invaded our country and not as soldiers of an allied army.

We were between the front where we were fighting the Germans and the Russian army which was pillaging the villages. How we succeeded in maintaining ourselves and came out of this situation alive was a miracle.

Our Western allies, the French and English could no longer help us. Supplies lines, that started from the far Russian northern port of Murmansk, allowed the French to send ammunition, food and medicine. There they were loaded onto trains which were supposed to arrive in Moldavia but all these precious goods were unloaded and left in fields near Russian railway depots inaccessible to our armies. The Russian Revolution had stalled all activity.

Then, too, there was also a French-led allied army at Salonika commanded by General Maurice Sarrail. This army was supposed to attack Bulgaria when we entered the war. But for many reasons, this army did not move for two years. Knowing of this, I could not give genuine encouragement to my soldiers. The best I could do was not to speak of the future. Somehow, somewhere in the heart there was the hope that we would come out well form this mess.

By a Royal Decree of November 11, 1917, I was awarded the "Star of Romania" with "spades" (for war service) for "the remarkable bravery and élan" with which I advanced with my platoon at Coșna on August 8, 1917, through the dense fire of an enemy who had entered the trenches of Poiana lui Boboc.

"Attacking with the bayonet one company after another, thus holding the enemy back until the arrival of the reserves. He was especially distinguished on the 9th of August when he executed an exceptionally dangerous reconnoitering mission and from which he returned with a painful wound in-order-to bring valuable and precise news."

Later, on the basis of a recommendation made by General Mircescu, who had commanded the Cavalry Division, King Ferdinand wanted to give me the "Order of Mihai Viteazul." having heard of this intention, I refused this honor at Oituz as I believed that every man there deserved the medal and not just a single individual.

King Ferdinand found a new formula. He agreed to give the "Furajeră" Medal of the Order of Mihai Viteazul to all those who fought at Coșna. Amongst those I was included and only many years later in 1931, through Royal Decree was I given the right to wear the Furajeră. By this time I was no longer in the army so I did not have the pleasure of wearing this distinction.

The Russian Tsarist Government had awarded me the medal of the "Order of St. Stanislas" with spades. The amusing detail of this order was that it carried a monthly pension of 7 rubles. Six months later, I did not receive any rubles but a rather pretty medal and a Royal Decree from King Ferdinand giving me the right to wear it. On January 21, 1917, King Ferdinand had also awarded me the "Virtutea Militară" for the courage and devotion to duty shown during the night of 16-17 November, 1916. This was usually given to soldiers and noncommissioned officers which I was at that time, my commission not having yet arrived. This meant that when I was finally promoted, I was one of the few officers to have been decorated with the "Virtutea Militară." The Decree was signed by Vintilă Brătianu, War Secretary, who earlier had expedited my promotion.

I was now 21 years old.

❧

1918

At the beginning of 1918, there no signs anywhere that our fate would change. At that time, the Romanian Government's attitude towards the Russian troops still on Romanian soil, was very well expressed in a manifest printed in Russian and Romanian and signed by the 1st Army Commander, General Eremia Grigorescu. This manifest was to be distributed to the Russian troops by their Generals. As I was liaison officer I took printed manifests to the Russian Commander and left him the task of distributing them to the Russian soldiers. The Commanders were a bit hostile and often reproached us for brutalizing the Russian soldiers who were committing acts of violence on our peasants. At first they did not want to distribute the manifests but after I insisted, they distributed them to the officers who sympathized with us. The text of the manifest read like this:

To the Russian troops

It is brought to the attention of the Russian units that the measures taken by the Romanian Command are not taken to stop the manifestation of Russian political beliefs of freedom neither nor to change them.

The reason for these measures have been erroneously understood by some troops thus giving our mutual enemies and ill wishers the opportunity to interpret them differently thus undermining the good friendship that always existed between the Russian and the Romanian people.

These measures have been taken not against the Russian Army but against those individuals either isolated or in groups isolated who terrorize the population by pillaging or stealing its last means of existence, against those who take control over trains without authorization and oblige the railroad employees to start the train at any unscheduled hour, against those who oppose the execution of orders given to assure food, lodging and transport on certain roads etc. with the aim of fulfilling everything in the best of conditions and with full order.

Just as it is a loss to the Romanian army and its people, it is also to the Russian army if the measures are not respected because the transportation of the Russian soldiers could only be possible by foot and food transports would be delayed and everyone would suffer.

The Romanian Command believes that real soldiers will understand the meaning of these measures and is convinced that they will stop and punish as deserved those who hide under the soldier's uniform but now act as teams of criminals, vandals and disturbers of the public order.

Do not listen to the interpretation that the enemies want to give and be sure that all has been done for the assurance of mutual interests that concern both the Romanian Army and the Russian Army.

Commander of the 1st Army
General Grigorescu

The numerous events that took place in our country and in Europe did not give historians the opportunity to write justly about our relations with the Russians. It could easily be argued that, thanks to Romania, the Russian Revolution was saved from disaster. The strong resistance of our armies in 1917 prevented the Germans from entering Moldavia and from there into Russia. Under our shelter the Russians had time to decide the political administration that suited them. We did not mix at all in their internal affairs.

༼ལྦྱ༽

ARMISTICE

At the end of January 1918, the 1st Division had orders to leave for a destination unknown to junior officers. We tried all manner of guesses. Finally we were told to go up the left bank, of the River Prut. Every night we slept in a different village. I was ordered to go ahead and find lodgings for the 'cyclist' company. One day, on leaving a village, I saw an old man and woman running after the Captain of our regiment. Both were crying and the woman howled as if for a funeral. I went to ask them what had happened and I found out that our sergeant-major had taken by force a barrel of wine they were saving for their daughter's wedding. They had saved it from theft by the Russians and now it was taken by a Romanian. I went immediately to find our commander, Captain Bădulescu. I pleaded with him to order the return the barrel of wine to the owners. I had a heated discussion with him, and for the first time he warned me that I could be arrested and court-martialed. Still I persisted and proposed on the first occasion to buy a barrel of wine and give it to the company if the other was returned. Finally, he agreed and the horse cart with the barrel was turned around taken back to the old couple with their wine.

When we arrived at a border point with Russia, the Division crossed into Bessarabia on to the left bank of the River Prut at Sculeni a short distance north of Iași. There lodgings were found with great difficulty as this small town was overflowing with refugees. I managed to lodge everyone, except my brother and myself. Someone told us that outside Sculeni, there was an empty house which a long time ago had been the Russian custom house. In the dark we went there and found a house with three rooms but with no windows or doors! To us it looked palatial. We installed the stretchers which we had adopted as beds. Years after, in London I found an engraving of this house in Demidoff's famous volume of his travels published in 1837. From then until 1918, it had not changed at all.

Illustration of Scalene in Demidoff's Travels Volume

A few days later, the division received orders to enter the heart of Bessarabia and to go to the small town of Bălți. Bolsheviks were causing unrest and a new Nationalist movement was attempting to announce a free Moldavia. Our government was itself maneuvering to absorb Bessarabia back into our nation. We now knew what our mission was. Our relations with the new Soviet Government had hardened and we were menaced by an attack. While in the past we had fought on the western front, now we were menaced from the North. Though we had not been bothered anywhere on our march, we were told to expect strong resistance.

As we approached Bălți 50 km north of Sculeni, the Divisional Commander called a meeting of the officers of the units under him. It was decided to surround Bălți assigning to each regiment a specific zone. We, the *cyclists* were given the zone "Calare" on the main road running through open fields. Seeing my advanced platoon tightly grouped right on the road, I scattered the soldiers wide apart and made them ready to fire.

As we approached the town, two cannons started shooting at us. Then a number of machine guns were aimed in our direction. For the first time in the war, I found myself in an open field in front of an enemy whose strength I did not know. Quickly I realized that these weapons were in the hands of inexperienced men. They were shooting in our direction but could not fix the range accurately. So far I had no casualties. My tactic was to advance a little distance as-soon-as I could guess the firing range of the enemy.

Much to our surprise, when we arrived near the outskirts the enemy raised white flags and offered to surrender. With great care I contacted their leaders thinking it was perhaps a trap. At the same time we continued to advance slowly into the small town, street by street. Expecting to hear an order to stop fighting, instead a patrol from my left flank came to report that a group of men were trying to set fire to military stores. I went there and sure enough there were Russians throwing petrol soaked rags through a broken door and setting fire to them. Naturally we arrested them immediately and managed to put out the fire.

This storehouse was in a huge barn with stacks of military clothes reaching to the roof, evidently left behind by the withdrawing Russians. All kinds of military equipment had been left behind including almost one hundred horses. I took my platoon to the barn with clothes and let them go in four at a time. They were told to strip and redress themselves in new clothes. Each man was to take two bags and fill them with spare clothes and a pair of boots. In short order each man had a Russian fur hat without insignia. When the ceasefire finally came, soldiers from the other units took them for Russians as I was the only one wearing a Romanian uniform. This equipment, taken under enemy fire in a military zone, was not illegal as we were entitled to take all we wanted as military loot. When we were all gathered in the center of the town, officers from other units congratulated me but could not duplicate my action as the Divisional Command had taken control of the stores and put them under military guard.

Once again finding lodgings for everyone was my responsibility. The best house was reserved for the commander, General Mihai Schina, who came to see the house. He looked right and left and refused to stay there. He said in wartime he did not like to live in such luxury. Given his refusal, other officers were able to claim it and my brother and I settled in. But I found that there was no way to heat it and nowhere I could buy a stove. Eventually I found a more modest house where the owner gave up his bed for me.

Our presence in Bălți was precarious. We did not know if we would be attacked by the Russian Bolsheviks or even by the local population. At the same time there was some rich landowners, Russian refugees from the revolutionary turmoil, who overnight came out of hiding and re-established their way of life on an elegant scale. Night after night, one of these families would give a rich dinner with the best wines. I did not know where they had hidden their best china and silver but the dinners were perfectly arranged and served by valets in uniform.

All the officers from the division and the cyclists company were invariably invited to these dinners. This was the first chance I had to be served a meal with so much luxury. The host did not sit at the table with the guests. Instead, he acted as *Maitre d'Hotel* and went from guest to guest to see that everyone was well served and their glasses continuously refilled. These dinners were hard to understand given the poverty all around Bălți. There were very few women present because the majority had gone to Constantinople (Istanbul) "for the duration." There they had become part of a large colony of pro-Tsarist "White Russian" refugees.

A return to reality came when the Divisional commander decided to send the *cyclists* and the Dimancescu brothers to the head of a bridge over the Dniester River which the Russians from the Ukraine were trying to take control of. At the last moment there was a change. I remained in Bălți and my brother was sent to Ribnița on the Russian-Ukrainian border one-hundred kilometers to the East. I was ordered to be attached to the Military Police and made a sort of third class commissary. My job was to maintain order in the town. Nobody was allowed to gather in groups of more than three and everyone had to respect a curfew by ten o'clock at night. The Military Police settled into a two-storied house. On the first floor was my office and in another room was the office of Colonel Poienaru, who had been wounded when we advanced on Bălți. In the basement there were two rooms. One served as a bedroom for four guards and the other as a prison.

On the main street, which may have been 100 meters long, there was a bakery, a jeweler and next the entrance to a movie theatre. This was of the kind of place that showed the first half of a movie for one month and the next half for the following month, and so on. Over the door was a bell which started to ring at noon and continued until sunset to remind people to come for the movie. The jeweler had nothing to display in his window and nothing in the shop. After many visits when he finally gained the confidence of a buyer, he would promise to find a gold or silver ring.

From my window I could see into a field where a daily market was held. Here were sold food, furniture, clothes and even the very precious Russian tobacco of the "mahorca" quality. In spite of our orders to stop this market as being contrary to our rule that people could not gather in groups of more than three, the market grew day by day. It became more and more populated and disorderly. A sub-lieutenant who shared the job with me went there and through an interpreter he asked the people to leave. Nobody listened to him. Then he brought the four guards and warned the crowd three times more. He then ordered the guards to shoot first in the air and the second time at the crowd.

In a few seconds the field was clear except for a poor old Jewish man who had been shot in the head and killed. With the same speed the field was filled with the deceased's relatives and friends. Their cries were heartbreaking. With difficulty I found out who was the most immediate relative of the deceased and offered to help them with the cost of the funeral. This offer was interpreted as an admission of guilt. Nothing was resolved from this difficult situation.

Meanwhile while fighting Russian troops at the Dniester bridge, my brother was wounded and sent by ambulance to Iași. He had a bullet above the knee and another from a Russian machine gun that had lightly grazed the his left tibia. I asked for and got permission to go to and see him. When I arrived at St. Spiridon hospital my brother was not registered there. So many wounded had been brought in there had not been time to count them nor to find them beds. A doctor told me to go up and down the corridors and look on all the stretchers for him for there were not nearly enough beds.

Finally I found him, looking very pale but cheerful. He described the fight in which he had been wounded. While leading his platoon, he had pushed the Russians from the right bank across the river and up the left bank. Though wounded and losing blood, he refused to leave until a replacement came. He said that all the time he was praying his replacement would not be me.

Everyone was worried that our troops would be influenced by the undisciplined ways of the Russian troops. The division had a so-called Royal Commissioner who fulfilled the function of a civilian judge. Our Royal Commissioner was Petre Dragomirescu who had his degree in law from Iași. At Bălți he suddenly became very active. During the fighting we had not seen him but in Bălți he wanted to create a performance record for his promotion. He had about ten soldiers from various units to attend him and he sent them out to find from their colleagues what officers could be impeached for some punishment.

Around us there were so many things left by the Russian army. There was not yet an inventory and there was no control. Each officer had taken five to ten horses without thinking what he would do with them at demobilization. Others had taken furniture from abandoned houses of Russians. By Petre Dragomirescu's standards almost all the officers should have been judged and sent to prison. There was great disorder as he collected information through his agents. I protested against his system which could only be bad for discipline.

Next to my room in the house where I stayed was another room occupied by Colonel Erbiceanu. He was commander of the horse-drawn artillery. All during the war he was a true hero and especially at Oituz where many times, thanks to his cannon barrage, the Germans were pushed back. But now the Royal Commissioner, Dragomirescu, had accused him of having stolen twenty horses, three carts and believe-it-or-not an airplane without an engine. Soon after, whilst I was resting, I heard a gun shot from the other room. When I hurried in I found Colonel Erbiceanu stretched on the sofa dying. He had killed himself.

I was revolted and immediately asked to be received by General Schina, the Divisional Commander. I told him how the Royal Commissioner had accused Colonel Erbiceanu and sent him to court and that such an action would have disqualified him from his post as leader of the horse artillery. I reported in detail to Schina the way Dragomirescu's agents were insinuating themselves amongst the soldiers and were encouraging them to accuse the officers of irregularities. Schina did not completely agree with me and defended Dragomirescu whom he praised as a very efficient Royal Commissioner. The next day I was called to the Commissioner's office questioned closely about the materials which he said I had stolen from the warehouse to clothe the soldiers. He said the situation was so serious that with regret he had to send me to be court-martialed.

Threatened this way, I asked permission from my Commander to go to Iași and I went directly to Prince Carol to whom I reported the same details presented to my Divisional Commander. Prince Carol told me there was no reason for me to worry and I should return to Bălți. I told him that the first thing I would do would be to ask for my discharge and return to live under German occupation. Carol told me it was not necessary to punish myself alone. To my great surprise he asked me if I did not want to re-enlist in which case he would take me as one of his adjutants.

DISCHARGE

His offer was very tempting but before I made a decision I managed to see my mother, sister, brother and brother-in-law. Mother advised me to get discharged, return to Bucharest and register immediately at the University in the Law Department. My sister and brother were inclined for me to register for architecture. My brother-in-law was neutral.

As-soon-as I returned to Bălți, I submitted my request for discharge from the army. This was immediately approved by General Schina. I had told him about my meeting and my talk with Prince Carol, who meanwhile had told him through his adjutant to give me satisfaction in anything I would ask. I told Schina that to remain in Bălți wearing the uniform and to be laughed at by Dragomirescu would have resulted in a big scandal with loud repercussions. In-Order-To bypass a scandal I thought Schina was glad to help me leave Bălți promptly.

By this time the political situation in Romania had become very complicated. In the north, we had been abandoned by the Russian army and in the south we were still under the German military occupation. Though an armistice had been agreed to, we were technically at war although no major attacks were in the works. The Bratianu Government had been replaced with a government presided over by General Averescu who had accepted in principle peace clauses discussed with the Germans. This peace treaty would go into effect once signed by King Ferdinand. But he refused to sign. His refusal did not stop the Germans from applying the provisions of the treaty. One of the provisions was to oblige Romania to discharge from the army all soldiers from Wallachia and Oltenia and send them to their homes. I availed myself of this clause when I asked for my discharge.

At this point, the country was divided into two. We in Moldavia were named "The gentlemen from Iași" and were considered pro-Allies. Those in the occupied zone were nicknamed "Germanophones" which was largely unjust. This nickname could have only been applied to a few, who had the protection of the German authorities and who acquired unjustified publicity. Our enemies with whom we were treating for peace, allowed the politician Take Ionescu to leave Iași and go to Paris and to take with him two hundred Romanians.

I knew that wherever I went I would be asked what I had done during the war and that I would be asked to show honorable discharge papers and a "certificate of good behavior." I obtained this from Captain Badulescu, the Commander of the cyclists company. This is how he described my activities from 1915-1918.

I, Commander of the Cyclist Company, Capt. Horia Badulescu, certify in this present, that Mr. Dimitrie Dimăncescu, born July 7, 1896, in Titu village, a graduate of Gheorghe Lazăr High School, enrolled as a volunteer in the 2nd Regiment of Hunters in the year 1915, that on July 1st 1916 he graduated from the school of officers in reserve being attached as N.O.C. with reduced term to the first company of cyclists, that on October l, 1916, he was promoted to Sublt. and on September 1. 1917, to Lt., that he was wounded on August 8, 1917, at the Oituz battles for which he is entitled to wear the distinction sign and for bravery in the in the army has been decorated with Virtutea Militară Second Class, the Star of Romania knight's class with St. Stanislas same class.

"The fact that he was a reserve officer implies unquestionably good behavior and this act has been given to him in-order-to use it to register at the School of Architecture. All the time he has served in the army he has not been punished."

Commander of the Cyclist Company
Captain Badulescu
Sculeni, Bessarabia, 20 August 1918

The day I was discharged from the army, I realized that except for my family no one else was interested. The crossing of the German control point at Focşani was humiliating for everyone, soldier or officer. Because in Moldavia we had suffered an awful epidemic of exanthematic typhus and recurrent fever, at Focşani all who arrived were fumigated independently whether they had lice or not. After this physical purgatory, we were interviewed and given an identity card: "ausweiss," indispensable for those in the occupied territory. After all formalities had been fulfilled, we were put in freight trains and sent to Bucharest. We did not arrive at the North Station but at the freight station. From there we were left alone to walk all along the Calea Griviţei into town carrying our bags and luggage.

I went directly to our family house near the Faculty of Medicine. To my great dismay, I was not welcomed. When my Mother left Bucharest, she had ceded the house to a friend, Mrs. Popovici with her nephew and her niece, the mother of a schoolmate of mine. There was not a bed or a sofa in the house where I could have slept. Mrs. Popovici, having no income whatsoever during the occupation, had sold everything in the house, even the kitchen utensils.

All day long I walked the city to find a shelter. I finally met my former "cercetaşii," the Danielopol brothers, who immediately offered me a roof and food at their home. The Danielopol brothers were extremely intelligent and very independent. Their father had died and now their mother found it impossible to discipline them. There were three boys, their mother and her brother, Mr. Peretz. In the kitchen there were special dishes prepared for each one of them. Meals ended chaotically with the breaking of glasses and plates. It was such a scandal that I was unable to eat anything. My arrival, she thought, might bring some order and discipline. Because I did not contribute anything towards my room and board, I could not raise my voice with authority. Her hope was hard to accomplish. However, I did have a shelter and the Danielopol brothers were splendid potential players in the resistance that I wanted to lead against the Germans.

❧

END OF GERMAN OCCUPATION

In the occupied territory, the population knew only the news given by the officials of the army of occupation. This news was always calculated in such a manner as to sound favorable for the Germans. In Bucharest there were two newspapers printed in Romanian, *Lumina* directed by C. Stere and *Gazeta Bucureştiului*. Stere was the protagonist of the idea that we should be incorporated with Germany. Stere thought King Ferdinand should abdicate and the Kaiser or maybe one of his sons be declared King of Romania. But King Ferdinand and Queen Marie had become widely accepted as the genuine symbols of independence to Romanians.

The spring of 1918 began with partial success for a German offensive on the Western Front in France. This demoralized Romanians. At the main Post Office[18] on Calea Victoriei there was a blackboard on which the General Quarters of the German Army stuck a daily official communique.

I had befriended an Austrian soldier, originally from Czechoslovakia. This man sympathized with the Romanians and was convinced that in the end we would win the war. He received the Hungarian newspaper *Buda-Peşti Hirlap* in which the Hungarians published the official communiqués of the Allies. My Czech friend translated it into French for me and I then distributed it in Romanian all over town. It was an activity both easy and difficult. In the beginning, this effort was kept a secret known only to me and my cousin, Bebe Ciricleanu. We had found a copy machine and paper which could not be identified as a Romanian product. Bebe Ciricleanu had stolen it from a German Office where she worked as a typist. I printed about 500 copies a day and our communiqué was embellished with news from here and there or on occasion invented by me.

We knew in occupied Romania that in Austria-Hungary and especially in Austria, there was a shortage of food becoming worse daily. We knew that each German soldier in occupied Romania was allowed to send one food parcel home per week. The majority stole the food from the people often by force. Special trains ran every week to Germany. I did not know how many German soldiers were in Romania so each week I in-

---

[18] The Post Office building is today the home of the National History Museum.

vented a number of food parcels going to Germany while we, Romanians, were strictly rationed.

After announcing the Peace Treaty still unsigned by King Ferdinand, and the coming of the Marghiloman Government, the Germans tried with difficulty to impose censorship on all Romanian newspapers coming from Iași. They carried Allied news shared by some foreign diplomats who remained posted there. When circulated in Bucharest, Iași papers often had entire columns left blank which had been censored. The one paper they did not have the courage to censor too often was Nicolae Iorga's paper *Neamul Romanesc*. He knew how to write articles with hidden truths as seen by him. Besides the news I received from the Czech soldier, I also received by liaison Iorga's paper which could not be sold in Bucharest.

At some point the German daily communiqué at the Post Office ceased to appear, so my communiqué had no rival. Two large maps in shop windows in the Calea Victoriei which had shown by a red line the advance of the German army disappeared.

Eventually the fate of the war began to shift decisively in favor of the Allies. On the Western European Front the French Marshal Ferdinand Foch faced the famed General Erich Ludendorff who was beginning to realize he could no longer win the war. In the Balkans, the southern Allied army of Salonika, now under the command of General Louis Franchet d'Esperey, had been re-equipped. After two years of waiting, it finally started moving north entering Bulgaria and Serbia.

Sunday November 3, 1918, was a beautiful sunny day. The Calea Victoriei was crowded with pedestrians. A rumor was spreading fast that at the Athénée Palace Hotel, where the General Quarters of Field Marshal August von Mackensen's army were located, were French military representatives sent to discuss the withdrawal or capitulation of the German army of occupation. The public realized that the German situation was critical for the French army was on the Danube and roads of withdrawal were closing due to the withdrawal of Austria and Hungary and preparations for their own internal social revolutions. As a result the rumor was easily believed. In front of the hotel, a large crowd gathered to greet the French soldiers. The women brought flowers and the men cheered.

This story of the French officers that everyone knew about, and the rumor about them, was invented and circulated by me. It was distributed in my bulletin copies dated November 2. My cousins, the Danielopol boys and I spread it all over town.

A Romanian officer came out on a Hotel balcony and announced on his word of honor that the rumor was not true: "No French officers were in the Capital." What he said hardly mattered. The crowd remained to cheer for the idea of victory that was near after enduring two years of occupation and had "the right to celebrate the coming down of liberty."[19]

The next day, Sunday, I went with the Danielopol boys to the Athénée Palace Hotel. A large crowd had again gathered by eleven o'clock. Behind us in the Atheneum Gardens there was a German band playing heroic marches. A German officer appeared at a small window of the hotel and menaced us loudly. If we did not disperse he said he would be obliged to call the army. As nobody moved and as everyone was yelling to see the French officers alternating these calls with "Vive la France," the military guards came out of the main doors of the hotel with bayonets on their rifles calling out "Zurück! Zurück!" (Back! Back!).

The crowd started to withdraw into the Atheneum Gardens where the band continued to play. We asked them to play the *Marseillaise*. I do not know how it started but within seconds the crowd jumped on the military band and trampled their instruments. The players ran away without offering any resistance and we, the crowd, were pushed into the Calea Victoriei by the soldiers advancing with their bayonets. From the Athénée Palace and beyond as far as we could see was a mass of people. We started to sing the *Marseillaise* as we were going towards the Military Club where German authorities were also installed. From the side streets crossing the Calea Victoriei from where the crowds had come were now German troops in military trucks. The mass of people was pushed from behind as well as from both sides towards the Club. There it was met by another crowd coming from the direction of the Post Office. Gathered along the two boulevards, the mass of thousands sang the *Marseillaise*.

The square in front of the Military Club was now completely blocked. German guards were left on the terrace where in haste they had brought a few machine guns. A German officer told the crowds to disperse quietly. Nobody heard him. Some could see him making signs with his hands for them to go. He then ordered his platoon to shoot three times in the air over our heads. Nobody moved and everybody continued to shout "Vive la France" and to sing. There followed several shots aimed directly into the crowd. Some people were killed, others wounded. The rest ran in great disorder.

The Danielopol brothers and I were in the center of the crowd. We took shelter at the entrance of a movie theater. The German troops coming

---

[19] Quote from V.C. Kiritescu, *Istoria Razboiului pentru Intregirea Romaniei 1916-1918*, Vol 3, page 311-312.

from the Athénée Palace to the Post Office arresting people who had not run away. I managed to go by back streets to my cousin's house on Boulevard Elisabeta and the Danielopol boys safely reached their own home.

Immediately after the disorders by the Military Club, a curfew was imposed and no civilian was allowed on the streets after 6 p.m.. About ten o'clock at night, I thought it would be better if I returned to the Danielopol house. Then suddenly, I found myself face to face with a military patrol. I was arrested me and sent me in a "Black Maria" (police van) to the Military Club where on the top floor there were several cells with iron bars. I was locked in one of these without any explanation. The next morning I was taken to a military tribunal. There I was presented to a German military judge and a German sergeant who was a self-appointed prosecutor.

Outside of giving my name and age, I refused to answer any other questions saying that I was a Captain in reserve in the Romanian army. I stated that the German prosecutor should have the same rank as mine. This objection was somehow discussed by the judge and the prosecutor. They telephoned various authorities and I had the impression that I had won my argument. Awaiting the arrival of another prosecutor, I was returned to my cell where the German soldier who guarded it spoke fluent French. He told me that all the arrested men at the Military Club were most likely going to be sentenced to death. I asked him what I was accused of but he did not know. He thought that all those arrested were thought to be guilty of the disorders the prior Sunday and of having distributed an allied and clandestine communiqué.

During my second session facing the judge I could not understand all that was said in German. And I pretended not to know anything they were saying and a civilian interpreter was brought in. From the beginning I denied everything or that I spread any clandestine information. All I had done was to walk on Calea Victoriei as I usually did every Sunday. The worst lie I told them was that I liked to go to the Atheneum Gardens to listen to the German military fanfare.

For some reason the session was suspended by the Judge and I was sent back to my cell. In spite of the expected German severity, those of us in cells were brought newspapers and we were served three meals a day. Reading between the lines, we could guess that the Germans and the Austro-Hungarians were not doing very well and were now preparing a defensive position on the Danube River to resist rapid Allied advances from the south.

Around 5 p.m. on November 10th, we heard a noise of rolling tanks which intensified. The guard on duty outside my cell approached to tell me that the German army had been ordered to leave Romania. To my amazement, he took off his belt with the bayonet passed it and his rifle to me through the bars of the cell. And then he gave me the key so that I could get out. For a while I thought it was a trap to kill me trying to escape. But suddenly the guard knelt and begged me to take him under my protection. He did not want to return to Germany. He even declared how much he loved the good, kind Romanian people.

My fast changing emotions from facing the probability of being killed to complete liberty was hard to describe. I did and did not believe my luck. Before I left the cell, I looked out of the window and saw military trucks overcrowded with soldiers, all going in the direction of the Calea Victoriei where the people were crowding the streets. Some were cursing the Germans openly whilst others vainly tried to stop the trucks. They were pushed back by soldiers pointing their rifles at the crowd, ready to shoot.

Not knowing where to go and trying to protect the German soldier following me, I went to a friend Gica Riegler whom I found in front of his family's pastry shop cursing the Germans as loudly as he could. Shortly, another friend, Richard Tătaru, joined us. Riegler took my protégé inside and gave him civilian clothes and I never saw him again. Meanwhile, we three realized what a chaotic situation would arise in Bucharest after the Germans withdrew. The French army was not far off. It had crossed the Danube and was about 70 km away from the Capital. Its commanders awaited the arrival of the Romanian army from Moldavia led by the King and Queen so that they could be the first to enter the liberated Capital.

We knew there might be a few days with nobody to assume authority or the responsibility for order in Bucharest. So we decided to act. I remember getting on the roof of a streetcar which had stopped at a crossing and making a short speech asking the people to maintain order. I announced that the three of us had assumed the leadership of the town and that any claims were to be brought to the Police Station where we would be at any hour of the day or night. Richard Tătaru, who was the most aggressive and revengeful of us, wanted to find Constantin Stere and shoot him with his own hand. When we arrived at our self-declared Command Post, to our great surprise we found Stere installed in the armchair of the Chief of Police. Gun in hand, Tătaru advanced towards him intending to shoot him. But Riegler and I were against such a simple execution believing it would trigger many others. Stere without standing up, told us that he understood our decision, but like any man sentenced to death, he wanted permission to speak his mind. With a very elegant gesture, he invited us to be seated facing him. Then he started his "last words" which continued at great length. We were very impressed. Tătaru put his gun back and told Stere he would look for a guard to take him to his home in Bucor, near Ploiești. He led him into another room and asked him to wait patiently there. I eventually became friendly with Stere and it became an intellectual pleasure to listen to him.

The people of Bucharest remained orderly during this interval when nobody was in control. The Germans had maintained all the police stations with Romanian personnel. Actually, this personnel was used whenever they wanted to requisition something. Through these police stations they had requisitioned all copper utensils, mattresses and blankets and all woolen articles. Because of this, police stations had become despised. However, the men remained at their posts to maintain order. The only excesses were at food and clothes deposits left behind by the Germans and which were quickly looted. No one tried to stop them.

When I had first returned to German-occupied territory in Bucharest, I registered as a first year student at both the Schools of Law and Architecture which were near to each other. But I did not like the University atmosphere which seemed far too frivolous. One came or not to classes. There was no record of attendance and most students bought the courses notes in shorthand to then be typed by more resourceful students.

Knowing that the French army was only one day's march from Bucharest, I was impatient to see them. I took with me a team of "Cercetaşii" who put on their uniforms. Then I went to two confectioners to buy candies as gifts and we went to meet the French. When we met the first advancing unit in a village, they responded with great joy especially after discovering that many Romanians spoke French. They asked us for a meal. Secretly after lunch, we took two French soldiers and brought them to Bucharest.

When we arrived at the center of the town in front of the National Theater, they received an unexpected ovation. Because their first wish was for a hot bath, I took them to the nearby Continental Hotel. Then we all went to the Capşa restaurant where a regal meal was prepared. Only plain soldiers, they had never seen anything of this sort before. The cooks rivaled each other in preparing French dishes. There were only a few people dining but outside large crowds quickly gathered shouting that they wanted to see the French soldiers. When the meal was over, I took them outside where they were acclaimed. That evening, we returned them to the village in a horse drawn carriage. They were absent from roll call but I assumed that any sort of punishment might only be "pro-forma."

At last came the day of the King Ferdinand and Queen Marie's entry to the Capital. They mounted horses at the Villa Minovici. Escorted by the famed French General Berthelot and commanding generals of the different Romanian armies, they descended Kisseleff Avenue then followed Calea

Victoriei. Behind them were detachments from various divisions and regiments which had now entered Bucharest. The populace lining the streets was jubilant.

As I waited to see them as one of many in the crowd, I met a group of students and with them we planned to give a reception at the National Theater for King Ferdinand as a welcome by the Youth of Romania. The King accepted the invitation for the next evening after his arrival in Bucharest. That day I wrote a draft of our welcome speech and written on parchment by another colleague. We decided that the committee to receive the King on the stage, should wear formal tails and a white tie. All day long there was a wild search to find such a costume, mostly from big-restaurant waiters. I found an uncle who had such a suit that fitted me perfectly but less lucky in finding find a pair of black shoes, instead they were yellow. The reception was a great success. The King, apparently very moved and in a response quite out of the ordinary for him, thanked me in a short improvised speech.

࿇

The War over, my life entered into a regular routine. This was not necessarily true of the country. Now about to be enlarged with new provinces and especially Transylvania, it was entering a difficult period of reintegration and adaptation. The new union with Transylvania was the biggest problem. Romanian leaders there had their own ideas on integration. Meanwhile, in Bucharest preparations were being made for the post-war Peace Conference. For that I had no direct interest, I focused instead on getting a university degree. Without it I would not be a complete person or ready to participate in national affairs. Unfortunately, the Law School was intimidating. There was a professor, Tocilescu, who taught Roman Law and demanded that the students learn his course word by word by heart. Only a "bookworm" could memorize his courses. After so much time in the army, I could not memorize anything and I was certain I would fail in any examination. I could see Tocilescu marking my exam with three black balls.

The School of Architecture seemed more inviting but did not turn out that way. Courses followed a traditional program that was based only L'École des Beaux Arts in Paris. And no student was allowed to give vent to his imagination. At a semester exam we were told to make a plan and a drawing of a teahouse in the garden of a rich man. All my colleagues were encouraged to make a pavilion covered with plaster angels and flowers. I made a simple cube with no ornaments. The professor asked me why I had not foreseen any ornamentation. I told him that nature, the plants and trees in the garden, would be the decoration. None of the people who would drink tea inside would put their heads out to look at plaster angels. Furiously and feeling insulted the professor crossed out my drawing and told me to start again using my imagination. I answered him that my imagination could not think of imitating others who, in my opinion, were in bad taste. This answer, I now realize, was disrespectful coming from a student and led to my getting a black mark. I knew then that I would not pass any examinations at the School of Architecture in Bucharest.

This was probably too severe a judgment of the Law School or the School of Architecture. From the age of eleven when I was a scholarship student at St. Sava and Gheorghe Lazăr schools, a student at the Military School of Infantry, and then a soldier in the Romanian army, discipline was taught. Everything was done according to the rules. When I enrolled at the University and the School of Architecture, I did not realize that I had entered a system also based on some fixed rules which I had no right to ignore.

All the while, my brother had remained with the 1st Division in Bessarabia. Given leave, he came to see me in Bucharest. We decided that he should ask for a transfer to the "Hunters" Regiment. I do not know how it happened or who helped him but a month later he was transferred. The 1st Division thus lost both its "Jamborei." But to our surprise, on March 24, 1919, I received an official order through my brother,

The "Hunter's Regiment"
The Commander's Office

URGENT
NOTE

Notify Sub Lt. Dimancescu from the 2nd Company that he should be present tomorrow morning and his brother, Lt. Dimancescu, at 9.15 at the place the parade (Place Victoriei). Lt. Dimancescu will report to me to receive orders.
s.s. Carol
Principe R

I discovered that decorations were to be awarded by King Ferdinand. Though I was demobilized, my brother told me that the Prince wanted me to come in uniform. Not knowing why I was called, I rushed to a tailor to put back the epaulettes taken off my uniform which I had turned into a civilian suit. When the day came, my mother, my sister and brother-in-law accompanied us to the front of the Geological Institute on Kisseleff Avenue. Already lined up were ten officers and soldiers. Prince Carol sent my brother and me to join the line. Our family took their places directly behind us.

On both sides of the Avenue there were detachments from various regiments. Soon after, King Ferdinand arrived to be greeted by the singing of the Royal Hymn. Prince Carol gave the report of the troops and then the King came towards those of us summoned to attend. Starting from the left, he shook hands and gave each officer a foreign decoration. My brother and I were in the middle of the row. When the King came to me he said:

"My cousin, the King of England (George V) is sorry he could not come to decorate you but he asked me to give you the British "Military Cross.""

The Military Cross, I learned later, was an exceptional honor especially since it was rarely awarded to foreigners. My participation in the sabotaging of our Ploieşti oil wells in December of 1916, was considered by Great Britain to be have been important to the outcome of the war. He pinned it on my breast, congratulated me and went to my brother who was next to me. Surprised the King said: "You are the Dimancescu brothers, Carol's "Cercetaşii."

That very instant my mother, from behind us,

shouted:

"They are my sons, Sir."

The King smiling, answered back:

"They are good boys, I congratulate you."

In his turn, my brother received The British "War Medal" because at the date it was awarded he was still a non-commissioned-officer. Shortly after this event, the Romanian army went to war with the Hungarians, whose army commanded by the Communist leader Bella Kuhn had attacked us along the Tisa River. My brother had hardly left Bessarabia when he was sent away again with the "Hunters." Our armies reached and occupied Budapest and managed to dislodge Bella Kuhn from power.

In turn, I found myself "re-mobilized." But this was not to fight but to help organize a military sporting-group being sent to represent Romania at the post-War Inter-Allied Games in Paris. This happened in a way quite unforeseen by me. I had met with a certain Colonel Bădulescu (no relation to my former commander) who happened to show me a letter lying on his desk. The invitation had been signed by General John J. Pershing, Commander in Chief of the United States Expeditionary Forces, and was addressed to General Constantin Prezan, the Commander of the Romanian army. Our country was invited to participate in the athletic Inter-Allied Games in Paris, France. Received a few months before, it had not been answered. Bădulescu mentioned he had no time to see to such matters and that he had no answer to send to Paris. From his office I went directly to Prince Carol, who served also as the President of the National Federation of Sports and Athletics. I told him that Romania must participate no matter how modestly.

Carol immediately telephoned Bădulescu and said "If you cannot find the time, Dimancescu has nothing else to do." From the moment it was known that Prince Carol was taking a personal interest in the Games, things happened. We had no trouble in finding military sportsmen. This group was put under the orders of General Găvănescu, and as is the habit in the army orders were not discussed but executed. Bădulescu himself quickly took seriously getting the job done. The teams soon counted one hundred-and-ten sportsmen and athletes beside military personal in charge of medical help, food, equipment, as well as those caring for the necessary horses. I designed a new uniform with a coat that had open collar with lapels similar to British ones. For most of the contestants this would be their first trip outside Romania.

American military leaders working with the civilian Y.M.C.A., wanting to leave France with an event memorializing the common Allied fight, initiated the idea of an Inter-Allied competitive sports event. The French offered a military training field in the Bois de Vincennes in Paris. The

American army engineers built the Stadium for 22,000 seated and 40,000 more standing. All this was completed in ninety days in preparation for competition between 29 countries that would participate in the first games between June 22nd and July 6th.

View of Pershing Stadium in the Bois de Vincennes (Paris). The Stadium and support facilities were built in 90 days by US army engineers. There was seating for 20,000 and standing room for 40,000. It remains in use in Paris.
Source: US National Archives

Traveling on a special train with horse wagons attached, we arrived at the games site outside of Paris. We were taken northwest of the city to the Stade de Colombes where the football and rugby competition would take place. The main events were southeast of the city at the newly built Pershing Stadium. Tents were pitched for us to use during all the competitions. The cavalry group was taken to another suburb of Paris where there were stables for the horses. For the American organizers who were in charge of the lodgings, it was huge achievement. No detail was too insignificant and everything needed was plentiful. For us Romanians, they procured a special corn-flour which was used for making 'mamaliga.' The Romanian detachment put up a very good show. We won a number of prizes. The rugby team in which I participated was one of only three country teams to play. We came in third after the much more experienced French and American teams.

So it was that in Paris my war years were brought to a close.

Romania's Rugby Team: front row middle DDD, right front Ioan D.

NOTE: Forty years later, quite by chance and feeling restless one evening in New York where was working, I had a sudden impulse to go to a bookstore. I walked to one selling second-hand books nearby. I reached it just before closing hour. Inside, the first book to attract my attention was with the title: Inter-Allied War Games, Paris 22nd June 1919. Immediately thumbing through, I came to a group picture and immediately recognized myself and my brother at the front. Our names were also listed among all the contestants. Buying it, I spent nearly all night reading it.

Dimitri and Ion Dimancescu at the Inter-Allied Games

PART III ⁓ AMERICA

The end of World War I meant a new and bright beginning for Romania. Doubled in size and population with the absorption of Transylvania into its national territory, European and American oil companies exploiting and refining its oil riches, and investors fueling a new industrial pace of development, the country's economic prospects looked bright. New money meant the beginnings, too, of a wealthy middle class ready to invest in new homes and a blossoming 'western' way of life. Bucharest, and other Romanian cities, became a hotbed of new internationalist architecture marking a sharp turn away from the monumental Beaux-Arts and Romanian-styled Brancovenesc buildings. King Ferdinand and Queen Marie sustained fashionable royalty into an era rapidly turning away from aristocratic legacies. The Queen would make her own imprint as a pioneering modern-woman on the western world greeted and headlined as the 'Lady Diana' of her time. All the while complex politics marked difficult times for a burgeoning democracy still not well-grounded in parliamentary politics and still wedded to long traditions of corrupt 'under-the-table' practices fueled in many ways by centuries of Ottoman practices.

England maintained its imperial facade though weakened by its war debts. On the continent, Republican France recovered its footings and strengthened its colonial outposts while Germany reeled from its post-war reparations while Austria and Hungary were now relegated to second-tier national status. Meanwhile Russia turned busy building its own 'communist-fueled' Soviet Empire The roaring twenties would quickly flow into the global depressions of the early thirties and the rapid rise of fascist movements in Germany and Italy. As Charles Dickens wrote of another era in his first words of The Tale of Two Cities, one of his most famed novels set in revolutionary France of 1789:

"It was the best of times, it was the worst of times, it was the age of wisdom, it was the age of foolishness, it was the epoch of belief, it was the epoch of incredulity, it was the season of Light, it was the season of Darkness, it was the spring of hope, it was the winter of despair..."

In 1919, it was the best of times for Romania.

World War I reshaped the world. The Treaty of Versailles settled the score between victors and vanquished. The Treaty of Trianon in 1920 settled the boundaries of Europe new young states including Romania.

The American industrial economy was thriving under the influence of industrialist like Rockefeller (oil), Carnegie (steel), Morgan (banking), Vanderbilt (railroads), Ford (cars). Inventors like Edison were becoming folk heroes. A car-driven economy was about to burst open from coast to coast. Immigrants flocked to the North American shores. A proverbial golden rainbow welcomed all comers ... though not all would find the pot of gold.

The end of the 19th-century had lured thousands of Romanian immigrants especially in the mid-western heartland of Ohio, Indiana, Michigan where smog-spewing steel and metal-based industries were rapidly growing. Pittsburgh was at the heart of this new industrial-era boom time. Thousands of ethnic Romanians, many having escaped oppression under Hungarian rule, were now choosing to return from America with savings to invest. In Washington, D.C., Prince Antoine Bibesco, appointed Minister of the Romanian Legation in 1922, launched a study to document Romania's presence in the United States. Authored by Serban Druțu, the research was carried out by two staff people including Dimitri Dimancescu, then a freshly minted young diplomat.

Romanians in America - 1922

SOURCE: "Romanii in America (1922)" - 200 page report published by the Romanian Legation (Washington, D.C.) and recently offered as a reprint by the US Library of Congress. Excerpts:

Referencing varied sources, the study reached an estimate of 230,000 Romanians living in the United States in 1920:
- 110,000 were Romanian citizens,
- 70,000 were Jewish Romanians who had attained US citizenship,
- 50,000 were ethnic Romanians who emigrated from Transylvania then under Austro-Hungarian rule. These same individuals were quick to claim Romanian citizenship documentation after Transylvania was absorbed into 'Greater Romania' by the terms of the post-WW-I Treaty of Trianon in 1920.

....During the same quarter century, 57,800 returned, more than one-half in the post WW-I wave of the country's enlargement into Greater Romania and rapid economic growth as oil, gold and wheat became major exports fueling rapid and large investments in infrastructure and industry. In 1919 as few as 60 returned; in 1920 and 1921, 30,000 returned.

....The peak in-migration period were the years 1906-07 and again 1913-1914 when a total of 30,500 and 37,500 emigrated from Romania respectively. Most were farmers and predominantly from Transylvania and the Banat; others from Dobrogea. About 10% arrived with higher education skills or professions. The primary motive, other than constrained opportunity to advance or buy property under Imperial rule over Transylvania, they sought the 'American dream' of higher income. At the time, wages for men were paid at a rate of $20-25 per week in industrial (machine tools, agricultural machinery, railroad engines, steel-works, or mining jobs); women were $12 to 18 per week and many found employment as domestics. This was equivalent to about $200-250 or $120 to 180 in present-day purchasing power. Room and board in lodgings in those days cost $4 to $5 per week.

....As the accompanying map indicates, the main destination were nine states: New York, Ohio, Pennsylvania, Illinois, Michigan, New jersey, Indiana, Minnesota and California.

....By the 1920s, New York City counted 38,000 citizens of Romanian origin of whom 90% were Jewish. The study made special mention that most arrived penniless. Four-out-of-ten became merchants. Many others found their way into the garment industry. Of the overall total of 70,000 Jewish Romanians in America, twenty per cent arrived as professionals in medicine or dentistry, law, engineering or architecture. Their principal parent organization in 1920 was The United Roumanian Jews of America based in New York with 12,000 members.

....The study noted in particular special qualities of ethnic-Romanian. They "did not object to hard physical work and lacked any self-pretense." And it added, "few were interested in joining the burgeoning union movement." The earliest Romanian social organization was the Uniunea Societatilor de Ajutor si Cultura din America (The Social Union for Assistance and Culture in America) that represented 120 local organizations in various American cities. Of those, thirty-two were in Ohio, seventeen in Pennsylvania, eleven in Indiana, and five in Illinois. The Social Union published a newspaper entitled AMERICA: The Only Roumanian Daily News. Forty churches were established of which 24 were Orthodox and 16 Greco-Catholic. A student group of 20 in Pittsburgh (Carnegie Institute of Technology and University of Pittsburgh) established the first Association of Romanian University Students in America.

DDD at the end of the War

CHAPTER FOUR

CROSSING THE OCEAN

I n Paris, my brother and I visited all there was to be seen. We almost relived the history of France. Then once the Allied Games were finished, my brother returned to Romania with the team. General Gavenescu kindly gave me two months leave before my being decommissioned. My salary as a Reserve-Captain was paid by the Military Attaché. This allowed me to afford renting a small apartment.

Now that I was there, I had decided to continue my studies in France by entering either the École des Beaux Arts for architecture or the École Polytechnique for engineering. But I felt unprepared and wondered if there was another place in France that would be easier for me. I found a book listing all the schools in France that gave degrees. The list was long and it was hard to make a choice. All required difficult entry exams with a strong emphasis on mathematics. That was one of my weak points. Finally I found a small school in Grenoble which granted engineering degrees. The admission requirements seemed easy, but I felt that I could not return to Romania with a lesser engineering degree.

Then one day on Boulevard de la Madeleine, I ran into a former "cercetașii" friend, Ionel Andronescu. He had not been in the war and had taken his Ph.D. in law at the Sorbonne. His father, a well-known doctor in Bucharest, after divorcing, was given custody of Ionel who now received sufficient support money from both his parents. At the Café Victoria,[20] which was almost empty at 5:00 p.m., we took a table in the basement. He ordered a bottle of Champagne to celebrate. We talked until about 4:00 a.m. I tried to convince him how lucky he was with Doctorate in Law, good income, and the freedom to do whatever he wished. He answered just the opposite. He said he was most unhappy and hated the idea of returning to Romania to live in the same house as his father who had remarried. He envied me because I had nothing, or so very little, and four years of study ahead of me before I started my life. We left the Café when the waiters re-

---

[20] Café Victoria still operates at 64 rue Charron its decor largely unchanged

fused to serve us any further. I accompanied as far as his apartment near Park Monceau and said goodbye.

At about 7:00 a.m. that morning, a mutual friend of ours, Virgil Cherciu, who worked at the Romanian Legation in Paris, came to tell me that Ionel had committed suicide. When we went to the apartment, I found a matchbox on the back of which were written the words: "It is finished." Stunned, I walked the streets of Paris wondering how a man who had so much could take his life.

Later while on Boulevard St. Germain, a window display of books caught my attention. One publication had the title *Comment Devenir Ingenieur* and next to it lay a pamphlet entitled with the question *Were you born in July?* Yes, I was born in July. Intrigued, I went inside and bought the book and the pamphlet. I immediately found a bench along the boulevard and sat there to read them.

The pamphlet was styled as a horoscope. All those born in July were supposed to have a beautiful future ahead of them. They were men of will and action. But to attain their goal, they had to cross a large expanse of water.

The book was more practical. It compared the French Polytechnic Institute in Paris with the Carnegie Institute of Technology in Pittsburgh, Ohio. The American school was described in glowing terms. The annual fees were $150; room and board were $30 per month. The school also had an employment office for students who needed a job during their free time. I decided right then to cross the "large expanse of water," which was the Atlantic Ocean, and make my way to Pittsburgh. That I did not speak English did not occur to me. I dropped everything else and determined to leave for America as-soon-as possible. I started by informing my mother. Then I wrote a few farewell letters to friends and relatives as though saying goodbye forever. This, I knew, meant taking a big step that would tear me away from my past, my country, and my family.

When I went to the American consular office, with few questions the officials easily issued me a student visa. At our Legation they were delighted because I could be charged with carrying a 'diplomatic pouch' full of books for Captain Vasile Stoica, a Transylvanian patriot, who was in New York preparing to make a tour of the United States to promote interest in Romania.

Equipped with a document describing me as 'diplomatic courier,' I used most of my money to book passage on the French transatlantic liner *France* and to buy three suits and some French linen. On the day of departure, I went to the Romanian Legation at 6:30 a.m. for the diplomatic bag before catching the 8:00 a.m. train for the Le Havre harbor. The 'pouch' was actually several trunks that would not fit into a taxi. I sent the Legation doorman to find a truck which took so long that when I got to the station the train had departed. Knowing nothing about transatlantic travel, I was never told that I could have gone to the Transatlantic Company where my ticket would have been canceled and my money returned. The *France* left without me and the money I had paid was no longer refundable. With little left, I had to look for a cheaper passage.

At the American Embassy it was suggested that I go to Tours 200 kilometers away where all post-War U.S. military transport arrangements were made. Once in Tours I couldn't interest anyone in my dilemma. I was Romanian and they only took care of Americans. However, they did tell me about a boat due to leave from Bordeaux in two days. So with my extra 'diplomatic trunks,' I went there by train and found, the New Zealand registered *S.S. Niagara*, a smaller ship on which I was able to get a third class ticket entitling me to a bunk on the lowest decks of the vessel.

Before sailing from Bordeaux the boat was delayed for three days. But though they had loaded my diplomatic trunks and my suitcase, I was not allowed to board. Without enough money for a hotel, I spent three nights on a bench in the central market of Bordeaux. The first evening while I was walking down a street, I saw a Romanian officer coming towards me. He suggested that we dine together in a summer garden which also had a floor show. He let me pay for the dinner, which was quite a setback for me, but said he would pay for the show. During dinner I tried to guess who he was because his face now seemed particularly familiar.

He wore a colonel's uniform and his breast was covered with medals, but they were not arranged in the proper order and there were some school medals mixed in with the military ones. This was decidedly not normal. When we went to the show, he asked for two tickets in the third balcony. I told him that it was not appropriate for a colonel to sit in the gallery to which he replied that at the first intermission we could take empty orchestra seats if there were any. All through the show I kept trying to remember where I had seen this man who now more obviously did not have the right to wear a colonel's uniform.

At last - and to my consternation - I finally remembered him as a young man who had once worked for my father! Of that I said nothing and after the show we parted and "my friend" suggested that we meet the next morning for breakfast. I immediately went to the police station where I reported the story of the fraudulent "Colonel." The policeman on duty told me that several days earlier they had received a notice from the Paris police who were looking for the chauffeur of the Romanian Military Attaché. The chauffeur had apparently vanished with the attaché's car, a suitcase of uniforms and a large sum of money. We decided at the police station that they would send some detectives to the cafe where I was to meet the "Colonel" for breakfast. So-as-to avoid a public scene, it was agreed that they would ask me for my papers and invite me to accompany them to the police station. When this took place, the "Colonel" gallantly offered to accompany us, protesting that I was an honest person. At the police station the colonel was told that he was under arrest. He was indeed the man that the Paris police were looking for.

Such incidents closed the first great chapter of my life. I was breaking from Europe and going to the New World. I had read all that I could find about the United States, but these books presented a different image than I had formed. While they described the hardships of the early settlers or their search for religious freedom, I was going to America to continue my education.

When it came time to board the 6,000 ton *S.S. Niagara*, it was nothing like the *France*. Instead, I was directed to a dark cabin. Already occupying it was a young Frenchman headed to the St. Pierre and Miquelon Islands to work in a cannery. There was also a young French woman with a baby which she was breast feeding. She was going to America to search for the child's father, an American soldier. She did not know where he lived but knew that his first name was "Henry." While there was discomfort for two men to be sharing the cabin with a woman, we soon helped her as by taking turns caring for the baby.

S.S. Niagara

The rest of the boat was full of American soldiers returning home. They looked like millionaires to us. They could walk on the deck, breathe fresh air and see the ocean. The long crossing took eighteen days. Luckily, I managed to befriend the cook who gave me some of the better food that he generally prepared. As a distraction the Americans organized a festival. A highlight was a boxing match in which my cabin-mate the Frenchman and I were enlisted to fight as light-weights. During my boy-scout days I had had a few boxing lessons from a well-known Romanian boxer named "Cotrus." This helped me to demolish my inexperienced opponent who had no idea how to box. For my victory I received a $50 prize which made me feel like a newly rich man.

As the ship approached the American coast it followed the shoreline for a long way. As it grew dark, I was able to see electric lights along a highway. We entered New York harbor during the night and stopped somewhere to await boarding by American authorities. All night I stood on deck looking at this unique glimmering scene of Manhattan and its tall sky-scrapers from the entrance to the Hudson River. Morning arrived at last and a small boat finally approached with all varied inspectors from health, customs and immigration. After we docked, of all the passengers I was the first one to be called. As a diplomatic courier I was given priority. The day was August 23, 1919.

✥

NEW YORK

The heat was tropical and my hair having grown long during the crossing bothered me. Being a complete stranger, I had no idea where to go. I left the wooden trunks and my suitcase at customs and followed the first street that I saw ahead of me. Suddenly I came face to face with a young man who asked me if I was French. To escape a long explanation I said, "Oui!" He took my arm and invited me for a drink in a bar. The man started asking me awkward questions. "Why are you coming to America?" "Where are you going to stay?" "How much money do you have?" I began to doubt his intentions and I told him that I was in a hurry to go into town. He said that I had to pay for the drinks so I took out of my pocket the $50 boxing prize. After a long conversation with the bartender my 'friend' returned with a handful of coins the value of which I did not know.

We parted in a friendly manner, he happy to vanish and me happy to enter a barbershop next to the bar. I was installed in a large revolving chair, typical of American barbershops. I had a shave, haircut, and a facial mas-sage with some kind of mud. The barber kept asking me things and as I

101

could not understand him I kept saying "Yes!" not knowing that I was agreeing to a variety of tonsorial services. When finished he invited me to step down from the chair. I held out my only handful of coins. He took $4.50 so that of my winnings I now had only $.50 cents.

In Paris I had purchased a map of New York that I now knew by heart. It was easy to remember as the streets are parallel and crossed perpendicularly. From previous inquiries, I knew that the center of town was at 42nd Street and 5th Ave which divides Manhattan into East and West halves. From the 14th Street pier where we moored, I headed there knowing that there was a YMCA information stand and nearby a hostel for Frenchmen. Walking around the center, I passed famous hotels, the Biltmore, the Commodore, the Roosevelt. From European experience, I had learned that if you go to a small hotel you have to pay in advance but a large hotel is glad to receive you and not asking for settlement of a bill to later on. So, with great courage I entered the Biltmore, asked for a room, and signed the register as Captain Dimancescu coming from Paris. At that time visitors from Paris were treated with special admiration. When they asked me where my luggage was, I told them it was at the port and I would give them instructions for retrieving it. With no more discussion I was taken to the elevator and escorted to my room. Actually it was a suite with a bedroom, living room and bathroom on the 14th floor. Looking down from my window, I was frightened by the great distance to the ground. Beyond was the great metropolis in full activity. What a spectacle! In quickly occurred to me that amongst all those millions of people working for a living, there must be a place for me.

What a transition I had just made from the below decks cabin of the *Niagara* to a luxury suite of the Biltmore in New York. The clerk who took me to my room spoke perfect French and said that if I needed anything to just telephone and ask for it. He gave me the key and left, wishing me, "Bienvenue aux États Unis." In such large hotels, I knew too, one could ask to have any items purchased. So I telephoned for a white shirt, pajamas and toiletries. Then I ordered lunch. A Maitre d'Hotel arrived with a long menu in French from which I ordered a steak and a bottle of French red wine. Then I took a bath. When I came out of the bathroom I found the white shirt that I had ordered and my lunch waiting for me. I ate well, drank half the bottle of wine, put on my American pajamas and went to bed hoping that sleep would inspire some good advice.

When I awoke the next morning, my first concern was to get rid of the 'diplomatic trunks' and deliver them to the Romanian Consulate. I planned then to request being formally discharged from the army. When I called Captain Stoica, to whom the books were being sent, he said in a very friendly voice that he was busy but invited me for lunch at the Biltmore where he too happened to be staying.

From a guidebook I discovered that there were many employment agencies on 6th Avenue. As there was still time until my lunch appointment I went there and indeed there were store-front-after-store-front employment agencies. With my English limited to few words, I recognized the word "restaurant." There was a long queue there, so I took my place in line. The processing was quick and I was hardly inside before I was given a slip with the address of a restaurant that was looking for help on First Avenue. Going there, I found a Greek establishment in a poor, dirty section of Manhattan. Inside the air was foul. An elderly man sitting at the cash register took my slip and asked me my name. When I said "Dimancescu" he threw his arms around me and asked me if I was Romanian. Two Turkish coffees appeared. He was the owner of the restaurant and although of Greek origin he had lived for many years in Brăila, a port city on the Danube River in Romania. He had earned a-lot-of money as the owner of a restaurant and coffee shop. Then someone persuaded him he could make more money in New York. Unfortunately this had not happened and his only wish was to return to Brăila.

As I explained to him that I intended to go to school in Pittsburgh, he said he would advance me the necessary amount to finish school. All this he told me with tears in his eyes. He said that of all the people that had come to his restaurant I was the only young person who wanted to go to school. He had neither children nor relatives in Greece. His real country was Romania. With touching generosity he told me he would give me as much money as I needed. I told him that I had come to America with the sole thought of finding my way on my own and could not accept his help. But I felt reassured by his encouragement that I could come to him if I needed help.

Once back at the Biltmore Hotel, Captain Stoica found me. I sensed that he took pride in impressing me on how well he was doing in the United States. To start lunch he ordered an avocado salad. I had never seen avocado before and did not know how to start. Stoica explained how. After that came an abalone steak which also something new to me. Stoica explained that it was a sort of large oyster found only on the Californian coast.

But the most important thing Stoica said was that he would take care of my hotel bill and that he would send someone from the consulate to get the wooden trunks. He advised me to look for a furnished room but said if I wanted to stay at the Biltmore he would take care of my bills. I thanked him and told him that that my first objective was to get to Pittsburgh. Quite generously, he told me he had some business to do in Pittsburgh and would take me with him, paying my fare. Accompanying me to the hotel's reception desk, he asked that my bill be transferred to his account. We parted on very polite terms not knowing exactly how long I would be in New York.

As-soon-as I was alone, I went to the YMCA information center and told where to find an inexpensive rooming house in what turned out to be another miserable neighborhood. The landlady showed me the lodging that was along a fourth floor narrow passage between two rooms for $2 a week. As far as the rent was concerned, Stoica promised that I would be reimbursed in dollars for a good part of the expenses I had incurred in bringing the trunks.

Before leaving New York I had to go and present myself to the Commissioner of the Romanian Government, a Mr. Pantazi. He was responsible for the formalities involved in my discharge from the army. The meeting in the Consular offices, a converted private house at 666 Lexington Avenue, was confrontational. Nobody had warned me that he was nervous and gruff. Hardly had I entered his office than he told me that I must be mad to have come to America.

"Sir," he said, "you had a very good social position in Romania. What are you doing here? You want to go to school? To study what? Engineering? They have better schools in Europe! But this is your own business. I will give the discharge from the army, but I will keep you here in my New York office."

I thought of my Greek friend and his warm welcome and then of Commander Pantazi's rough manners. Eventually I came to realize that Pantazi was a very brave man and that his arrogance was a front to cover his own insecurities.

The first night in my new lodgings not at all pleasant. It was so hot that I could not sleep. When I heard horses neighing, I thought I was having a nightmare. But going to the window to look out, I stared right at a horse's head. The neighboring building was a stable five floors high where the horses were taken up and down by elevator. To aggravate things, an "elevated" railroad ran near my window. This was a sort of steel-roadway over the street for trains to run on. Every half hour a train passed by with a thundering noise. I could only imagine that thousands of inhabitants of New York were accustomed to these infernal nocturnal symphonies.

At daybreak, and to my surprise, I heard a flute that sounded like a Romanian "doina" and then someone shouting "Let me sleep!" in Romanian. Realizing that my neighbors were Romanian, I quickly dressed and knocked on their door. It opened to a miracle! They were Mihnea Socec, a former colleague of mine from Lazăr High School, and Serban Druțu whose family lived on the same street in Bucharest as mine. When in Paris, we had met in the street and they had told me that they were going to America where they were expected by a rich uncle who had a big house. The "uncle," it turned out, was imaginary. When they arrived in America, Commander Pantazi latched on to them and hired them as clerks at the Consular office.

Happy to be in their company, we went together to the Consular office. This was advantageous as later they introduced me to the rather unusual employees who worked in the basement as "writers of passports." There was a long queue of people extending from the door of the passport office out onto Lexington Avenue. They were the "clientèle." In name only, the boss of this section was a Macedonian who spoke "Cuto-Viaha" and had difficulty speaking pure Romanian. Next to his desk sat another Macedonian who had the same language difficulties. Both of them dealt with applicants from individuals originating in what had been Austro-Hungarian Transylvania, the Banat, Bucovina, Bessarabia, and Macedonia. They referred to them as "wooden-headed" and were quick to tell me that I would have a lot to do with the "wood-heads."

Above the passport office were three rooms where Pantazi's assistants, Matila Costiescu-Ghyka, Professor Cadere from Oradea, and Vasile Stoica. The three had completely different personalities. Stoica was the most active and Cadere the least active. Ghyka spent most of his time at the New York Public Library doing research for his work on metaphysics.[21]

They were part of a "Commission" created by the Bratianu government at the urging of Stoica who claimed correctly that thousands of Romanian in America wanted to return to Romania. Many were from Transylvania and now that it was not longer Austro-Hungarian territory, they needed Romanian passports. Those from Bucovina had Austrian passports, those from Bessarabia had Russian passports, and those from Macedonia had Turkish passports. To confirm them as Romanian citizens required a legal writ from the Romanian parliament either on an individual basis or "en masse." Prime Minister Bratianu decided to send a Commission to New York authorize the issuing of temporary passports that would be confirmed when individuals arrived in Romania. But without authorization, Commander Pantazi imposed a $10 fee for each "passport" that was nothing more than an officially stamped sheet of paper. In the basement office, Tascu Tănasescu, the Macedonian, and Druțu and Socec, both from Bucharest, could arbitrarily issue passports without asking for verification papers from the applicants. They obtained their passports after interviews with one of the two Macedonians. Many of these emigrants had come from

---

[21] Matila C. Ghyka was a novelist, mathematician, historian, philosopher and diplomat. He was born in Iași, the former capital of Moldavia, of the Ghica family of boyars. On his mother's side he was the great-grandson of Grigore Alexandru Ghica, last reigning Prince of Moldavia before the union of the Danubian Principalities. Source: Wikipedia

Cleveland, Detroit, Chicago and Youngstown. Tired of staying in New York and lining-up in the street, were ready to pay up to $100 for a passport. In fact, many of them were slipping various sums under the table thus contributing to the well being of the two lowly Macedonian clerks. Inexperienced travelers, these same 'clients' fell into the hands of people who knew how to profit from their situation. A few would become prominent in the Romanian diplomatic service. These were profiteers of Romanian origin who opened special lodgings known as "Romanian Houses" where the emigrants could get room and board for exorbitant sums. That was not all. Some of these "patriotic" hotelkeepers also opened travel agencies to sell return tickets to Romania.

Many of the returning immigrants had with them large sums of money that they had saved while in the United States. Some had as much as $10,000 or $20,000 in cash that they kept in a belt under their coat. The Romanian travel agents advised them to change their dollars into lei and to send this money ahead to Romania. The exchange was made at much lower rate than the official rate. In this way, many lost half their savings. There was no one to impose any control over the boarding houses or travel agents. Some of the agents were on very good terms with Commander Pantazi's two basement clerks, who would process passports faster when they received under-the-table bribes. It did not take me long to realize that the Lexington Avenue office was a great mistake.

To Stoica, I suggested that consular offices should be opened in other Romania centers and that Ghyka and Cadere - whom I respected - should head up the offices in Detroit and Cleveland. Stoica, though very young, considered himself qualified to look after the Romanian colony's business. Since Commander Pantazi was his boss, he was polite with him but he generally ignored him. The same situation prevailed between Pantazi and everyone else in his office. They all considered him crazy. The impressions given was that authorities in Romania were not interested in the problems of Romanians in the United States. Greater Romania had other problems.

Stoica, though the son of a peasant from Avrig in southern Transylvania, came to the United States young and in public dressed himself in a self-styled Romanian army uniform. He became popular in "good society" in New York and was often invited to the homes of wealthy families on Long Island and Newport, a wealthy resort-town in Rhode Island. He took the question of American-Romanians as one of great importance. But he had an exaggerated conception of the problem. Without any statistics, he concluded that there were a million emigrants from Romania and that their return home would contribute to the national economy.[22]

୶୬ଓ

STUDENT IN PITTSBURGH

Dimitri D., Capt. Vasile Stoica, Mihnea Socec at
Carnegie Institute of Technology (1919)

I did not know who was financing his expenses, but I imagine that Commander Pantazi was giving him money from the fees for passports issued in New York. There was plenty of money. Stoica went to the best hotel in Pittsburgh, the "William Penn," and of course he took me along. I was

---

[22] He fought in the Romanian Army against invading German forces in Oltenia, and followed the Romanian troops in their retreat to Moldavia. In March 1917, Stoica (by then a second lieutenant) was a member of a group of exiled Romanian Habsburg subjects who were sent as a delegation to the United States to campaign for Romania's cause. The envoys also established close contacts with the Czech Tomás Masaryk and the Polish Ignacy Jan Paderewski.

He was instrumental in the creation of the *Romanian National League of America* in July, some months after America joined the Entente forces; among other things, the *League*, centered in Youngstown, Ohio, helped direct the war effort and participation of the Romanian-American community towards the US forces on the Western Front.

He eventually returned to Romania. After WW-II he was imprisoned from 1948 to 1954 and in 1957 was arrested again and sentenced to 10 years in prison. He died in Sighet prison in 1959. SOURCE: wikipedia < en.wikipedia.org/wiki/Vasile_Stoica >

starting my student life in this large industrial city in a luxury that did not correspond to my financial situation. Together we called on Mr. McClung, an American who was serving as Consul for Romania and was married to the millionaire Andrew Mellon's sister. Without forewarning me Stoica told him I would be appointed his assistant with the rank of vice-consul. All the needed expenses would be paid by Pantazi's passport fees. The same day we rented two rooms at 3 Wood Street in a commercial office building overlooking the Monongahela River that joined the Allegheny River to form the Ohio River as short distance away.

The offices had a lovely view towards the river and across to Mt. Washington. I promptly went to the Carnegie Institute of Technology[23] where even though I only spoke French I was able to obtain all the information about registering as a student. Though I was supposed to pass an entrance exam, I was introduced to the Director of the Institute, Dr. Arthur A. Hamerschlog, a German hired by the famed steel magnate Andrew Carnegie and the Institute's founder. We conversed in German and French and he was very understanding especially of the value of a European "baccalaureate" (high school diploma) and admitted me on the spot as a second year student even though I could not speak English. He said I could learn the language in two or three months just by listening to others. He advised me to take Management Engineering and sent me to the Dean of that department who gave me a student card and a room in a dormitory. Moreover, he found part-time employment for me to help me cover my tuition fees. I was fortunate, too, that Carnegie had decided that tuition costs should be very low so that even poor students could attend. In 1919, when I was admitted, the yearly tuition was $110. My first job was to wash dishes at the student restaurant. This assured me of three good meals a day. I had to collect the dirty dishes and bring them to a room where there was a mechanical device for washing the plates, glasses and cutlery. I was also given addresses where I could mow lawns, rake dead leaves, and shovel snow. For these services I was paid generously by the hour.

The classes were not larger than thirty students, the average was about twenty. There was a friendly feeling between the professors and students. We were addressed by our first names. At the beginning of class we were given a ten-minute test of ten questions to be answered *yes* or *no*. This test was given every day for each course. This gave the professors an idea whether we were up to date with the subject. Sometimes the test would take place at the blackboard, when each student had to solve a problem in ten minutes. The blackboard extended all round the room with the exception of the windows. After the test the professor would talk for 20-25 min-

---

[23] Later renamed Carnegie-Mellon University

utes explaining the current lesson and allowing us to put questions to which he offered a precise answer. The school year was divided into three semesters and at the end of each one there was a long written test, which lasted all 55 minutes. We were allowed to use our own books or any other information. The theory was that it was more important to know where to find the answer than to memorize it.

The courses at the Institute were divided between classes with professors in class and afternoons in workshops with special instructors. The workshops equipped with tools and machinery similar to those in factories. We had a foundry, a mechanical carpentry shop, and one for ironwork where each student worked with a hammer and forge. In three years, thanks to these workshop, I learned the factory routines of the metallurgical industry. In one shop we had a collection of new 1919-1920 car engines. We had to dismantle them completely and then put them back into perfect working condition. In another shop, the students had to build a four-room house out of bricks and complete it in one term with kitchen, bathroom, water, and electricity installed. Class sessions lasted one hour and we had to go to the room assigned each professor. Our attendance was marked on a seating plan so that each student had to sit at the same desk every time.

For the first three months I was like a Chinese person in a Greek school. I understood nothing of what the Professor was saying. The first word I recognized was "plus," and later "minus." With great perseverance I began to read the textbooks and gradually to understand phrases. Somehow after three months I started to speak a little. A colleague named Braverman, a Jew of Russian origin, devoted himself to helping me learn English. He corrected my pronunciation of the letter "a" and "i" which were pronounced differently in Romanian.

Life in an American school of engineering is completely different than in a European school of the same type. In America the students are treated as high school students are treated in Europe. Their presence in class is absolutely obligatory. Unjustified absences can result in suspension. Only two weeks were permitted for sickness per semester. I adapted fairly easily to this life. I was going to bed at midnight and getting up at 4:00 a.m. I believed that four hours sleep were enough, particularly because I had read that the inventor Thomas Edison managed only four hours of sleep each night. Between 4:00 a.m. and 8:00 a.m. when classes started, I reviewed the lessons for the day. There were evening classes from 7:00 to 9:00 for students who had jobs during the day. One needed 52 credits to graduate. My wish was to learn as much as possible, so I registered for both day and evening classes also, not knowing that it was not allowed to do both. I was the only student to do this. Their logic was that it was physically impossible to attend both the day and evening schools. When the university discovered what I was doing it was too late to change anything.

Democracy is supposed to dominate all aspects of life in America. But inside universities there are many non-democratic activities. Students with A and B marks were invited to join fraternities. For reasons that I could not understand I was not invited to join a fraternity, so I surprised everyone by creating my own fraternity. Nobody could stop me. I designed a gold key for my fraternity that was called "Delta Chi Rho." At the beginning we had only three members. After I left Carnegie my fraternity was invited to merge with one of the oldest and largest fraternities. My successors accepted the invitation. There were many other organizations that restricted their membership. Some had a professional character. For instance we had student societies for mechanical engineering, chemistry or mineralogy. Most of these had limited activities and a small number of members.

The most important and popular was the International Club whose members were foreign students and a few of their American friends. I joined this club. Each year there was a congress of international students held at a large university. For three years in a row, I was sent as the representative of the Carnegie International Club and in my last year I was elected president of all the international clubs from schools and universities in America. This helped me meet a large number of foreign students.

CARNEGIE INSTITUTE OF TECHNOLOGY, PITTSBURGH, PA.

The group of buildings at the Carnegie Institute of Technology included the schools of Industries, Mechanical Engineering, Machinery, and Arts. These buildings were around a large square. Some students took courses that were given in more than one building. When the weather was bad, they could get from one building to another through tunnels. All these departments accepted only men, with the exception of the School of Arts where women could enroll. In the Arts building there was a theater with seating for 1,000 people. Every week the drama students put on a show with open attendance. There was also a concert once a week given by music students. There was also a daily non-sectarian Christian service in the theater. In my three years there I never missed one.

Near our buildings was the Margaret Morrison Carnegie College, one of the four colleges of the Institute. Girls studied basic domestic and livelihood skills. Girls in the fourth year had to prepare lunches and dinners for four, eight or twelve people. They were allowed to invite senior students from the Carnegie Institute. There was great competition among those who wanted to be invited and I was lucky to be a regular invitee

Across a small vale, west of the Institute there was a huge building that was the main Carnegie library and a much larger theater for 3,000 people. This had the largest organ in the United States and several halls with an international collection of paintings and sculptures. Andrew Carnegie had managed the sale of the organ after World War I from Notre Dame Cathedral in Paris. There were free organ concerts two or three times per week. I did not miss many of these concerts which became a musical education. Besides what I had seen in European museums, exhibitions at Carnegie introduced me to contemporary plastic arts as well as technical arts. The Institute was a complete setting within which to shape one's individuality.

"Commencement Day," when diplomas were distributed, was the culmination point for every student. My emotion was great, but none of my relatives were there to share my happiness. Dr. Hammershlog shook my hand heartily after handing me my diploma and telling me that my marks had justified his decision to accept me in the Institute.

There was a special honorary fraternity, Alpha Tau, for the School of Industry students. Without guessing that I would be selected, I was initiated into this fraternity at a ceremony where the participants wore black hoods over their heads. I was brought in the hall where the initiation took place with my eyes bound and listened to the various speeches without knowing who was talking. At the moment when the fraternity president, Professor Leighow, announced that I was a member he and the others took off their hoods and my eyes were unbound. He gave me the "Key" and congratulated me.

When I received my diploma in 1922, I was the student with the highest marks in the entire school. My diploma gave me the right to the title of "Engineer." It had been my father's wish for me to become an engineer. While I had satisfied his wish I now wondered what to do with the diploma. Engineering had many branches and the one I had specialized in was quite new. I was among the first "Taylorist" efficiency engineers. Carnegie Tech was among the first schools to teach the breakthrough "scientific management" theories of Frederick Winslow Taylor. Claiming that factory workers should be compensated on-the-basis-of the "Time Element," Taylor had developed a system for measuring the exact time it took a worker to produce one specific item again-and-again. He also demonstrated that workers often wasted too much time by making useless movements and that tools had to be arranged in ways to save motions. We "Taylorists" had been taught to measure time and to organize work logically. I did not know then that this was the start of a revolution in production efficiency in America. Later this changed to "Industrial Engineering" and then to "Management Engineering."

In my last month at Carnegie, the Dean had called me to his office and told me that he was going to resign and start an industrial engineering company. He wanted to know if I would like to work for him. This was a great honor for me and would resolve the dilemma of what I was going to do when I left school. I told him that I was very honored but asked for some time to think it over before making my decision.

Then another unexpected visit occurred. It was just a few days after I had received my diploma, that the Romanian Minister in Washington, Prince Antoine Bibesco, came to Pittsburgh to meet the Romanian students there. Besides myself, newly graduated, there were eleven other students at the neighboring University of Pittsburgh, all of them studying oil engineering. They considered themselves superior to me and still had one more year of studies. Bibesco invited us all to dinner in his suite at the William Penn Hotel. He seated each of us by age. On his right was George Anagnostache, a quiet person with slow reactions, and on his left, Ionei Gardescu who was at home anywhere. I was at the end of the table though I was not the youngest but no longer a student. Bibesco's style was to pose questions and expect very short answers. He assaulted the group with questions that were at first personal and then jumped to other subjects. One of the questions was which was the better of two universities: Carnegie Tech or Pittsburgh University? The answer, in chorus, was "Pittsburgh University." In fact it was a much larger school with a large faculty and more buildings. And behind it was the house of its founder, the multi-millionaire Andrew W. Mellon. Carnegie Tech was a newer and relatively small school with only engineering and arts departments. It was backed by the wealth of Andrew Carnegie who wanted a "school of intelligent, but not necessarily rich boys."

At the end of the dinner, Bibesco invited each one of us, one at time, into the next room for a confidential talk. Each was asked: "Do you need any money and how much?" In parting, each student received from $300 to $500. These interviews were short. When my turn came, he asked me the same question to which I answered that I did not need money. Despite his insistence, I refused. He said, "You must he an extraordinary person. Your colleagues told me that you have six mistresses and are an embarrassment to the Romanian students." Without letting me answer to confirm or deny the accusation, he said: "Is she pretty? Have you kissed her yet?" And without waiting for an answer, he congratulated me. I explained that in America any student or single man can have a girlfriend and the notion of a mistress does not exist as it was commonly so in Europe.

My interview ended and Bibesco returned to the other room where the others were waiting. He told them a curtly "Good-bye" and opened the door through which they quickly left. As I left he said "I hope you will come and see me in Washington." Of course all the students wanted to know how much money each one, including me, had received. We all parted on a false note of friendship.

◈

CHAPTER FIVE

DIPLOMAT

The day after my encounter in Pittsburgh with Minister Bibesco,[24] I received a telegram from him inviting me to dinner at the Romanian Legation in Washington. I was inclined to decline because of the cost of the round-trip train fare. However, after I accepted he mailed me money for my travels and I arrived in the Capital. At the train station I was met by Serban Druţu, now the Chancellor of the Legation whom I had met by chance in New York. Bibesco had given him a free hand to manage the diplomatic Chancellery.

The next morning, Bibesco phoned to say that Princess Bibesco would be delighted to have me for lunch. Full of excitement I went into town and bought a new suit, a shirt and a pair of shoes. When I looked at myself in the mirror I appeared ridiculous. However, at the due time, I went to the legation where I was ushered to the Minister's office by a uniformed valet. As-soon-as he saw me he rushed over and started feeling the collar of my jacket. He asked me where I had bought it and how much I had paid for it. He told me a similar suit would have cost much more in London. This sort of reception seemed odd to me, but as I was going to find out, Bibesco had an odd personality.

Meanwhile another guest arrived, the first secretary of the French Legation. I was introduced to him as "Mon grand ami Dimancescu." Shortly after, Princess Elizabeth Bibesco came in and I was introduced to her as "Mon ami Dimancescu" without the 'grand.'

Lunch was served in the legation dining room and I remember that it started with a soufflé. I do not remember what followed. There seemed to be a number of questions for which I did not have answers. Elizabeth Bibesco asked me how I liked Washington, a banal question to which I replied that I liked it. For the rest of the meal the conversation was dominated by the French diplomat who had a bag full of news of interest to diplomats. I listened in silence as I could not contribute anything. The first one to leave was the Princess in her Rolls Royce. Soon after, the French man left too and

---

[24] Prior to WW-I, Romania was represented in Washington through its Legation headed by a Minister. Senior members were called Counselors. After WW-II they became Embassies headed by an Ambassador.

when I was ready to go, Bibesco asked me if I would like to work at the Legation. I told him that I had never thought of entering the diplomatic corps. Quite simply, I did not have the qualifications. The minimum requirement was a Law Degree. I explained that I had been asked to join an engineering firm for which I had to give an answer.

Bibesco said he would not insist and did not want to influence my choice, but added that between being an engineer in Pittsburgh or any other industrial town in America, and a diplomat in Washington, the choice was not difficult. As for the degree in law he said that was an easy matter to settle. He said he would wait for my answer. As I left, he gave me an envelope with money for my round-trip train fare. I tried to refuse but with the same persistence he would not take the envelope back.

Washington tempted me, even though I had barely had a glimpse of how diplomats lived. The Legation was in large house overlooking Sheridan Circle. Pittsburgh was waiting for me with a good salary but with a room with windows which could hardly be opened because of the persistent smog from the steel factories. I found myself at a great crossroads in my life. I had to make a choice between two kinds of lives. Which one to take?

By the time the train reached Pittsburgh, my decision was made: Washington. From the station I telegraphed Bibesco:

"Greatly honored. I accept your offer."

An answer was delivered soon after:

"Delighted. Come when you want."

When I went to see Dr. Hammerschlog to tell him that I had accepted a small job in the Romanian Diplomatic Service, he very kindly told me that he would have done the same and described to me the monotony of an engineer's life in an office.

It was not difficult to leave Pittsburgh. All my clothes fit into one suitcase and the books into a large trunk. I did not know where I would live in Washington and did not want to burden Bibesco with my small problems. Washington was a city with innumerable government employees, many of them single living in simple furnished rooms. Easily enough I found a room on Church Street near Dupont Circle, a five-minute walk to the Legation. My new hosts, a family of three, offered me a bedroom, living room, bathroom and American breakfast for $30 a month.

When I had everything in order, I telephoned Bibesco who asked me to come to the Legation right away. He took me to the Chancellery to meet with Druțu and Miss Helen Fitzpatrick, who had worked there for years. After a short introduction, he left us alone and Druțu assumed his role as my chief. He did not care that I had an engineering degree and told me coldly that I was not a diplomat but merely an office employee.

He kept a register in which he meticulously recorded columns of entries of all the legation's incoming and outgoing correspondence. The correspondence files were kept in small parcels and filed in numerical order. It was impossible to locate a document if one did not know its number that had been recorded in the register. Only Druţu knew the numbering system by heart and could locate anything. He showed me my work place, a large mahogany desk with empty drawers. Daily assignments would be given to me. To begin he put the register on my desk and told me that from then on I had to keep him posted. He provided me with an eraser, saying that no errors were allowed and everything had to be neat and clean. And although there was a phone on my desk, he said that I was not to use it for personal calls. Fortunately his phone gave me direct contact with Bibesco, who often called me to his office. After showing me the files, Druţu invited me for lunch.

When Bibesco was appointed Minister to Washington in 1920, Commander Pantazi's mission in New York was called to an end and he and his assistants were recalled to Romania. Pantazi had accumulated over $100,000 in fees on passports. Collecting them had not been authorized in Romania and no one there wanted to accept responsibility for accepting the money. Pantazi put the sum in Bibesco's name thus resolving one illegality with another. These monies were then used to buy a large house in Washington for $75,000. It was nice but not ideally suited for a Legation. The entrance to the first floor was on 23rd Street. A large hall on the right was the dining room and the living room was on the left became the chancellery. Though large as a living room it was too small for all the administrative personnel. From the hall, paved with large square of white marble tiles, there was a semi-circular stairway to the second floor where Bibesco installed his office in the former library. He had brought beautifully bound books from England. Across from the library was a large living room furnished with rare items and a piano. Between these two rooms there was a large hall turned into a living room from which another circular stairway led to the third floor with five bedrooms each with a small bathroom and a small living room. This became the personal apartment of the Minister, his wife, their daughter, Priscilla, and her English governess. One floor higher were several rooms and bathrooms for three servants who had access to the basement via an elevator. In the basement were the kitchen, the servants' dining room and the cook's apartment. There was also a room with a bathroom for the chauffeur who was a Romanian gypsy called Marin.

My diplomatic career began in these surroundings. It had nothing of the luxury that I had imagined and I was now consigned as a 'copyist.' There were, however, some benefits. Bibesco did not treat me as a copyist and always addressed me as "Dear Friend." From the start he introduced me to some of his colleagues and invited me to dinner two or three times a week.

Monthly the U.S. State Department published a small booklet, called the "Diplomatic List" in which were listed all foreign diplomats currently in the Capital. In the beginning, my name was not on the list, which was a great handicap. However, one day I received an engraved invitation to a ball for embassy and legation personnel. On the appointed day, I went to the ball dressed in tails and white tie but was rather surprised when the doorman told me the ball was being held in the basement. When I entered, I discovered that the ball was for the servants of the embassies and legations? Of course, I stayed and danced with the cooks and maids. Later I found that my name was listed not on the diplomatic list but on the servants' list.

Without telling me, Bibesco had requested Bucharest to grant me the title of "Chancellor of Legation." And after some difficulty the modest title was confirmed and my name soon appeared on the official Diplomatic List. I did not know that this would throw me into the social whirl of the Washington elite. Now I received three or four invitations every day and did not know how to divide myself. In those days, the Washington working season was from October to March-April. Every day there were three or four luncheons and dinners of importance. In between there were 5 o'clock cocktails and there were late suppers, some starting at midnight. At first, I accepted a lot of invitations but soon realized that they meant very little. Slowly I became more selective about the invitations I accepted.

The years I spent under Bibesco's tutelage in Washington became a course in diplomacy that I could not have received anywhere else. He was born in Paris where he was raised among the social elite. Despite his quirks, Bibesco was an extraordinary man. He came to Washington from London with an established reputation enhance by his marriage to the daughter of the British ex-Prime Minister Herbert Asquith and a social life amongst England's own upper classes. For a short while, he had been the legation attaché in Petrograd, but was obliged to return to Bucharest because of a personal incident. He had been at lunch in a restaurant with a friend, when suddenly a Russian noble came to his table and slapped him without reason or provocation. The Romanian Foreign Ministry, informed of the incident by telegram, forbade Bibesco to challenge the nobleman to a dual. And to avoid a "diplomatic incident" refused to lodge a protest with the Russian Foreign Ministry. Bibesco retired from public life for a while until the incident was forgotten.

The Bibescos' had a passion for the theater. They never missed premières presented in New York and Washington. They had many actor friends and used to invite them for dinner. Bibesco took a great liking for the actress Ann Harding and whenever he had the opportunity he would send her flowers with a card or a word. He sometimes asked me to deliver the flowers. Eventually, Miss Harding concluded that the flowers were from me! She gave me an autographed portrait with a nice dedication.

He read English and French literature and had cultivated contact with many intellectual friends. He corresponded with them by postcard. To a long letter from a friend he would reply by postcard simply "Received letter of such date. Thank you." and would sign *A.B.* His handwriting was impossible to read. Sometimes he would call me and ask if I could guess what he had written. With the Romanian Foreign Ministry, he corresponded via very short telegrams explaining to me that reports he sent to Romania were never read by the Ministry.

Under him, the Legation staff grew. The first to come after me was Frederic 'Nanu' Nairn, First Secretary of the Legation and soon promoted to Counselor of the Legation, He was the son of another Romanian diplomat who had married a Belgian woman while stationed in Brussels. Nanu was more of a Belgian. He spoke and wrote perfect French and spoke Romanian with an accent but with an outstanding knowledge of Romanian grammar. He had me write some of the Legation's reports and then would check them as meticulously as a teacher would. Sometimes he would have me rewrite a report three or four times. Working with him was an educational experience. Besides his good work, he had two great qualities. He was an excellent bridge player and was in great demand around Washington for bridge games. The second was his wife, Rose, born in Mexico and educated at a Catholic school in London. With hair the color of copper, she was very beautiful. She was admired and courted by all the men. Some as celebrated as the Duke of Sutherland had asked her to marry him. And Senator Peter Gerry[25] of Rhode Island, himself married to the widow of George Vander-

---

[25] His name was given the process of 'gerrymander' which meant fixing voting district geographical to ensure victory of an incumbent politician.

bilt, had begged Rose, sometimes in front of her husband and sometimes in front of me, to marry him.

With Bibesco's and Nanu's contacts, our Legation was ahead of all the others in gathering political news. Bibesco was an honorary member of the Metropolitan Club where he mingled with leading American politicians and members of Congress. He did not smoke or drink. At the Metropolitan Club bar he would ask the waiter to fill a cocktail glass with water which he would occasionally sip. At Legation dinners he served the best French wines for he had a cellar of rare wines and champagnes. In contrast, Elizabeth had sometimes to be restrained in her drinking. Many distinguished British personalities would make a courtesy call to their own Embassy and then come to the Romanian Legation to relax.

It became a habit that if some guest could not come at the last minute, I would be routinely asked to take their place. I remember that at one lunch where Lord Balfour had been invited, I was brought in at the last minute as a stand-in for a cancellation. Bibesco and Balfour had a tennis date, so I had to attend both at lunch and join them at tennis. Bibesco whispered to me to lose balls because Balfour was an old man. Actually Balfour was an excellent tennis player and for two hours made me run from one end of the court to the other.

Bibesco set out to resolve several problems. One was the recognition of Bessarabia[26] as part of Romania by the United States, and the settlement of inheritances of Romanian immigrants. The United States held to the position that Romania had annexed Bessarabia after WW-I at a time when the Russian people could not express their views. Though various writers and newspapermen supported the Romanian position, the State Department would not budge. The second issue involved mainly Romanian immigrants who had died in industrial accidents and whose insurance policies left amounts of $10,000 to $25,000 to their heirs. Bibesco would have liked the 600 pending cases to be treated together and the total sum remitted to the Romanian government which would then determine who were the rightful heirs. The United States denied any responsibility, arguing that the inheritances were a legal matter between the state in which the immigrant had resided and his relatives in Romania. For lack of a solution, Nanu Nairn took on the responsibility of studying each case individually making this

---

[26] Bessarabia had fallen under Tsarist Russian rule prior to WW-I. But at the War's end was returned to Romania by the terms of the Treaty of Trianon in 1920. Much later, after WW-II, the Soviet Union took it back by force though Romania never formally acknowledged the return by formal treaty agreement. It was turned into the independent nation of Moldova after the disintegration of the Soviet Union.

one of his main activities. All the details and questions were passed on to me and I had to do all the leg work.

At the same time, Andrei Popovici left his editorship of the paper *America* to accept the job of attaché at the legation. Unfortunately, he devised a solution to the inheritance issue that appeared easy but which soon turned into a disaster. His solution was to turn the cases over to a Mr. Lupear, a poorly-trained lawyer of Romanian origin from Indianapolis. Lupear created powers of attorney which gave him the right to represent the interests of the deceased immigrants in his name or that of Romanian authorities and without restrictions. He rented a whole building and thanks to Popovici was named Honorary Vice Consul in the State of Indiana. Any amounts of money that were collected were in Lupear's name and were deposited in his personal account in an Indianapolis bank and spent in his own interest. This situation provoked a scandal in which the Legation was implicated because it appeared to be covering for Lupear. The powers of attorney were finally canceled and all the files returned to Washington.

Another important question that needed to be resolved was the matter of war debts owed by Romania to the United States. At the end of World War I, all the European allies owed money to the United States. Though Romania had not needed a loan, it accepted one and spent it on useless items acquired from the surplus of war materials that the Americans had in France. [Note: *I write later about the widely acclaimed modern-dancer Loie Fuller and more details about the way in which the loan was authorized.*] In the U.S. Treasury accounts the Romanian debt was listed as $7,500,000 and Romania was asked to pay it immediately. In Bucharest, on the other hand, it was anticipated that all war debts would eventually be forgotten. Only one country, Finland whose debt was about the same size as ours, was believed to have paid its debt promptly but in reality took more than 55 years to so.

Bibesco discussed the question of the War Debt with his friend Andrew Mellon, who was Secretary of the Treasury. He assured Bibesco that the debt could be settled on friendly terms and without publicity. Bibesco informed the Romanian Minister of Finance, Vintilă Brătianu, that he was in a position to settle the matter quietly in Washington. But there was in Bucharest at-that-time an ambitious young man, Nicolae Titulescu, who was looking for a cause that would give him international visibility. He convinced Bratianu to send him to Washington with the mission of resolving the "very difficult" debt problem. He arrived in Washington with several Romanian experts and about four secretaries. Their mission occupied an entire floor at the Wardman Park Hotel, one of the best in Washington. Bibesco sent a telegram protesting against the mission, but Brătianu replied that he should tend to the diplomatic affairs of the Legation and leave financial matters to Titulescu. Thus immediate friction between Bibesco and Titulescu was to be expected. Unwittingly I was the spark that set it off.

As-soon-as I finished my work at the Legation I would go to the Hotel to visit friends who were members of the Titulescu mission. They had brought four large trunks from Romania with papers containing statistical data and details about Romanian state expenditures. It was out of the question that the Americans would take on the task of translating these papers. Yet, on meeting the U.S. Commissioner of War Debts, Titulescu planned to present him with all the material contained in the four trunks. More or less casually I told him that it would better if we had photographic copies of all the material. Titulescu answered, "Bravo, you do it."

At the same time, he telephoned Bibesco to ask him to let me work with the "Titulescu Mission." Bibesco answered that he needed me and could not let me go. Furious, Titulescu replied with an outrageous insult: "You are crazy and have always been crazy." Relations between the Legation and the Mission were interrupted. Titulescu then sent a coded telegram to Brătianu, saying that he would not start negotiations with the United States until Bibesco was recalled. In less than 24 hours, Titulescu had a reply from Ion G. Duca, then Minister of Foreign Affairs, that Bibesco would be recalled. Bibesco and Titulescu never spoke again, the former canceling a dinner he had arranged in Titulescu's honor.

Titulescu had a way of insulting his colleagues with harsh words, but without any real meaning. Mr. Ciotori, who was his shadow, was accused at every step of being "stupid," "an idiot," or "mad." So it is possible that when he told Bibesco he was crazy, he did not really intend to offend him. However, Bibesco was obsessed with thought that he would die insane because his mother had died from a nervous breakdown.

The negotiations for the liquidation with the American World War Foreign Debts Commission was led by Senator Reed Smoot on the American side. He had a very simple political philosophy. "We gave them money, now they must return it." It was agreed that the meeting would take place at the Treasury Department where a large room had been prepared. A long table was the middle and at one end sat the American delegation and at the other the Romanian mission. Titulescu had brought five solutions. They differed only in the way payments should be made, the length of the term and the amount of interest to be paid. Though the Americans were early risers and wished to start at eight o'clock, he managed to impose on them his own time of eleven o'clock. At the Wardman Park Hotel he would stay awake until two or three o'clock in the morning, though there was no need for these late nights. His mission members had to keep him company. Sometimes he would rehearse the speech he had to make the next day. He would shake his hands, raise or lower the tone of his voice and try all kinds of expressions. Those present listened with supposed admiration and Ciotori would show his admiration in a loud voice.

At the first meeting of the Treasury he arrived with his so-called experts. He also took me along, not that I was a financial expert, but as an interpreter. That proved unnecessary as the Americans had an interpreter who spoke perfect Romanian and knew all the financial terminology. Titulescu's opening remarks were spoken in French. He presented the Romanian situation, which in his opinion, was not obligated to pay the debts but one had to find a place in the national budget in which to enter the payment. A lot of time was spent on translations from English to French and back to English. The first day his presentation lasted until lunchtime when we all went to eat. Talks resumed at two o'clock and went on for two hours spent mostly translating his words. The following day came the first of Titulescu's proposals. Relatively short the translation was quickly done for the Americans who answered immediately that they didn't accept it. Titulescu told then that he would make another offer after consulting with experts. After lunch we met again in the reserved room where we were supposed to discuss a new offer. After the translations was made another refusal followed immediately. Thus continued our negotiations until he had no more formulas to propose. At the end he was obliged to accept the American formula. In closing he made a pathetic speech describing the sorrows that would fall on poor Romania. Bucharest newspapers, of course, published long articles saying how difficult it was for him to negotiate and described him a winner in the outcome. Upon his return, the mission was received with great ovations.

On rainy week-end days I stayed in Washington rather than visit a small house I bought in rural Maryland. I had a small rented apartment in the city where my mother had come to visit at the same time as the Titulescu negotiations were occurring. In this apartment, one evening I had a surprise visit from Titulescu. His mother and mine had been good friends in their young days. As-soon-as he came, Titulescu dramatically knelt down at my mother's feet saying, "I come to ask you forgiveness because I did not go to my mother's funeral. Until she closed her eyes for the last time my mother kept calling me that she would not die until she saw me one more time." He started to cry and both mother and I felt very uncomfortable. Apparently, he had been unable to attend the funeral due to a mission out of the country. He calmed down and told mother that he had brought her a case of rare wines and a case of canned foods that he had intended to send his mother before she died. Mother took a small icon from a table and gave it to him telling him: "Nicolae take this as a gift from your own mother, to guide and protect you." For years to come whenever I met him, he would remind me of this icon which became his precious amulet.

After the war debt negotiations were completed, only one member of the mission, Eftimie Antonescu, remained behind because he wanted to visit Niagara Falls. I was assigned to accompany him. At Niagara, besides the dramatic waterfalls, there were numerous tourist gift shops. He was delighted by the Indian craft items and bought all kinds of moccasins and leather items. Back in New York we spent part of a night wrapping his souvenirs. Then came a shock. Antonescu discovered that most of things he had purchased were *Made in New Jersey* and were not genuine Indian handcrafts. He yelled at me saying that I should have known. I was angered, packed my suitcase and left for Washington. Antonescu chased me down at Pennsylvania Station, apologized and begged me to stay with him until his departure. Back at the Ritz Hotel we removed the *Made in New Jersey* labels. We remained good friends for many years after.

Through Bibesco, I met Ian Hubrecht, the Dutch Minister, and his wife who was a talented painter. Their legation was quite modest and one could only seat six people in their dining room. Their dinners were more like a family gathering. We were often invited by them to meet a prominent visitor from Holland. I was surprised that when the guests were from Holland the dinner conversation would be in Dutch a language of which I only knew about three words. Mrs. Hubrecht specialized in painting flowers, mostly magnolias that were in profusion in Washington in early spring. Her house was filled with magnolia branches. Bibesco admired one of her best paintings, a magnolia branch with four flowers, and offered to buy it. She refused to sell it to him, but ended up giving it to me. It remained with me for many years and a reminder of my years in Washington.

I was also welcome at the Spanish Embassy, Ambassador Riano and his wife did not have any young diplomats among their embassy personnel. They sometimes organized dances after dinner and I would have to dance with Mrs. Riano who was not a good dancer The best I could do was keep her from bumping into other dancers. She was always out of step and stepped on my toes. They used to let me bring friends, but I did not want to expose my friends to the ordeal of dancing with Mrs. Riano.

I also used to visit the home of the Italian Ambassador, Gelasio Gaetani, who was later named Ambassador to Japan. Gaetani lived in a three-apartment building on Massachusetts Avenue at the corner of 18th Street. He had the first floor. Mrs. Henry K. Brown, a millionairess, lived on the second floor, and Andrew Mellon, the aluminum king who was the U.S. Treasury Secretary at-that-time, lived on the third floor. Mellon's daughter, Elsa, lived there too and there was speculation that she might marry Gaetani. She was often invited to dinner at Gaetani's and brought along a friend from Pittsburgh. I was invited so-as-to make a foursome. The conversation was at the level of two young American girls. The meals were outstanding because Gaetani was a gourmet. Once a year, Gaetani would give a cotillion party in his spacious apartment and would give each guest an expensive gift. Mrs. Brown competed with Gaetani in giving parties at which she hired an orchestras from New York to play. She was not in much sympathy with the Washington elite. To be invited to one of her parties was quite a social honor.

Andrew Mellon

Unlike, his neighbors, Mr. Mellon led a quiet life. I had met him in Pittsburgh through our honorary consul, Mr. McClung. I also met his brother, Richard. These men, though extremely wealthy, lived relatively secluded lives. They had no friends and many acquaintances. I was surprised that I was accepted in their narrow circle. They played bridge at home or went out to play golf among themselves. At the beginning of the century golf was a rich man's sport, played at exclusive private clubs. When I was introduced to Richard Mellon, he invited me to play golf with him on a certain day. I did not have the courage to tell him that I had never played. To prepare, I got several golf books from the library and learned the rules and theory of the game. I also went to a sporting goods store and bought all the necessary equipment. At night I practiced golf swings in my apartment. Unbelievably, I beat Richard Mellon who praised my "European" style of play. This "European" style simply involved hitting the ball as hard as I could in the direction it was supposed to go. He often invited me to play with him. His conversations were limited to the businesses be was interested in. I was invited to Andrew Mellon's home several times. There was nothing in his spacious apartment from the doorknobs to the chandeliers that was not an art piece. He had acquired some paintings by the great masters from the Soviet Government. Born in riches and living a sheltered life, he wanted to know my reactions to everyday Americans that I don't think he knew much about himself.

When I came to Washington, Andrew Mellon, the head of the Mellon family, was named Secretary of the Treasury. He befriended Bibesco and often came to the Legation with Charles Curtis, who later became the U.S. Vice President (under President Hoover), to play poker with the Bibesco's. These were private affairs with me the only witness at a distance. If I was free on one of the evenings when they gathered at the Legation, Bibesco would ask me to come and help him. My job was to see that they had drinks and to call the butler when drinks were needed. They played for stakes that were not high for them but seemed high for me.

Once Bibesco was invited to dinner with Calvin Coolidge at the White House. He took me with him. There were just the three of us at the table - Coolidge, Bibesco and me - and hardly a word was said during the entire meal. I do remember him asking at the end whether we liked the fresh strawberries.

Bibesco had in his den an antique map engraved by Abraham Ortelius in 1570. Nobody took any notice of it until one day I asked him why he had hung it on the wall. This induced a discourse on cartography and how Ortelius and Mercator were two of the great cartographers of the 16th century. His lesson inspired me to go to the Library of Congress where I discovered a "Map Room" and a large collection of maps and atlases. This section had been founded by Philip Lee Phillips who had spent a lifetime compiling a catalog of maps and atlases. This induced a passion that endured for the rest of my life as a collector of old maps and eventually built a large collection.

Antoine Bibesco, as my chief, was preoccupied with the idea that I should make a good marriage in America. He wanted me to marry a millionairess and even tried to coach me how to court American girls. I have no idea how he knew about these things or how he would know more than I who lived among young people. Every morning he would ask me what girl I had met and if I had won her heart I would answer that I had other interests and then he would tell me not to waste my time.

≈≈≈

ENGAGEMENT ANNOUNCEMENT

My days in Washington took a personal when turn when I met Madeleine Couzens. Introduced through the small social circle of diplomatic connections, we soon developed a close friendship. Her father, U.S. Senator James J. Couzens of Michigan, was highly respected and influential both politically and as a businessman. This was in part due to his early friendship with Henry Ford and a small investment of $2500 in the Ford Motor

Company in 1903. Sixteen years later Ford bought him out for the then enormous sum of $30 million.

Madeleine's home being in Detroit, I made frequent nightlong trips north. During those drives I would almost hallucinate at the sight of white crosses along the narrow roadways marking where accidental car deaths had occurred. Our friendship turned into a serious announcement that D.C. papers headlined: "Washington's Richest Heiress Announces Engagement." But that meant that I had to announce myself to the Senator, a stern man, to ask his approval.

"You want to marry my daughter?," he asked.

"Yes," I said.

"Then I can only approve on two conditions." For this I was not ready. "You must change your name to Couzens." And," he added, "you must become a Catholic"

Left to answer, I could only tell him that as a Romanian I could not do as he asked as hard as it would be for Madeleine and me. In this way ended a wonderful and happy relationship.[27]

Press photo of Madeleine Couzens and DDD at Washington, D.C., event

---

[27] Editor Note: Almost 85 years later, I met Ambassador Roger Kirk (posted to Romania 1985-1989) and his wife. To my surprise came an unexpected coincidence when I found out that she was the daughter of Madeleine Couzens. She kindly shared the photo above.

The four years I spent in Washington was a school of "savoir faire." I graduated without a real knowledge of American life with only a vague sense of normal working class life. All those who lived in the Diplomatic Corps were in an unreal world. We stayed in the best hotels and ate at the best restaurants.

Several times Bibesco asked me how my father had died and who my ancestors were. My ancestry seemed to interest him a lot. I could not understand the significance of these questions until one day he asked me if I would like him to adopt me. He said that after the birth of their daughter, Priscilla, his wife refused to have another child. The Bibesco family, headed by Antoine and his cousin Valentin, did not have a boy to inherit the name. Bibesco and his wife thought of adopting me in-order-to carry on the name. It was a tempting proposition. Bibesco was rich. He had two houses in London, one in Paris and another on the Grand Canal in Venice. He also had property in Corcova, the southwestern Oltenian region of Romania. He used the title of Prince, even though the Romanian constitution had abolished all princely titles except for members of the ruling royal family. King Ferdinand and later his son, King Carol, did however tolerate the fact that some Romanian families that were descended from ruling Princes could use their titles outside Romania.

Bibesco told me that before I could accept his proposal, it would be necessary for his mother-in-law, Lady Margot Asquith to meet me. As a future adopted son of her daughter, Elisabeth, I would have entered the Asquith family. She had only a vague idea about Romanians and judging by her son-in-law thought they were "all a bit odd." When I went to London, I was invited to see Margot Asquith, who lived in a simply furnished house in Bedford Square. She had only the strict necessities. There were no paintings on the walls, but the table in the dining room was overloaded with silver. In the end, Margot Asquith found me "charming" and told Bibesco that she was not opposed to the adoption.

But I was neither attracted by his wealth, nor his title of Prince. I told him that I needed time to think over his proposal. My father had the name "Dimancescu" for two generations and, like him, had worn it with pride and did not wish to change it. I kept stalling an answer and never gave one. Bibesco was hurt by the fact that I did not want to become his heir. After he left Washington in 1926, I decided it was time to leave the Diplomatic Service and awaited the right moment to announce my decision.

CHAPTER SIX

QUEEN MARIE IN AMERICA

I t was only from newspapers that I read of Queen Marie's plans to visit the United States in 1926. I immediately took a short leave and returned to Bucharest where I asked for an audience with the Queen. As usual she received me very graciously. I told her that I wanted to do everything possible to contribute to the success of her cross-country.

"My visit has been planned by my good friend Loie Fuller," she said. "Miss Fuller lives in Paris and on your way back to America stop and visit her. I will write and tell her you are coming and advise her to make use of the services you are offering."

When I arrived in Paris I went to see Miss Fuller in Neuilly. I had no idea who she was other than she was a friend of Queen Marie. I had heard that she was a famous dancer and a friend of the great French sculptor Auguste Rodin and that she had organized a ballet company in Paris. Before going to see her, I envisioned her as a young woman. I dressed in a summer suit with a green shirt and pink tie. When I got to her apartment I was surprised to find myself in front of a much older woman. She extended her hand saying if the Queen had faith in me, she would too. During my few days in Neuilly, she told me about her life story and explained her friendship with the Queen.

Loie Fuller in younger days on stage

She was born in 1862 in Fullersburg, Illinois, a small hamlet 20 miles west of Chicago. "My parents were modest people," she told me. "The moment I could walk I felt the urge to dance. My dream was to become a dancer. With the help of friends, my parents sent me to Paris where I took a course in classical dancing." Continuing her story she spoke of her vivid imagination. "I could see dancing combined with brightly projected lights and veils. Thus I created my own style. I appeared on stage wrapped in many veils and under many colored lights. I was the first to have electric lights on the stage. I became an immediate success." During the 1890s, the Loie Fuller Ballet created a great sensation on the Parisian stage with thirty ballet dancers she had recruited from a Paris orphanage and trained. "They slept and ate in my house," she said proudly.

One of her admirers was Rodin who wanted to marry her. They eventually agreed that marriage would not be compatible with their artistic occupations. From Rodin she had a collection of hands of different French personalities sculpted in white marble. These were displayed on several shelves in her living room. It gave one an eerie sensation to see all these vertical white hands. She also had a small head of herself in marble that Rodin had sculpted when she was in the bloom of her youth.

"Ballet was in great demand and I earned a lot of money," she told me. Everywhere she went in Europe her ballet was financially successful except the three days spent in Bucharest where the staging and equipment costs were very high.

"Princess Marie came to all three of my ballet performances," she told me. "At each intermission she came backstage to my dressing room to congratulate me. When we parted on the second evening she told me that if I ever needed help to come to her.

"The last evening," Fuller recalled, "she had barely arrived when I trailed after her in tears. I could not leave Bucharest because I could not pay my hotel bill. Without questioning me any further, she went into the next room and returned with a box full of gold coins that she put in my lap. She said there was no hurry to repay the loan.

"In turn, I told her very solemnly that I would never forget her kindness and that I would do anything in my power to help her." Returned to Paris, Fuller paid off the debt to the Queen but remained obligated. Between her tour in Bucharest and World War-I, she and the future Queen corresponded frequently. "In me she found a person to share her secrets," Fuller said. "I've kept her letters in a locked steel trunk.

When Romania entered the war and overwhelmed by German armies in 1916, Miss Fuller worried about what would happen to the Royal family. Now removed to northern Moldavia, all correspondence was interrupted.

One day a young American woman brought her a letter from Queen Marie. The letter explained that the Germans were about to conquer Moldavia and that people were advising the Royal Family to take refuge in Russia, but that they had decided not to desert their people. The Queen wrote that Romania lacked medicines for the wounded.

"Could you find someone to buy medical supplies?" asked the Queen.

"When I finished reading the letter, I cried," said Loie.

The young woman who had brought the letter said that she was the niece of William Gibbs McAdoo, Jr., son-in-law of U.S. President Woodrow Wilson and his Secretary of the Treasury, and would ask her uncle to help Romania.

Three days later Miss Fuller and the woman sailed together for New York. Before leaving Paris, Miss Fuller went to a store on Place Royale that sold medals and decorations and bought the Star of Romania. She thought that if she had the opportunity to meet President Wilson she would present it to him on behalf of the King of Romania even though she had not been authorized to do so. Miss Fuller went on to tell me about the success she had in Washington, first at the White House where Wilson listened to "the Romanian story" and then at the Treasury Department where Secretary McAdoo offered to lend Romania more than Miss Fuller intended to ask for. An American mission was formed and sent to Romania by way of Murmansk. A good part of the medical supplies including Ford built ambulances[28] managed to get to Iaşi where Queen Marie herself supervised their distribution.

During her visit to the U.S., Miss Fuller met with several American millionaires to whom she described Romania's plight. This resulted in many gifts coming for Queen Marie's charities. Miss Fuller told me that these donations continued years after the war was over. In thanks, Loie Fuller suggested by letter to the Queen, she should consider visiting the United States and personally meeting the donors. Thus was born the idea of the visit to America. The Queen accepted Miss Fuller's suggestion and gave her a free hand to organize the visit.

General Alexandru Averescu, who was then Prime Minister, confirmed that the government agreed to the trip and had allocated funds to pay the initial costs of travel to New York. In a letter to the Queen authorizing the trip, he added that the government was not opposed to Loie Fuller accompanying the Queen and helping with the arrangements. The Queen sent a copy of Averescu's letter to Miss Fuller, which she showed me to

---

[28] When I was wounded at Oituz in the Summer of 1917, one of these Ford ambulances carried me to the hospital.

confirm that she was officially authorized by the Romanian government to organize the visit Miss Fuller outlined the details of the program to me.

In the first place, the visit was not supposed to be an "official" one. Miss Fuller's most devoted friend, the millionaire Samuel Hill in Portland, Oregon, agreed to pay all the expenses in the U.S. including arrangements for a special train to take the Queen cross-country as far Seattle, Washington, and then down to Portland, Oregon. He also deposited $200,000 in a New York bank in the Queen's name. The purpose for these fund was to allow the Queen to make donations to charitable causes in the various towns that she was to visit. The Queen would not have accepted any personal gifts or free lodgings in hotels. Sam Hill ultimate goal for the Queen's trip was to inaugurate the "Maryhill Museum" which Hill had built high on a barren cliff-top 40 miles east of Portland on along the Columbia, River. Actually he had the idea of building a fort that could be used as a stronghold against a potential Japanese invasion in case of a war with Japan. It was a solid concrete building with underground food stores that could have lasted a long time in case of an invasion. At the time of Queen Marie's proposed visit the fort-museum was still under construction. Only two exhibit rooms, containing some art items and items donated by Queen Marie, were ready.

Miss Fuller had a list of persons who had helped the Queen and places where she was supposed to spend a day or two. After I received all the details, Miss Fuller said she would write to the Queen to have the Ministry of Foreign Affairs assign me to the Queen's escorting suite. At the legation I found an unpleasant situation. After Bibesco had left, Radu Djuvara was sent to serve as Chargé d'Affaires until a replacement for Bibesco was named. Djuvara was transfixed on the memory of his father, Trandafir Djuvara who had a distinguished diplomatic career. Any conversation with Djuvara, started and ended with "My father says..." For every situation there was a Trandafir Djuvara solution.

Radu decided that he could not as a patriot allow the Queen to travel under the protection of a "dancer." Consequently he started to plan a program in which the Queen would travel under the supervision of the Romanian Legation. He did not realize that in Loie Fuller's program, all expenses were to be covered by Samuel Hill. The Djuvara program had no funds whatsoever. A familiar name came into the scene, Andrei Popovici. Still at the legation and now serving as Djuvara's aide, he had his own plan. Queen Marie would call on mayors in various towns and they in turn would feel obliged to offer her accommodations. Djuvara himself would wire the biggest hotels suggesting that they offer her free lodgings.

I was apprehensive about the Djuvara program and sent a telegram to the Queen to let her know that Djuvara was trying to change Miss Fuller's plans. In so doing I was being loyal to the Queen but disloyal to my chief in Washington. A copy of the telegram found its way to Mr. Ion Mitilineu, the Minister of Foreign Affairs, who agreed that Djuvara should have a free hand. Djuvara reprimanded me severely and said that I was to be disciplined by being transferred to the consulate in Cleveland. I presented my resignation which he refused and said I was prepared to leave for Cleveland.

Loie Fuller traveled ahead to New York and stayed at the Plaza Hotel where Mr. Hill was also staying. One day, the two were confronted by Djuvara, who told Miss Fuller that he could not allow the Queen to travel under the auspices of a dancer. At that moment, Mr. Hill jumped on him, grabbed him by the collar and invited him to step outside for a fist fight. Djuvara said he did not know Hill and had nothing to settle with him. I was present at the scene and tried to calm Mr. Hill. Loie Fuller was in bed crying. Suddenly, Mr. Hill stepped forward. Addressing Djuvara he said, "You can take your Queen. I'm not interested in her visit any longer," and then left the room. He canceled the $200,000 account and had the special train sent back to Seattle. Djuvara left the room feeling triumphant.

Queen Marie's cross-Atlantic trip in October 1926 was to be made on the liner *S.S. Majestic* along with her son Prince Nicholas and daughter Princess Ileana. In New York, William Nelson Cromwell,[29] a well known lawyer and a friend of Romania and the Queen, took things in hand. He had with some reservations agreed to be the Queen's host and was against the Djuvara-Popovici approach of begging for help.

Fifth Avenue Ticker-Tape Parade for Queen Marie (New York 1926)

---

[29] William Nelson Cromwell's firm eventually became Cromwell & Sullivan, one of America's leading law firms.

Popovici did manage, however, to get a Ford dealer to place twenty cars at the disposal of the Queen during her stay in New York. A rival dealer, offered thirty cars. The two sets of vehicles lined up side by side at the pier. No one knew which would be chosen. Djuvara decided that his personal chauffeur should drive the Queen's car. The driver chose the Fords and seated himself in the first car. The drivers from the other group started a rumor that there was a bomb under the lead Ford. This scared the chauffeur who ran off and was not seen for several hours.

At the port the Queen was received by the Mayor of New York, other local officials, and the members of the Legation. Accompanied by her daughter and son, Princess Ileana and Prince Nicholas, two ladies in waiting, and a representative of the Ministry of Foreign Affairs, Queen Marie settled into the other group of cars for the ride to the Ambassador Hotel where an entire floor had been reserved. She was treated to a uniquely New York welcome, ticker tape parade down Broadway on her way to City Hall for a greeting by the recently elected Mayor Jimmy Walker. Her arrival soon became to the social talk of the press. A new star had been found.

In her honor, Mr. Cromwell organized a reception and dinner at the Plaza Hotel. Hundreds of invitations had been sent out and there was such a crowd that no one knew who was really there. Mr. Cromwell led the Queen to the dais from where there were speeches that no one could hear.

Next was a stopover in Philadelphia for an official welcome. There was also a special "Ballets Fantastiques" with fifty dancers arranged by Lois Fuller and sponsored by the Queen. The Philadelphia Orchestra played.

Although it was clear that the Queen was not coming on an official visit to the United States, the State Department discretely informed our Legation that it was hoped that the Queen would not visit Washington. But Djuvara had already arranged the trip with plans for the Queen to stay at the Legation and to make a short visit to the White House. After her arrival where she was met 'unofficially' by Secretary of State Frank B. Kellogg, there was a State Dinner at the White House with President and Mrs. Calvin Coolidge who later called on the Queen at the Legation. There was also a wreath-laying ceremony at the World War-I Tomb of the Unknown Soldier.

From Washington, the Queen left for the Pacific Coast, planning to stop in different towns. She had a personal train car belonging to the president of the Baltimore Railroad Company and there were two more cars for the rest of her entourage as well as a press car. After reaching Chicago, there was an unexpected delegation at the train station with the men wearing morning jackets and silk top hats. They were Socialists who had come to protest. They greeted the Queen by telling her that she was not welcome in Chicago. While visiting the Chicago Art Museum, the Queen fainted while going up the stairs.

Another incident made her begin to realize the error of choosing the Djuvara-Popovici program. In Chicago, another train-car was attached to the Queen's train. This was the personal car of Mrs. Alma de Bretteville Spreckels, a wealthy Californian friend of the Queen. On board was also Loie Fuller. Shortly after leaving Chicago, the train stopped and Mrs. Spreckel's car was unexpectedly detached and left behind. This was done on the orders of Mr. Laptev, the Foreign Ministry's representative, who had assumed the role of director of the trip.

On the West Coast and in Portland, Oregon, she was greeted to another gala event at the Multnomah Hotel hosted by Samuel Hill. Then there was the thirty-car procession headed forty-miles east along the Columbia River. Sam Hill had built a Mansion dedicated to her as the Maryhill Museum. Though only half-finished, the Queen dedicated the oversized mansion-fortress on the barren Washington-state side of the River.

Maryhill Museum on the Columbia River in 1926

On the return trip, there were more unpleasant events. On arrival in Cincinnati where she was supposed to stay for a few days and visit the Romanian community, she was advised to leave immediately for New York because of planned protests. She was warned by the U.S. authorities that there was a plot to kill her and that it was better for her to leave the United States quickly. She departed without fanfare though the Queen's visit from beginning to end was a great headlining subject for the American press. The visit made for sensational news. All kinds of article were written, some bizarre, some fantastic in imagined details. Regrettably, when the Djuvara-Popovici team tried to grant exclusive rights to only one reporter, the rest of the reporters turned hostile towards the Queen.

In short, the visit was controversial both for the Queen and for Romania. During the Queen's visit, I collected all the clippings I could from the

American press about her visit. This cost a small fortune to copy as there were hundreds and hundreds of articles. After her departure, I asked for leave and went to Bucharest with my large collection of clippings. I went to see the Minister of Foreign Affairs, Ion Mitilineu, to whom I handed my resignation. He did not want to accept it and said he would put me on a "reserve" list that meant that he could call me back into active service at any time. He said he knew I had a file of unfavorable press clippings and did not want anyone in this country to know the contents. I agreed though telling him that I kept the right to show the file to the Queen.

I then went to Ion Duca, the ex-Minister of Foreign Affairs, and gave him copies of the press clippings. He was furious about the errors committed by the Foreign Ministry's representatives in Washington. I told him I was going to leave for a while and go to Paris and London. He said that when he returned to the foreign ministry he would recall me.

PART IV · CHANGES

Carol II of Romania renounced his title of "King" in 1925 as a result of controversies ensuing from his affair with Magda Lupescu. His four-year-old son Michael replaced him though under the tutelage of a three-person Regency. In 1928, Carol's wife, Crown Princess Helena, divorced him. Then in June of 1930, with the support of the Peasant Party Leader and its leader Prime Minister Iuliu Maniu, he secretly returned from France to Romania and reclaimed his title. All the while, Maniu had worked hard - and in vain - to try and break the bond between Carol and Lupescu. This relationship continued to cause dissension and international scandal in ensuing years.

The following is excerpted from *King Carol, Hitler and Lupescu* by A.L. Easterman, 1942.

"Maniu had been largely responsible for Carol's return to Roumania, though he had objected, at first, to his assuming the Crown. I inquired of the obviously disappointed statesman if, in the light of events, he would have acted otherwise. Deliberating at some length before replying, Maniu said, carefully: "I do not regret at all having brought the King back to the Throne. What I do regret, most strongly, is that certain groups and personalities are exploiting certain defects of character which are common to every man, but which must be restrained in a king. As a consequence, the King's high personal qualities cannot be used for the benefit of our people because the real forces and personalities of the country are cast aside and eliminated from the conduct of State affairs.

"When I insisted, politely, on a clearer indication of what he meant by 'certain groups and personalities', Maniu hesitated, but finally agreed that he referred to 'Madame Lupescu and those associated with her.' He added: 'On this point I regret also that Roumanian statesmen do not follow the attitude of British statesmen, in similar circumstances.' He referred, obviously, to the severe standards of personal conduct required of Royalty in Britain, where the influence of a Lupescu would not likely be tolerated.

"In the autumn of 1928, Ion Brătianu died. With his death, and in face of the now powerfully consolidated opposition and the parlous disintegration of national affairs, the feudalistic Boyar governing clique was struck a mortal blow. Without the dogged old tyrant, the faction which had depended on him for its influence and hold on the nation, was leaderless and fell to pieces. The Regency became still less of account. For a few months, Ion Brătianu's brother, Vintilă, continued the family

political dynasty as Prime Minister, but he had neither the ability nor the strength of Ion to combat the powerful new forces ranged in hostility to him and his faction. He resigned in November.

"When Maniu, the natural successor of Brătianu as leader of the country, with the strongest party behind him, quickly took control of the situation and became Prime Minister, the bulk of the nation hailed him as the saviour of Roumania. For a time he ruled with almost undisputed authority, and it seemed as if the country was destined to a new era of order and restored self-respect, as well as to a revival of the national fortunes. Maniu instituted a cleansing of the governmental machine, and essayed to purge political life of its traditional corruption. He ventured on a program of reconstruction, introducing reforms in the conditions of the peasantry, his chief love, reorganising the general economic system and improving transport. On the whole, Maniu's government performed a valiant task and did it well. There was a perceptible over-sweep of general contentment and a wave of relief that the days of the Brătianu tyranny had gone.

"This placid reaction did not last, however. The first flush of unquestioning acceptance of a new type of government passed, as is the way of men... As long as Ion Brătianu held the reins of power, these forces were, for the most part, driven more or less underground. The sudden relaxation of his grip emboldened these forces to emerge.

"Conservatives, Liberals, 'National Christians', the Iron Guard, and a host of other political denominations rose and prated vociferously. The Iron Guard, particularly, grew arrogant. Its leader, Corneliu Zelea Codreanu, began to indulge in 'messianic' antics, utilising a natural, if uncultured gift for demagogy, to inflame passions and inculcate ideas of terrorism as the method of securing 'national regeneration' towards the ideal of a 'Christian state'.

"New men arose as national figures of importance and influence, at home and abroad. Chief among them was Nicolai Titulescu... A man, powerful, able, to be reckoned with and feared. These were some of the human factors which wrought a change of attitude towards Maniu and his government...

"In this situation, thoughts of the exiled Carol in France were given more and more expression."

CHAPTER SEVEN

PARIS & PRINCE CAROL

F rom Romania I went to Paris and naturally went directly to see Loie Fuller, who lived in Neuilly in a beautiful large house that belonged to Prince Oleshweski, a Russian immigrant. She shared the house with Gabrielle Bloch, the daughter of a Parisian banker. This woman had divorced her husband the day after their wedding. Gabrielle was taking care of the household and Miss Fuller, who though only 63 years-old was now quite ill. When I went to see her, I found her in an armchair in her bedroom. Some of the orphan girls, who had been members of her ballet company, lived with her in Neuilly. Most them had matured and had lost their ballerina figures. She invited me to stay there, but I declined because I didn't like the atmosphere in the house.

A symbol of her past, a Rolls Royce, was kept in her garage but was seldom used because she could barely afford the cost of gasoline. Every day three doctors came to care for her. Even though she was an invalid she would come down for the noon meal, where she always had two or three guests. Despite these shortcomings, Miss Fuller thought she could still stage some shows with what remained of her troupe. The husband of one of the ballerinas now managed the ballet and was constantly touring Paris and provincial theaters hoping for an engagement. She even suggested that I might take over the management of the ballet, but this did not interest me at all.

When Rodin died he left a clause in his will authorizing Miss Fuller to identify and authenticate his works whenever there was doubt concerning authenticity. His former assistant lived in Miss Fuller's house. This man started to produce copies of Rodin's work that even Miss Fuller could not distinguish from the originals. He quickly developed a market for his fake works, many of which ended up in European and American museums.

Even though she was immobilized, Miss Fuller still tried to think up various schemes to make money. Every time she needed money, an elderly Canadian woman, who also lived in Neuilly, helped her out. One of Miss Fuller's ideas was to make an *avant-garde* film. The idea was to film scenes through a pair of glasses. With support from the Canadian woman, a studio was rented, two cameramen were hired and the actresses were to be girls from the ballet. When she recuperated somewhat, Miss Fuller went to the studio with the Canadian lady and Gabrielle Bloch, who was trying her hand at directing. I was invited to join this venture, thinking that it had great possibilities.

Miss Fuller and Miss Bloch were so sure of success that they formed a company and sold shares to investors. The famed World War-I Maréchal Joseph Joffre was among those who bought some. I did too. The shareholders met two or three times a week at Miss Fuller's house and the Maréchal was one of the most enthusiastic among us, even though he knew nothing about filmmaking. At each meeting he asked how much money was due to him. But soon after the production company closed its doors. I later found out to my great surprise that Prince Carol was also a shareholder. He was living in exile in Neuilly after the scandal of his affair with Magda Lupescu who was said to be Jewish which led to his being forced to leave Romania. Because of this scandal, Queen Marie was firmly against the return of her son. But the situation was much more complicated. No one then or even now, knew who Mme. Lupescu really was. According to an account by a friend of hers, she may have been a blood relative of Prince Carol.[30]

It was reported that his great-uncle, King Carol I, had had an affair with a local school teacher that resulted in the birth of a baby girl who had to be given a legal identity. The solution was to marry the teacher to an apprentice pharmacist from the Bucharest suburb of Buftea. The newborn was then registered as the daughter of the pharmacist, under his family name 'Lupescu.' When the child was of school age, King Carol I had her sent to the Diaconese Boarding School in Bucharest. This secret was never known in Romania and Mme. Lupescu was always considered the legitimate daughter of Lupescu. Many in Romania at the time could not conceive of Mme. Lupescu's return with the Prince because she was Jewish. That was seen as unacceptable in the event Prince Carol married her and she became the Queen.

While in Paris, I used to go and visit Prince Carol. Sometimes I helped him plan some of the projects that he had in mind for when he returned to Romania. One of these was to nationalize the Romanian subsoil and thus reduce the domination of foreign oil companies. He said that no one could see that decisions of the Romanian government took shape because of the influence of the oil cartel which was trying to prevent new taxes on oil.

[30] In 1942 a book appeared in London entitled *King Carol, Hitler and Lupescu* by A.L. Selling well, it alleged that Mme. Lupescu was the daughter of King Carol 1st, in other words Carol's aunt. Easterman had been told these details by Tanzi Gutava, a Romanian artist from the National Theater in Bucharest, married now to Ronald Adams the owner of a theater in London. Tenai Adams affirmed that she was an intimate friend of Mme. Lupescu and had been told by her all these details.

During this interval I went to Romania to meet various personalities and to gauge "the pulse" of the country. Ion Mihalache, President of the National Peasant Party, asked me to come and see him at Topoloveni, a village west of Bucharest near the city of Pitești. I was received in his modest peasant house and served lunch prepared by his wife. Mihalache said that everyone was accusing me of being a "Carlist." He said he could "not do any 'Carlism' without knowing if Carol wanted to return to Romania and under what conditions." I promised that upon my return to France I would ask Carol what his intentions were.

I also went to see Virgil Madgearu who was prominent in the National Peasant Party and who also wanted to know Carol's intentions. In my turn I asked him the intentions of his party and especially of Iuliu Maniu. He told me that they were opposed to Carol's return with Mme Lupescu. I also saw Octavian Goga, who was an open "Carlist" who declared that he would bring Carol back.

Back in Paris, I told Carol of my meetings with Mihalache, Madgearu and Goga. Carol answered very clearly that he intended to return but not under the auspices of any political party. "When I return, it will be by my own means. I shall come back when I shall be convinced that the Romanian people want me back." After this meeting, I went back to Bucharest and reported personally and verbally Carol's answer. During my talks with him, Carol did not mention Mme. Lupescu.

<hr />

Mrs. Alma de Brettelville Spreckels of San Francisco also had a large house in the Neuilly suburb of Paris where she spent part of the year. She entertained a lot with receptions and dinners with Miss Fuller a frequent lunch guest. Although very wealthy, Mrs. Spreckels did not know much about French social life and Miss Fuller was her advisor on such matters. Mrs. Spreckels, whose husband died in 1924, had been hoping for many years to find a husband and Miss Fuller was trying to find one for her. Sometimes I was present at these lunches, although I had no interest in participating in the conversation between the two ladies. Finally, Miss Fuller found a candidate for Miss. Spreckels, the American Ambassador to Spain, a widower who was apparently looking for a rich widow. Everything worked fine and a meeting was arranged. Mrs. Spreckels had a new dress made for her meeting with the Ambassador who was to arrive by train from Madrid. The two ladies took me with them to the train station and when the train arrived the Ambassador, Alexander Moore, was taken from the train on a stretcher. He had never revealed the fact that he was a very sick man and could not walk. Mrs. Spreckels had him taken to her home by ambulance. He stayed about three weeks before returning to Madrid ending any marriage prospects.

Meanwhile, at her lunches Miss Fuller would come out with a succession of fantastic projects. Invariably, she would end the lunch with the same advice to Mrs. Spreckels:

"Alma, your husband left you a huge fortune. Neither you, nor your children will remember him. One day you will be gone too and your name will also be forgotten. While you are still alive, you should raise a monument to honor the family name." Alma would answer that she would be happy to do something but did not know what sort of monument would be appropriate. One day, Mrs. Fuller said:

"Alma, build a museum in San Francisco and fill it with good paintings and works of art."

"But where would I collect such things," Mrs. Spreckels replied,

"I have an idea," said Miss Fuller. "If you name the museum 'The Legion of Honor Museum,' the French will give you all sorts of things worthy of the name. You give the money, and I will take care of the rest."

Without further discussion, Alma took out her checkbook and made out a payment to Miss Fuller for $75,000. She immediately went to the telephone and called Gaston Doumergue, the Twelfth President of the Third French Republic. Being a good friend of his she got through quickly.

"Mr. President," she said, "I have near me an American lady who has decided to build a museum in San Francisco which will be the Museum of the Legion of Honor. France has to contribute to this museum from the surplus stocks of its own museums."

The President did not seem the least surprised at the request and gave a satisfactory reply right away. He appointed Mr. Tierman, the Counselor of State, as his representative to search for art contributions for the San Francisco museum. On the second day, he came to visit Miss Fuller and Mrs. Spreckels and agreed to take them on tours in which I was included to identify and select items from French museums. For several weeks, Rolls Royce cars took this group to various Paris museums. I had never guessed that museums had hundreds of paintings and statues in storage because there was not enough space to exhibit them. Mrs. Spreckels was able to choose from these treasures. To this day most people of San Francisco do not know the origins of this now famous museum. Miss Fuller also asked

Queen Marie to donate objects for the museum. The Queen chose about thirty pieces of her own jewelry collection including pins and bracelets that she had received as gifts from various European royal families. She also gave a dress that she had worn at the Imperial Court when she visited the Tsar and the Tsarina. It was white 'noire silk' embroidered with wheat ears in gold thread.

Miss Fuller also asked Maréchal Joffre to give something. One day after a lunch at Miss Fuller's, he invited us to go to Verdun with him to show us the Trench of the Bayonets. This was a national monument and the grave of a French platoon which was ready to go into battle when all its soldiers were buried alive by an explosion. Only the tips of their bayonets remained above the ground. No one was allowed to walk over the trench where the soldiers were buried. Maréchal Joffre procured one of the bayonets for Mrs. Spreckels' museum. He also gave her the képi (cap) he had worn during the war. Eventually an organization was legally established for the museum and Mrs. Spreckels was named to the board of directors [though later voted off the board]. The plans for the Museum were a copy in smaller scale of the Palais de la Légion d'Honneur in Paris.

In Neuilly, I met Puiu Dumitrescu, who became Carol's private secretary after Carol's return to Romania. Dumitrescu was the nephew of a politician, Alecu Constantinescu. Through his uncle, Dumitrescu was introduced to many political figures. During his university years, he was offered a scholarship by the National Liberal Party to study in Paris. He was told, by Ion Brătianu, the leader of the Party, that he could have the scholarship on condition he got rid of his 'Carlist' ideas. Puiu told me that on hearing Brătianu's offer he swore, slammed the door, and left. After this he made his way to Paris on his own and went to see Carol, whom he had never met before and offered his services in any capacity.

At the time I met him in Neuilly he was serving Carol as a sort of advisor-usher-valet. Puiu had a lot to do with Carol's return to Romania. He had the idea of hiring a plane with a French pilot. In Paris he worked closely with our Military Attaché, Colonel Tătăranu. The colonel was of the opinion that Mme. Lupescu should remain in France. Dumitrescu, however, said it was his (Dumitrescu's) right to make this decision. Implied in this comment was that Carol lacked the will power. I left Neuilly without receiving any special role in Carol's return. Dumitrescu said, "I know that we can count on you." I do not know to what extent I could have helped, but I knew that I was regarded as 'Carlist' by many people in Romania.

CHAPTER EIGHT

THE RIGHT JOB

I went on to London where my sister, Dr. Octavia Dimancescu-Nicolau and her husband Dr. Stefan Nicolau lived and worked. Both had done biological research at the Pasteur Institute in Paris and were well-known in the French medical world. They had been invited to London to try to find a remedy for or a vaccine against polio. Their laboratory was in Hampstead, north of London. Everything that they needed, including clinical-test monkeys, was made available by the British Institute for Medical Research. They lived at the Conservative Club on St. James Street where they had an apartment on the top floor and where they were able to provide me with a room.

In exchange I offered to help them in their research. In violation of British laws, the Nicolau's were injecting a polio virus into monkeys through a hole the skull. An infected money was then put in a cage with a healthy monkey. In about 15 days the disease started to show in the infected monkey with paralysis in the legs. It was evident that the virus made its way from the brain through the nervous system to the legs. Nicolau and Nicolau, as they were called, were the first to coin the word, "septineuritis," to denote the transmission of the disease through the nervous system (as in septicemia that is transmitted through the vascular system).

My contribution was to keep index cards for each monkey or other animal and record the course of the disease and the results of the autopsy. This was an enormous task. After the autopsy, specimens were taken from internal organs and used to study cellular changes. All this information had to be recorded in detail on the cards. In some cases the monkeys were sacrificed after one, two, three or more days after inoculation so one could compare changes in their organs.

I had an idea that alcoholic beverages might hasten the course of the disease. So we tried this approach. Nicolau and Nicolau established the amount of alcohol that a monkey could drink without serious effects and we then started to feed the monkeys all kinds of alcoholic beverages from ordinary wines to whiskey and gin. Two monkeys one treated with alcohol and one without, would be placed together in a cage and then we would gradually increase the amount of alcohol each day. We found that the monkeys went through the same stages of drunkenness as humans. They started by being happy, then sentimental, then they would become irritable and finally would lose their balance and fall. We discovered that drinks made of fruit extracts did not have as much effect as drinks made of grains. Gin caused headaches. For 24 hours after becoming intoxicated on gin, a monkey would beat its head against the bars of its cage, which made us surmise that they were suffering from headaches. We would give them aspirins and the headaches would appear to be gone. We were pleased with our findings.

Nicolau and Nicolau wrote a report which they presented to the British Institute of Medical Studies. The director of the Institute came to visit the laboratory and congratulated them for their work, but said that the report must be considered highly secret and would not be made public. The reason for this was our conclusions about the unpleasant effects of gin. A contributor to the Institute was one of England's largest gin distilleries.

Nicolau and Nicolau discovered a great similarity between polio and a disease called "borna" that affected horses. They created a vaccine that was 80 per cent effective in the cases they treated, but it could not be considered a sure remedy.

Without a real job, and still on the diplomatic reserve list, I decided to look for work in the field of industrial engineering. I went back to Romania to see if I could find work. By coincidence I received a letter from an American, L. L. Briggs, who was staying at the Athénée Palace in Bucharest. He said that he wanted to meet as he needed my assistance.

Briggs owned a small arsenal in Philadelphia where he manufactured antitank guns and a light tank, called the "Christie," which could travel on rough terrain at speeds up to 60 kilometers per hour. He wanted to sell both products to Romania, but had not been able to see the War Minister, General Mircescu, a former commander at the Oituz battlefield with whom I had remained on friendly terms.

It was easy to obtain a meeting for Mr. Briggs, who appointed me export manager. Mircescu received us well and listened attentively to Briggs' presentation, documented with photographs and charts. The antitank gun could be disassembled into three parts, each of which could be carried by a soldier and quickly reassembled. Once the presentation finished, Mircescu told me in a friendly tone, "Listen Jamborel (as he knew me when I was in the army), we need neither antitank guns, nor Christie tanks. We hope to avoid armed conflicts. What we really do need is housing for our officers."

I translated what Mircescu had said. To my great surprise Briggs said that if the general did not want tanks and guns, he could provide him with houses, but wanted to know what type of house the general wanted and how much he was willing to pay. Mircescu said that if we were successful in providing the kind of housing he needed, the country would be grateful. Back at the Athénée Palace, Briggs started to draft an offer then left for the United States. There he hired architects to help plan a detailed project and returned to Romania with his offer that I translated into Romanian. He was offering to build twenty-five types of houses ranging from single-family units to multiple-family units. The houses would have to be paid for installments over a ten-year period. The buyer would have to purchase life insurance from Briggs so the house would be paid for in case of death. Briggs was ready to provide all the financing for the project. When described to the press, it was favorably reported.

When General Mircescu received the proposal he contacted Iuliu Maniu, the President of the Council of Ministers. Maniu said that he was very interested in the proposal but needed time to study it. I immediately sensed that there might be something unusual might be going on. Maniu appointed a national parliamentarian, Ghiţa Crişan from Oradea Mare in the northwest of the country, to analyze the offer. "The American Construction Company" was incorporated by Briggs who returned to the United States leaving me to work with Crişan. If needed he was ready to return to Romania.

The Presidency requested that the construction of housing be extended from the military to include civil servants. Briggs made clear he had the material and financial means to deliver what was needed. Meanwhile, I had endless meetings with Crişan. He seemed to be asking all sorts of irrelevant questions. He let me know that he was meeting with Maniu on a daily basis and that they were near to accepting the Briggs proposal. Finally, he invited me to lunch at his house. After the meal he bluntly said: "What will Mr. Maniu and I get?" I was taken aback by so blunt a request but asked him what each one expected. Without hesitation he said they expected at least 10 per cent of the total American investment in the project. I replied that I was not authorized to discuss the matter, but that I doubted that Briggs would expect to pay anyone in Romania a commission, especially such a large amount. I told him that Briggs and his associates were expecting to earn about three and a half per cent on the project. I contacted Briggs, who was even more surprised than me about Crişan's request that implicated the prime minister. Briggs said he would abandon the project and did not want to discuss it any more. He said he was going to Turkey where he hoped to get an order for his tanks and antitank guns. He fact he found a good customer in the Soviet Union. Thus ended my first attempt to bring a large and advantageous business to Romania. The most disappointed was General Mircescu, who had hoped to solve the problem of housing the military. He insisted that Briggs should come to Romania and discuss the matter with him personally, but Briggs refused to return.

As I was now free, my friend Paul Vidrascu asked me to join "PARID," the organization that administered state fisheries. Vidrascu had a big irrigation and flood control project in mind. The president of PARID was the ecologist and oceanolog Dr. Grigore Antipa[31] and the general administrator and chief engineer was Paul's father. Paul had studied the problem of damming the Danube to recover about 1.8 million acres for agriculture. However, the dam would have eliminated thousands of large and small lakes that were a rich source of fish. Each year PARID would hold an auction that would grant one-year fishing rights to certain lakes. The fishermen who were ultimately selected were those who passed bribes to PARID employees.

When I started working at PARID, I investigated the fraudulent auction system. I bypassed the chief engineer and with the help of Dr. Antipa I found a better solution for the lakes. I devised a system whereby each candidate was registered with a number that was used in place of the candidate's name. The selection of candidates was taken out of the hands of junior clerks and transferred to a committee of senior engineers. Dr. Antipa, pleased with this solution, appointed me as his assistant. Meanwhile, Paul Vidrascu pursued the dam project by visiting Ion Mihalache who was the Minister of Agriculture and enthusiastic about the proposal and suggested hiring a well-known Dutch engineer, van Konijnenburg to do a preliminary study. I was asked to accompany him during his survey of the Danube River along eight-hundred kilometers from the Iron Gates to the Delta.

Before he arrived in Romania, I spent a few months in the Delta with a team of engineers who were completing a project for Vidrascu father. This project involved damming some lakes which dried out in the summer and left millions of fish dead. Usually the lakes overflowed in the Spring from rain and melting snow, but the water evaporated in the summer leaving the lakes dry. The team that made the topographical measurements consisted of

---

[31] Dr. Antipa was the founder of the Institutului Biooceanografic din Constanta and Director of Muzeului National de Istorie Naturale in Bucharest.

the Vidrascu brothers, a young engineer and myself. We slept on a raft on which there was a two-room hut. We all shared one room and used the other one for meals. On the barge there was another large room for the workers who carried our equipment, and a much smaller one for an older woman who was our cook.

At sunrise, we would leave and do our measurements along the lake shores. At noon we stopped for a snack and after the afternoon heat at four o'clock we would return to our barge. We would all bathe in the Danube to cool off. In the meantime the cook would prepare dinner. When the weather was good she would prepare the meal on the shore, making a soup in a large pot with many varieties of fish from the Danube. Sometimes she would fry fish on skewers over an open fire. It was a pleasant life, except for the mosquitoes. We wore a protective net, but it was not sufficient. I had a remedy recommended by my sister. This required dissolving quinine powder in alcohol. I rubbed this liquid on my skin and it successfully repelled the mosquitoes. Sadly, the young engineer who refused to wear a net or use my repellent, caught a severe case of malaria and eventually died.

As we advanced with our work along the shore, the barge followed us. I found an abandoned hut on an islet and settled there to have more peace. I had a good supply of books, some by the popular French writer Paul Morand whose novels were then in vogue. Quite by coincidence, Paul Morand was visiting Romania and had been invited by the Minister of Public Works, Grigore Gafencu, to make a tour of the Danube Delta on a government boat and somehow both showed up at my hut. Morand was even more than surprised to find some of his latest books in this wild setting. I discussed with him the story of a Russian emigrant who yearned to return to his country and crossed the Danube to get there. Hardly back in Paris, Morand wrote a novel *Flèche d'Orient* in which he recounted the Russian's tale and described me under the name of "Muriano."[32]

When van Konijnenburg arrived, I was assigned to accompany him. He was one of the leading European experts in hydraulics. When he was not traveling in the country he stayed at the Athénée Palace Hotel in Bucha-

---

[32] Paul Morand, *Flèche d'Orient*, Librairie Gallimard, Paris, 1932, Page 105. "En 1915, Dimitri a quitté la Russie. Il vit à Paris, marié. Le reste de sa famille a été massacré. Dimitri a oublié sa langue natale, ses enfants seront français. Il n'a plus rien de slave. Mais un pari perdu va troubler l'ordre de sa vie tranquille. Affirmant qu'on ne peut joindre Bucarest par avion en une seule journée, Dimitri promet, s'il a la preuve du contraire, d'aller chercher et de rapporter le lendemain un kilo de caviar frais. Dimitri perd son pari et s'embarque sur l'heure. Mais l'anecdotique expédition va bientôt se transformer en un véritable périple. Dimitri, confronté à sa culture originelle, aux images, aux couleurs, aux accents de son enfance, va être emporté dans le tourbillon d'une nouvelle vie, comme à contre-courant, remontant le cours du temps jusqu'à sa propre source."

rest. He was a gourmet who was captivated by Romanian cooking. He loved the eggplant salad that he would mix with fresh, black caviar. He spoke English, German and French perfectly and without an accent and took pleasure in learning Romanian words.

Paul Vidrascu had already completed an experimental dam on Prince Carol's property at Mănăstirea near the town of Călărași along the Danube. but because of the height of the dam, the approach was too costly. He and his father did not want to recognize that the cost of their approach would exceed the profit from the cultivated land. They were hoping that the van Konijnenburg study would produce a less costly type of dam.

After finishing his work in Bucharest, van Konijnenburg traveled to the Danube River at the Iron Gates near Turnu Severin from where we started measurements along the Romanian left bank of the Danube. He would wade knee deep in the river and with my help from the shore would note the level of the water on that date. We worked our way slowly far downriver. When we eventually passed the royal property at Mănăstirea, van Konijnenburg told me confidentially that the dam built by the Vidrascu's was an enormous mistake. He said that not a single lake along the Danube should be dammed.

He described how dams would lead to catastrophic floods every three or four years when the Danube waters were abnormally high. He finished his work relatively quickly. Back in Bucharest, he completed his report illustrated with his own watercolor sketches. He took it to Mihalache whom he told that under no conditions should the Danube be dammed. He had statistics that showed that fishing production was greater than agricultural production would be. The result was a defeat for Mihalache.

When we finally parted, he quoted a Latin saying: "My house is also your house" and I regretted that I never had the chance to accept his invitation more so as he lived with a brother who was a well-known Dutch painter. I left the PARID project but remained as Dr. Antipa's assistant. He seldom came to the office and I had little to do. When he did come, we just talked to pass the time. He was also a director of the National Museum of Natural History which preoccupied him much. He was constantly searching for new specimens.

To have something to do and to get exercise after leaving the office, I took a long walks up Kisseleff Avenue toward Băneasa. During one of these walks a car stopped and the driver, Eugen Filotti, said he had been looking for me. He was the Director of Press and Communications and wanted to open a Department of Tourism.

"For a long time, I was stuck on your name," he said, "knowing that you might be the best man for the job."

I had known Eugen since we were in the second grade together in elementary school where he always won first prize. At the time we met on the avenue, I had written several articles complaining that no one was taking the initiative to publicize tourism. Though I used the pen name of "Mircea Baldovin" some of my friends, among them Filotti, recognized my style. Thus I became Director of Tourism. I already had ideas. We needed roads for tourists coming by car, and large and small hotels along the tourist routes.

As a first step I went to London to meet the President of the Thomas Cook travel agency, and to Paris to see the Director of the growing American Express travel agency. The head of Thomas Cook told me the secrets of tourism: "Allow a good commission for travel agents who sell tickets to Romania. If they know they will get a good commission, they will praise Romania. Advertisements for tourists will not produce much. No one will come to Romania because they saw a pretty picture." The director of American Express was more skeptical. He said the distance between Budapest and Bucharest was too great and too expensive to make either by train or car and even if anyone came there was nothing interesting to see.

My being an employee of an important government agency was an honor but it was also a great disappointment. The government officials may have been good men but seemed useless in their jobs. There were days when they did nothing but drink coffee.

Eugen Filotti's job was like a tennis ball. He was transferred in and out of the Ministry of Foreign affairs several times. Several young newspapermen were given high ranking jobs as press counselors for the services they had rendered the two political parties that alternated in power. Each of these men was eager to get jobs as attachés at some embassy abroad. However, their most important function in Bucharest as counselors was relegated to shepherding some important foreign visitor. In such cases the counselor was given a large sum of money to entertain the guest at the best restaurants or to take the visitor to Sinaia or Braşov.

One day I was told that an American newspaper woman, a Miss Baker representing the *New York Times*, was at the Athénée Palace Hotel. I went to meet her and found that she was a pretty blond traveling with a brunette just as pretty. She told me that she had been in Bucharest for two weeks waiting for an appointment to meet the King, but so far no luck. She had come from Ankara where she had a long interview with Kemal Pasha, the founder and first President of modern-day Turkey. Upon leaving he offered her an autographed picture and his cuff links. I managed to obtain the audience but the King gave her neither a picture nor a set of cufflinks. When I met her after the audience with the King, she was so happy that she gave me Kemal Pasha's cuff links and invited me to call on her if I ever came to New York. Many of these visitors came on their own and did not request assistance from the Press Office. In some cases, they would face difficulties and one of us would be dispatched to help them.

One day I was on the Orient Express on my way to Paris when I encountered Bruce Lockhart, a well-known English writer and journalist. We became friends and I soon found out he worked for British Intelligence. Two years later he wrote *Memoirs of a British Agent* in 1932 and eventually became highly influential during World War II. He told me that he had come to Romania to interview King Carol II, but in spite of the intercession of the British Legation he was not received at the palace. He was leaving Romania furious at being ignored and vowing to get back at this insult. Much later when Carol had abdicated and was bouncing from country to country, he was refused a visa to England because Lockhart, now an influential member of the British government, had opposed it.

The Press and Communications Department had many responsibilities that were not well defined. One of these was the promotion of cinematography. During the late 1920s, there was only one man in Romania, Dumitru Ion Suchianu, who was an expert on the subject. He was up to date on everything in the movie world. He wrote many articles on the subject and never lost an opportunity to accuse the authorities of doing nothing about it. He made the point that such a beautiful country as Romania with a population that still wore picturesque costumes could furnish hundreds of subjects for films. Partly to appease him the Press and Communications Department hired a German film director to make a film in Romania based on a script written by Suchianu.

The story was extremely childish and the location was the Bibescu Castle at Mogoșoaia. Martha Bibescu, owner of the Castle, gave permission for the filming on condition that the gardens and terraces not be damaged. The final scene involved a huge display of fireworks from the terrace. By the end the Castle and its surrounding looked as if they had been attacked by vandals. The film was a fiasco.

But Suchianu did not give up. He now promoted the idea of having another film made in Romania for which he chose the French film company, Gaumont. A Romanian dentist who had settled in Paris had written a novel in French based on a Romanian plot. It was called *Roumanie Terre d'Amour*. With Suchianu's help he came to Romania and signed a contract with Gaumont. The French film company imposed strict conditions: all the actors had to be French with the exception of the heroine, who could be Romanian. After visiting various sites, Gaumont and Suchianu selected the village of Rucăr in Muscel County.

I was chosen by the Press Department to supervise the filming and had the right to object to scenes that did not have an appropriate Romanian character. The French director was an old man of the old school. He would prance in front of the camera for half an hour before deciding the correct position of the actors. He went as far as telling the actors how far they should bend their heads and whether to bend to the left or the right. Much time was wasted staging scenes with all the costs were being paid by the Romanian government. All the French actors and personnel were receiving higher salaries than they would have received in France. Despite this benefit, they complained of the lack of comfort in a Romanian mountain-village. The subject of the film was the life of Romanian peasants that the French actors could not understand. Any suggestions that I made, were turned down by the director who would say:

"I know what the spectators want to see and they would not know if the actors were interpreting peasant life incorrectly."

I replied that Romanian spectators would criticize the film and accuse the government of having misspent money on a film that had nothing Romanian about it other than the settings.

Nothing substantial came of my days at the Department of Tourism. It was now 1930.

CHAPTER NINE

UNEXPECTED EVENTS

On June 8, 1930, Carol II, returned from exile and was proclaimed King. At the Ministry of Communications where I worked someone called saying: "Carol is back." The first question was "Where is he?" At the Press Bureau we were divided into two groups: one that believed that the news was not true and one that was convinced that it was true. We received hundreds of calls inquiring what the truth was. Mr. Maniu, the Prime Minister, told us to deny the news as he was convinced that Carol was not on Romanian soil. I learned that he had sent an order to the Bucharest police chief that if by any chance Carol should enter the capital he should be arrested and taken to Giurgiu on the Danube River from where he could cross over into Bulgaria.

My colleagues thought I knew Carol's secrets and they tried to press me for details. I left the office and went to the Royal Palace in Cotroceni. It was surrounded by members of my old "Hunters" brigade and no one was allowed inside the gates. The commander of the guard immediately recognized me and let me enter. There was no one in the Palace yard except for a guard and two civilians in front of the door to Prince Nicholas' apartment. As I advanced toward them, one of them ran over and embraced me. It was Puiu Dumitrescu. He told me that they had arrived by plane from Transylvania and had landed on the military drill field from where "Hunters" brought Carol and him to the Palace where Nicholas was waiting for them. Dumitrescu asked me to stay at the door and not to let anyone enter until he knew who the person was. The same order had been given to the guards at the entrance of the Palace. A short time later, he me took upstairs to Prince Nicholas' apartment where I saw Carol who was trying on a military uniform. He said simply: "I count on your support." I went downstairs and assumed the post of 'receptionist.'

A royal aide arrived having been sent by Queen Marie with the order that Carol should leave the palace grounds immediately. I called Dumitrescu who told me to send the aide away without an answer. Callers started to arrive. They were let in one by one from the Palace gate. The first was Mr. Grigore Iunian, the Minister of Justice, who was immediately received by Carol, but left after 15 minutes. The next was Mihai Popovici, who stayed only three minutes. He was followed by Professor Nicolae Iorga who met with Carol for over an hour. The great historian resolved the problem of what to do with King Mihai who was still King. He suggested that the National Assembly proclaim him Voievod of Alba Julia. He also suggested that a new government be formed under the Presidency of the great patriot from Ardeal, Vaida Voievod. There was still the Regency problem. The regents were Prince Nicholas, Mr. Constantin Sarateanu, and Orthodox Patriarch Miron. One by one they resigned. Mr. Maniu also sent his resignation and was followed by other members of the National Peasant Party. After Iorga, Carol received Ion Mihalache with whom he talked for an hour. Mihalache assumed the responsibility of convening the National Assembly.

Before Carol's return to Romania, though many were called 'Carlists,' there was no coordinated movement to bring him back from exile. The press had been ordered to avoid mentioning his name. When one referred to him, they used the expression: "the closed question." The day he arrived, a sentinel at the gate wrote the following on a small piece of paper: "The 'Hunters' battalion with the music in front and the 'closed question' in the middle are advancing toward the palace." This small piece of paper found its way to Carol who had it framed and hung in his study.

Yet, now that he was back on the throne, my friends and others called me "The King's man." I did not ask him for anything but he asked me if I wanted to be Palace Minister. I answered that I was greatly honored but that I thought I could better serve the King and the country without being one of 'his' men. And while during the first months I went to the Palace daily, it was not to see the King but to talk with Dumitrescu. I entered the Palace through a side door and went directly to the Private Secretary's office. In his waiting room there were usually many people with different requests. Every morning Dumitrescu would spend about two hours listening to various complaints. He was considerate and tried to satisfy everyone.

For the moment, King Carol's return to the throne, meant more or less normalization of life in Romania though not an end to considerable political maneuvering by the dominant parties It also meant the start of another chapter in my life. Growing signs of Nazism were beginning to gel and in my view England looked was a key to our security. Then too I looked to America as a possible next step in my life. And though I did not want to ask for Carol's help, I looked forward to being recalled into the diplomatic service.

ꬷꙻꙻ

When these events transpired, I had been supervising the making of a film by the French crew mentioned earlier. I was traveling back and forth between Rucăr in the mountains and Bucharest. My mother was accompanied me on some of these trips. My having been away from the country for along time, her great concern was to see me married and married to a Romanian woman. As we sat on the porch in the evening she would repeat the same refrain: "Do not go away again. Stay in Romania and get married."

I was now almost 35 years old and told her that after living alone for so long, it was difficult to decide whom to many. My friends tried to act as matchmakers attempting to find girls who were suitable for me. In Bucharest, as always, there were a number of fortune tellers. One day I went to one of them with my friend Lawrence Bungardeanu. He had finished his military duty in Romania and was ready to return to America where his father was a Romanian priest in New Jersey. Even if I had little interest, we went to the best-known fortunetellers simply out of curiosity. He asked me to stay with him while his fortune was told from cards. He was told that he was going on a long trip. When the fortuneteller finished with him she insisted on telling me my fortune for free. She said I would marry very soon. She said I should go to Câmpulung (about 100 kilometers north of Bucharest) where there were two rich sisters and one of them would be suitable for me.

After a few days I had to resolve a family matter with an uncle who lived coincidentally in Câmpulung. After that was settled, he told me it was time for me to get married and that - to my surprise - he knew of two rich girls in the town. I guessed that they must have been the two same girls proposed by the fortuneteller. I left my uncle and while waiting for the train I went to the station restaurant for a cup of coffee. While there a young girl came up to me mistaking me for my brother who looked much like me. She was also going to Bucharest and while we traveled on the train she told me that she had two very good friends in Câmpulung both sisters and one would suit me as a wife. Evidently the young ladies had advertised all over the country that they were looking for a husband. For me, at least, nothing came of it.

During my stay in Rucăr the main subject of my mother's conversation was marriage. She knew that during my stay in the United States I had been engaged and she feared I might return to the States. All the while, every morning in Rucăr at 11 o'clock, a lady and her daughter passed in front of the house where I was staying. The daughter of the peasant in whose house we were staying had already told my mother who the two people were. They were the wife of a general named Rădulescu and her daughter who went daily to bathe in the ice-cold rapid waters of the Dâmbovița River. My mother was told that they belonged to the Baștea family, the richest family in the village and owned the Berevoescu Mare Mountain in the Făgăraş Range. Their house was surrounded by large trees so one could not see what was going on in the yard.

I had brought my cocker spaniel to Rucăr with me. Mother took great care of him and would not let him go into village where he could be attacked by the fierce shepherd dogs. I do not know how he succeeded, but somehow he managed to get into the yard of the General's family. One evening as I was sitting on the porch, my neighbors passed by walking quickly as usual, out for the evening exercise. I told my mother that if I were to get married I would marry a girl like the one that passed our house. "If it's true that they have money," I said, "I am impressed that they are not spending their summer in Sinaia or Constanta like other wealthy people." I liked their modest behavior and style of dress. While I soon forgot about the subject, my mother did not. She confided in Marioara, the peasant's daughter, that I had fallen in love with the General's daughter.

Country Home of the Baştea Family in Rucăr

When my work in Rucăr ended, we packed and left for Bucharest. Shortly after mother received a letter for Marioara who wrote she had gone to see the General's daughter and told her that I had fallen in love with her. Marioara was told that she was a liar and that if the gentleman had something to say he would not have confided in her. Marioara begged my mother to persuade me to come to Rucăr one more time to see the General's daughter and tell her of my feelings. This way she would be absolved of being considered a liar and bring the matter to a close.

The letter served as an encouragement to my mother to push me to take the first step. Mother, sensing that I was getting close to leaving for America, implored me to go to Rucăr to save Marioara's honor and to meet the General's family whom we had ignored during our stay. She was so persistent that I felt it would cost me little to give her satisfaction by going to Rucăr. Thus I found myself on the train to Campulung and then by car to Rucăr high up a beautiful mountain valley.

I stopped at the peasant's house to tell Marioara that I was going to see the Rădulescu family and to ask her to prepare a room for me. While I was there the General's daughter passed and Marioara quickly called and we were introduced. Before going to her house, I asked her if she wanted to go for a walk and she accepted. The village of Rucăr lay between two hills covered with pine forests. A small river ran through the center of the village. Walls bordered both banks. On one side there was a road for carts and vehicles, on the other there was a pedestrian path. Several small iron bridges connected to the two sides. We started walking along the river and reached the Iordache Fountain, renowned locally for it pure fresh water coming from a mountain spring. It was named after a man who was cured from a serious illness by drinking the spring water. He erected a small monument with an inscription giving thanks for the miraculous cure.

Along the way we covered many subjects and discovered that when I was a schoolboy living on Strada Frumoasa in 1910 or so, my parents' house was back-to-back with the Rădulescu house on Strada Verde. My brother and I would climb the fence to look in the neighbor's yard and see a baby in a pram. As children are prone to do, we threw small pebbles at the pram. Little did I know that that baby would one day be my wife.

As we arrived at the fountain we sat on a bench and I started a sort of lecture saying that when she decided to marry she would have to choose a man older than herself who could also be like a father and a brother. I explained, that romantics believe that marriage should be based on love. Love at first sight is only a passing cloud and meaningless. True love is like a flower that grows with time. I had the impression that my listener was not impressed with this lesson so to entertain her I changed the subject. I said: "It is true that the way I see you now I like you very much and if we should get married our love would be like a the flower. If I propose to you to marry me and in case your parents object would you run away with me."

Quite to my surprise she answered, "Yes!" I continued on the same subject. "Would you be ready to go with me across the ocean to America?" She answered in the same curt way, "Yes!" I felt a sudden change was taking place in me and I started to seriously think about a plan for eloping and going to America.

I took her hand and kissed it. I felt a thrill as she put her head on my shoulder. As it was getting dark we decided to return home and we came back along the riverbank hand in hand. Both Getta Rădulescu, her mother, and her grandmother, Mrs. Baştea, were waiting for us on the porch and asking why we were so late. I was introduced to them and asked if could come and talk to them the next day. When I returned I was received by Mrs. Rădulescu on the porch of the large traditional country-styled house.

She asked me right away: "What is the reason for your visit?"

I answered: "I come to ask your daughter in marriage."

Her reply was short: "Just like that without knowing you?"

I told her that I had watched them for a whole month going on their way to bathe in mornings and going for their evening walks. She said that other men had made the same offer as mine. She said the matter could not be resolved over a cup of tea. The question was if her daughter liked me and if her husband would agree. "My husband is now in Bucharest," she emphasized, "where you can see him. But he and I have to find out about you. We never met you before and know nothing about your family." I gave her a few names for references, including my uncle Pompiliu Antonescu, who was a landowner in Barlad County. I took leave from Mrs. Baştea, Mrs. Rădulescu and their daughter, Zézé - a nickname she had given herself when she was small. I told them I would call on the General in Bucharest.

The day after I returned to Bucharest I went to leave visiting cards at his home. Just as I was ringing the front door bell expecting a servant to answer and take my cards, the General in uniform came out. I felt uneasy, especially as the General curtly asked me what I wanted. I told him I wanted to leave my visiting card. He took it and handed it to an orderly and without another word stepped into the street and climbed into the carriage that was waiting for him. I returned home rather perplexed about my encounter with General Vintilă Rădulescu.

My mother was now as happy as she could be about my visit to Rucăr, but not so happy about the reception I had received from the girl's father. After two days, the Rădulescu ladies returned to Bucharest and knew about my encounter with the General. When I spoke with her, she explained that her father did not know who I was but said that the general was expecting me the next day at six o'clock.

I appeared once again at No. 13 Aleia Zoe, dressed correctly and was received by both General and Mrs. Rădulescu in his den. He asked the reason for coming (even though he surely must have been told). I gave him a short answer and he gave me a lecture.

"Our daughter is our only child and we think she is too young to get married (she was 19). Admitting though that circumstances might be so as to encourage me to consider your request, first-of-all we have to know who your are. No one from our family has met you or your family. Give us a chance to know you better. You may have heard that many young men have asked our daughter's hand. They were refused because they were mainly interested in her dowry."

I interrupted telling him that I did not care how much money she did or did not have. I did not want her to have any dowry as it was the duty of the husband to take care of his wife and provide for his family. I told him: "I am sure that should she need help you would not hesitate to help her." I gave the General the names of persons I thought would provide information about me. We parted on cordial terms with the hope of meeting again soon. I went into the living room where I was left with Zézé Rădulescu for a short time. She said she hoped I would come for dinner after the house was put in order after the summer vacation. After this first formality, events occurred quickly. General Rădulescu told me that the worst references were given by my uncle Pompiliu Antonescu who told him I was an adventurer pretending that I had an engineering degree from a school in America, and that I was constantly traveling between Europe and the United States.

I was completely flabbergasted by my uncle's references. No one in the family had ever had any conflicts with him and he had been my father's best friend. I could not understand his reason, unless he had other plans for me. Luckily a person that I had not mentioned as reference, Mr. Stănescu, a Minister in the government and a friend of an acquaintance of the General's, had praised me highly. He said I was one of the best men in the Foreign Ministry and that I was known as a competent diplomat.

Finally we went to the General's library with Mrs. Rădulescu and he told me: "We give our approval to our daughter's marriage but with one condition, you must give your word of honor that you will remain in Romania and you will not go to America."

I answered affirmatively and gave my word of honor that I would not leave the country again. My wish was to settle in Romania and raise a family I told them that the wedding should take place as-soon-as possible and without fanfare. I would have liked to get married in Rucăr in one of the small churches built by the Baștea family. Their answer was that the General's position and the fact that they only had one daughter required them to invite army colleagues numerous friends and relatives.

There was now developing a group of "THEM" and "US". "THEM" included: General Vintilă Rădulescu, chief of the Army Veterinarian Service, Rector of the Veterinary Department of the Military College, and head of several organizations involved with the care of army cavalry. Mrs. Getta

Rădulescu, daughter of Ion Baştea, who had been president of the Court of Appeals and who had died of typhus in 1919. His wife Elena Baştea, born Zamfirescu, who through her husband was one of the heiresses of Paraschiv Baştea, one of the largest landowners in two or three counties. Also Mrs. Getta Rădulescu's sister, Mrs. Viorica Negoescu, married to General Ion Negoescu who personnel director at the Ministry of War. The Baştea-Rădulescu-Negoescu group lived in Parcul Filipescu (now the Dorobanţi embassy district) where they were among the first to build a large house in 1917.

The "US" group was smaller. It started with my mother, Elena Dimancescu, widow of the railroad engineer and daughter of Petre and Ecaterina Petrescu from Rămnicu Sărat. There was also my sister, Doctor Octavia Dimancescu, who graduated for the University of Bucharest Medical School as a doctor and from the Paris University of Medicine. She had been married to Dr. Weber and then to Dr. Stefan Nicolau, a scientist whom she also later divorced. Finally there was my brother, Major Ioan Dimancescu, a member of the Hunters' Regiment. The US group had friends and relatives in the literary and artistic circles, while the THEM group had ties to the military and judicial worlds.

ෳ

WEDDING

The day we went to order our wedding rings I was very moved. This was the sealing of our future. I gave Zézé a ring with a cluster of small diamonds that I had bought a long time ago and kept for my future wife. On September 21, 1930, the engagement took place in the Baştea apartments where General Negoescu exchanged our rings. Customary to the Greek Orthodox religion the future godfather puts the wedding rings on the right wedding fingers of the couple. These would be moved to the left hand on the wedding day. The engagement was followed by a wonderful meal and a group of musicians who played soft music.

The engagement over, wedding preparations began. The date was set for November 23, 1930. The number of invitations quickly numbered eight-hundred! "THEY" had the most invitees. Half were invited to the reception. I imagined that a wedding would be very simple. But now there were hundreds of guests and numerous things to do.

Zézé had asked me to give her a bridal bouquet of calla lilies, which were hard to find in Bucharest. To find them I went to the gardener of Queen Marie who told me he might have six in the hot houses. The day before the wedding I went to get them but was told they were not in bloom.

I then went to all the florists in Bucharest, but none had any white flowers left because of all the weddings. Only one florist had twenty white carnations, but without stems because they were prepared for buttonholes. I got these and made a bouquet by tying each carnation head to a white ribbon.

The wedding took place at St. Nicholas Church near the Royal Palace. It was a small church but Zézé had wished to be married in it as she had been christened there. The church was on one of the main streets of Bucharest, Calea Victoriei. Traffic that day in Bucharest was very heavy and the Chief of Police assigned extra policemen in the vicinity of the church. King Carol sent his representative, the Marshal of the Palace, General Ilasievici. I think that half the people in the church were military people including all eighteen generals of the Romanian army who were in Bucharest.

At the proper moment, General Rădulescu appeared with my bride. After going around the altar and praying before the icons with her mother, she was brought next to me in front of the altar. Our godparents were General and Mrs. Negoescu. We circled the table in front of the altar three times. At the end of the ceremony, people came to congratulate us. Many of them I did not know. Then quite suddenly I saw someone pushing his way through. It was Prince Antoine Bibesco who, after the usual congratulations, asked me why we invited so many military people.

By the time we arrived at the reception, it was snowing. We, the bride and groom, danced the "bride's hora" with the godparents and bridesmaids and ushers. This was a signal for everyone else to join the fun. The party ended at 7 o'clock in the morning. Over forty kilos of caviar had been consumed by the guests.

We left that morning for our honeymoon destination in Brașov but we stayed overnight in Sinaia because King Carol had asked me to come and see him. The next morning at 11 o'clock I went to the Palace where an audience with the King had been scheduled. In the waiting room I found Viorel Tilea who was then Chef of Cabinet for the Prime Minister. He had come to have a decree signed by the King and immediately asked me if I would let him go ahead of me as he wanted to catch the next train back to Bucharest. Tilea went in ahead of me but came out in about two minutes furious because the King had refused to sign the decree.

When I went in, Carol congratulated me effusively and told me that he wanted to give me a wedding gift. I could choose between Minister in Belgrade, Counselor in London, or opening a Consulate in California. I thanked him and told him that now that I was married, I wanted to consult my wife about the choice. We then talked until late into the afternoon. When I came back to our hotel, I found Zézé sound asleep under the blankets. I could hardly see her and feared that she had left. She reproached me that I had left her alone and had not sent word that I would be delayed. When I told her about the King's offer she immediately chose California. She said sensibly that we could see the other countries any time.

The next day I went back to the Palace and told the King about our decision. He showed me the decree that Tilea had brought him to sign. It was for a friend of Iuliu Maniu's who wanted to be appointed Consul General in San Francisco. Carol took a pen, crossed out the name, and wrote mine in its place. He said he could not send a man to America who could not speak English and whose only qualification was that he was a friend of the leader of the National Peasant Party. I told him I was very honored, but was in a very difficult personal situation, as I had given my word of honor to General Rădulescu that once I married his daughter I would not leave Romania. Smiling the King said: "Such a question is easy to resolve. As Chief of the Army and I will order him to give you back your word of honor."

This nomination brought me more enemies that I could imagine. Mr. Tilea accused me of being responsible for the rejection of his candidate and that Mr. Maniu was displeased. I talked to the King about a variety of things. Upon returning to the hotel, with Zézé it was decided to leave in the middle of December for Paris where another wedding gift was waiting for us. Antoine Bibesco had put his spacious apartment at 45 Quai Bourbon on the Isle St. Louis at our disposal for as long as we wished to stay. His cook had been notified that we were coming and was to prepare meals for us and for as many guests we wished to invite. His maid was at our service and we were told we could not only help ourselves to the best wines in his cellar but that we could take one or two cases with us when we left. We chose champagne. We spent two weeks including Christmas in Paris.

Before leaving Bucharest I had gone to see Mr. Tilea and asked for any instructions he might have. He told me he did not have instructions but an order. On my arrival in California, I was to go and see Mr. Randolph Hearst, the powerful and influential owner of over thirty American newspapers, and ask him to stop criticizing King Carol in his publications. It was useless to explain to Mr. Tilea that in America you cannot go to a publisher like Mr. Hearst and tell him what his papers can or cannot say. When I assured him I would try to do what I could, he repeated that this was not a matter of choice but an order. On December 30, we sailed on the *S.S. George Washington* from Cherbourg, France.

UNITED STATES LINES   S. S. GEORGE WASHINGTON   U. S. GOVERNMENT SHIP

CHAPTER TEN

CALIFORNIA

O ur December Atlantic Ocean crossing was unusually stormy. Our ship was like a nutshell on the mountainous waves. Furniture, torn from security bolts, was rolling about. Even the piano broke loose and had to be wedged with mattresses. The voyage turned unpleasant for Zézé as she soon was overcome by seasickness. On New Year's Eve at midnight I went to the cabin with two glasses of champagne and she could not even look at them. She said she would only cross the Ocean one more time to return home and never again. A six-day voyage turned to twelve. Finally, we arrived to see New York's Manhattan skyline. Happily, a few friends were waiting for us at the pier.

The next day we received a dinner invitation from Miss Baker of the *New York Times* who mentioned that she just gotten married. Miss Baker probably wanted to repay me for the help I had given her arranging her interview in Bucharest with King Carol. The dinner was to be at the Rainbow Room, one of the most elegant restaurants in New York. When we arrived there we found that the new husband was in his eighties and a millionaire. The dinner was excellent with caviar and champagne. Two days later, we were shocked to read the headline that the same man had committed suicide leaving his fortune to his new wife.

We did not stay long in New York and left for Washington to call on our Minister, Carol 'Citta' Davila. Coming back to the Capital city was like returning home. Many of my old friends were still there. The Legation was the same except for the arrangement of the rooms.

Though Davila had known me for a long time, he received me coolly. He was angry that the King had not consulted him about my appointment as Consul General in San Francisco. His relations with the King had varied between ups and downs. As young men they had known each other fairly well and they used to play tennis together. Davila chose a career in politics and joined the National Peasant Party. Upon his return King Carol never gave a thought about rewarding his friends and Davila was unhappy for having been ignored. This created an unpleasant situation for me. As minister he had to submit my appointment papers to the U.S. State Department. However, he kept my papers in his desk thus treating me as an employee rather than as a diplomatic official. Not wanting a big fuss about this, I let the situation to take its own course and matters were somehow resolved.

DDD & Alexandra 'Zé' at the Romanian Embassy (Washington, D.C.)

We had arrived in Washington in full winter. Now we were heading west in springtime. I had arranged to buy a Ford coupe and we chose to drive by a southern route that would give us an opportunity to see a big part of the United States. Averaging 300 miles a day, we would leave at 7 o'clock in the morning, stop for lunch wherever we wished and then finding a stopping place before sunset. New Orleans was a surprise with its old French atmosphere and crossing of the Mississippi impressed me. I was now entering my vast Consular jurisdiction that extended from the Mississippi to the Pacific. We passed through various historical places and through an area of Spanish influence, quite different from the Anglo-Saxon northeast. We reached the Pacific at San Diego.

As we were driving northward along the coast between San Diego and Los Angeles thrilled by the scenery, we suddenly came upon three men with guns. One was in the middle of the road, while the other two were on opposite sides. We stopped and Zézé quickly dropped her engagement ring on the floor. We could not turn around or run the men over. They ordered us to get out of the car with our hands up. They opened the trunk where we had our suitcases and were intrigued by my top hat box. I explained that I was a diplomat, a term that they did not seem to understand. As it soon turned out, they were policemen in plain clothes looking for a murderer who had killed a man in San Diego and had fled in a stolen Ford coupe. While they were searching our car, a police car arrived to report that the criminal had been caught on the inland road. I had been mistaken for the criminal, who had stolen a Ford of the same model and color as mine. The police apologized and let us continue on our way.

Before sunset we arrived in Los Angeles and headed straight for Hollywood. I was interested in Hollywood not so much as a tourist but because it would affect my work. All films that were brought into Romania until now had had to be approved by the Romanian Consulate in Chicago and provided with a certificate of origin. This now became my job. We reached Hollywood Boulevard, just a wide street of no particular interest, and went to the Roosevelt Hotel. Across from this hotel was Grauman's Chinese Theater where all movie previews where shown and attended by many artists, movie directors, scenario writers and guests. It was common for hundreds of people to crowd around the entrance to catch a glimpse of the celebrities.

As we planned to spend some time in Hollywood, we rented a furnished apartment in one of the tallest buildings in Hollywood. Here we saw for the first time a wall bed. One had to pull a handle and the bed came down ready for sleeping.

Quite fortunately in helping me was my friend Ionel Ghica who had spent a long time in Hollywood. He was contracting to have a plane built with which to beat the world distance-flying record. He provided me with a letter of introduction to Jean Negulescu,[33] an artist who became active in the movie world. In turn, he introduced us to John Villiers Farrow,[34] a writer and film director already a personality in Hollywood. We quickly became friends and we remained so until his death in the early nineteen-sixties. Thanks to him we met many famous people in Hollywood. I played a role in his second marriage to Maureen O'Sullivan who later became our daughter's godmother.

---

[33] Jean Negulescu (later Negulesco) was born in Craiova and eventually became famous in the Hollywood film world. In 1934 he entered the film industry, first as a sketch artist, then as an assistant producer, second unit director. In the late 1930s he became a director and screenwriter. He made his reputation at Warner Brothers. Negulesco's first feature film as director was *Singapore Woman* (1941). In 1948 he was nominated for an Academy Award for Directing for *Johnny Belinda*. In 1955 he won the BAFTA Award for Best Film for *How to Marry a Millionaire*. His 1959 movie, *The Best of Everything*, was on Entertainment Weekly's *Top 50 Cult Films of All-Time* list. Source: Wikipedia

[34] Father of the actress Mia Farrow.

From Hollywood we traveled up the California coast to San Francisco where I had planned to open the Consulate. The city's beauty immediately fascinated us but we were intimidated by the sight of its famously steep hills. Though we intended to stay at a hotel on Nob Hill, I gave up climbing it by car and went to another hotel at the foot of the hill. The first days I did not have the courage to drive the car in town and left it in a garage.

When it came to renting an apartment or a house, we did not know anyone who could give us information. Then one day we happened to stop in front of a thrift shop and saw an odd-shaped coffee cup. We went in to buy it. Inside a lady came towards me and after looking at me for a while she suddenly embraced me and said warmly "Welcome to San Francisco." It was Mrs. Alma de Bretteville Spreckels whom I had met in Neuilly through Loie Fuller. She promptly invited us to dinner as she wanted us to meet two persons who knew Romania. Her home was one of the most beautiful and large houses in San Francisco with white marble in a classic style and a lovely hillside view of the Bay. At dinner we were introduced to Miss Janet Peck and Mr. Jerome Politzer with both of whom a long friendship ensued.

Mrs. Alma de Bretteville Spreckels and her San Francisco home

Miss Peck had been to Yugoslavia where she had helped Serbian refugees during the First World War. Mr. Politzer, a well-known lawyer, had been to Romania to represent the Baldwin locomotive factory of Philadelphia in conjunction with money owed by the Romanian government for the purchase of locomotives. He had reached an agreement to receive wheat instead of cash. Janet had had no contact with Romania, but she was interested in European affairs.

Janet Peck had a large house in San Francisco as well as two houses on a ranch in Los Altos about 30 miles south of San Francisco. She often invited us to the ranch on weekends. She was the daughter of a rich tea importer who had been among the first settlers in California. At her parents' death, she and her brother, Orin, were left in the care of the Hearst family. Both children were sent to school in Europe. Mrs. Hearst would have wished Janet to marry her son, William Randolph Hearst, who later became the newspaper tycoon. Though he married someone else, he continued his friendship with Janet and was devoted to her. In her bedroom she had a telephone with a direct line to him at his San Simeon castle-mansion.

This was a wonderful and unexpected coincidence as I now saw the possibility of meeting Hearst through Janet Peck. This had been the principal order From Mr. Tilea before I left Romania - and something I never dreamed would happen. Also thanks to Janet, we were introduced to some of her long time friends including Dr. Philip King Brown and Mrs. Brown, a well known San Francisco family who had a beautiful oceanfront house in the Seacliff neighborhood with a breathtaking view facing the Golden Gate entrance. It was the first to have been built on the bluff. They made us feel very much at home. Mrs. Brown, whom we soon called "Mother Helen," invited us to join them for Christmas dinner, our first in San Francisco. Her daughter Phoebe immediately became Zézé's best friend and remained closely so their whole lives. The Brown family often comes into my life's story.[35]

Mrs. Spreckels advised us to rent an apartment on Nob Hill at the Huntington Apartments where she had once lived. We followed her advice, but the apartment was extremely expensive and after a few months we moved to a smaller apartment owned by an Irish widow. While we were at the Huntington, we had the unexpected visit of John Farrow. He was still an Australian citizen who had come to the United States on a tourist visa that had expired after several extensions. He had been advised to cross into Canada where he could apply for a permanent visa but the American consul in Vancouver refused to do so. Impulsively, John had rented a plane, landed illegally near San Francisco, and came by taxi to our apartment. As long as he stayed in our apartment he could not be arrested because my residence technically had diplomatic immunity. He worried that if he did go out he might be recognized and arrested by the immigration authorities.

We discussed what to do. He had to leave the United States again, but to where? I went to see Merique de Belfont, the French consul, who sug-

---

[35] In 1956, after difficult times for our family in exile from Romania in Morocco, Phoebe Hearst Brown took in both our young sons, Mihai age 16 and Dan age 13, in her home. They stayed with her in the Seacliffe house until our arrival at the end of the year.

gested that Farrow go to Tahiti but that meant a French visa that could only be issued in Paris. Consul de Belfont sent several telegrams and promised that the French authorities in Tahiti would be instructed to let him enter without a visa. The problem was now how to get him from our apartment to the pier where a ship, the *S.S. Makura* registered in New Zealand would soon be sailing for Australia with a stop in Tahiti. Luckily and quite by chance, a friend of John Farrow's knew the San Francisco Fire Chief, who brought a fire engine into the garage of the Huntington and with sirens sounding took John straight to the boat. The boat was ready to sail and John jumped onto the deck. As we waved good-bye someone found John's passport, which had dropped as he had literally jumped aboard. After a long exchange of telegrams and radiograms, de Belfont worked everything out for the traveler without a passport. This incident passed. However, I had informed Minister Davila in Washington that I wished to help a friend. His answer was that I was forbidden to get involved in the matter. By the time our communications crossed back and forth, Farrow had already arrived in Tahiti.

John Farrow's story brought me to the British consulate, where I met Cyril Cane, a distinguished diplomat who chose the post of British Consul General in San Francisco instead of minister to a small country. He thought that San Francisco was a much more vital place. At the time, he refused to do anything for John Farrow who though born in Australia was a British citizen. Cane told me that Farrow had a bad reputation in Hollywood. He was known as a "Don Juan" who made headlines with a scandal in San Francisco.

At the end of World War I, Farrow, a volunteer in the British Navy, was serving on a submarine that had moored in San Francisco. While on a 24-hour leave, he did not return to his ship but eloped with the daughter of a rich Californian family. After a few days, the girl's parents found them and though they had married, the girl was taken back by the family. Farrow was court-martialed for being absent without leave and was dishonorably discharged. This story, which Cane recounted to me, was published in the Californian press. In turn I explained how Farrow, when hiding in our apartment, saw a sensational news item that caught his attention. A sailor from a British ship had been enticed to a hotel and attacked. The sailor hit his assailant with a metal object hard enough to kill the man. The sailor gave himself up and was charged with murder. All this sensationalized in San Francisco press and public opinion quickly turned against the sailor. Moved by the story, Farrow telephoned a writer friend, Charles Morgan, and asked him to hire the best possible lawyer to defend the sailor. Thanks to a successful defense by the lawyer this led to an acquittal. All legal fees were paid by Farrow and Morgan.

All my efforts to portray the good side of Farrow could not persuade Cane to help him. Although Cane disagreed with me regarding Farrow, we became good friends for years and met many years later - in the 1950s - when Cane (now Sir Cyril Cane) was Consul General of Great Britain in Rabat, Morocco.

Through Farrow we met a number of well-known Hollywood personalities, including Edward G. Robinson who was Romanian-Jewish of origin.

Edward G. Robinson

He was my own size and would pass on to me finely tailored suits from his films. We also got to meet Eric Von Stronheim and the comic-duo Laurel and Hardy. They both acted like comedians even when off camera. They asked me for "one" photograph of the King of Romania. When I asked why only one, they answered that they would take turns keeping it. I eventually gave them a framed picture. They then pretended to fight over who would get it.

And thanks to my friend Jerome Politzer, I was accepted as a member of the Stock Exchange Club even though admitting foreigners was against regulations. The Club was on the top floor of a skyscraper. One day as I was going to lunch there I saw a rather stocky man on a scaffold in the hall starting to paint a fresco. Politzer introduced the artist who was the great Mexican painter, Diego Rivera. I asked who was the main subject of the fresco.

He said that the centerpiece would be a huge head of a woman, the portrait of Helen Wills Moody, a popular tennis star. In his opinion she had the most perfect face that he had ever seen. Years later, I discovered that Matila Ghyka also chose Helen Will Moody's head as it corresponded to his formula of the golden number, in his book *Le Nombre d'Or*.[36]

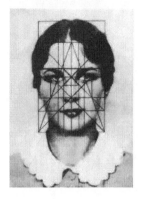 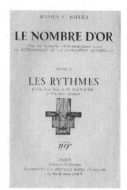

When the United States, under President Franklin Roosevelt, renewed relations with the Soviet Union, the Soviets sent a young man named Galcovici from his prior post in Tokyo to San Francisco as Consul General. I immediately wired to Titulescu, who had been appointed Romania's Minister of Foreign Affairs, asking for instructions on my relations should be with my new Russian colleague. Titulescu answered that I should be friendly and to give him help if he needed it.

Soon after his arrival in San Francisco, Galcovici came to see me and told me that he had also received instructions to maintain good relations with me. The first thing he asked me was to help him find a house for the Soviet consulate and one where he could also live. We went to see a large house for sale belonging to an American millionaire. Galcovici liked the house. The hall was in an octagonal shape and walls were covered with mirrors from ceiling to floor where he could stand and see his image repeated eight times. He stood there repeating "Galcovici, Galcovici..." eight times. I invited him to have lunch with me at the Stock Exchange Club, which had comfortable but not luxurious rooms. The fact that I had brought a "communist" into this capitalist Citadel offended the club members who came close to asking me to resign. Politzer's intervention saved me from the embarrassment.

---

[36] *Le Nombre d'Or*, Vol. 1, Photo p. 19-20, Librairie Gallimard, Paris, 1931.

Around the same time, thanks to Michel Weill who owned The White House, a large department store, I was admitted to the "Cercle de l'Union" where I often went for lunch and where only French was spoken. We became good friends with Michel and his wife Evelyn. Both of them were "refined" Europeans. Michel's uncle, Raphael, besides having donated to many charities and civic causes, had built a high school and had donated a statue by Rodin for a public square. As he had no children, he left everything to Michel including his department store. Each year the Weill's went to Europe for a few months and would bring back some unique items of cultural value. From England, one year, they shipped five tons of rare leather-bound books. These were put on sale at the "White House" where it was Michel's idea that younger people could buy rare items at a reasonable price.[37]

Although I badly wanted to meet Mr. Hearst, I did not want to abuse my friendship with Janet Peck. Occasionally during our conversations I would mention to her that I would like to meet him. She had heard my desire, but said nothing about it. One day I told here that Zézé and I were going to take a trip to Mexico and would be going by way of Los Angeles. She then asked me if I would like to stop at San Simeon to see Mr. Hearst. Naturally, I said yes. She immediately telephoned Mr. Hearst to tell him that two of her friends were going south and she would like him to invite them. He answered affirmatively and said that the only thing he needed to know was the date.

San Simeon was built as a sort of Citadel on top of a mountain dominating the Pacific Ocean. There was a guard at the main entrance to check each visitor. The road to the top wound through thousands of acres populated by wild animals. The guard instructed us not to get out of the car before reaching the main building. He watched us through binoculars as we made our way up the serpentine road.

Our car was taken by a valet and parked somewhere and at the main entrance, a lady was waiting for us and took us to an apartment that had

---

[37] The merchant Michel Weill, who was a nephew of Raphael Weill, was born in Paris and relocated to San Francisco (1904). With time, he became a president of Raphael Weill and Company, in San Francisco, which was known as the White House department store. He also was a president, vice-president or board member of the French Hospital; the Alliance Francaise; the City Planning Commission; San Francisco's De Young Museum; the Sigmund Stern Grove Music Festival; Californians, Inc. He also received military and other honors from France.

Source: http://magnesalm.org/notebook_fext.asp?site=magnes&book=156764

been reserved for us. There were accommodations for 120 guests, which were divided into three groups: close friends and relatives, business associates and newspaper men, and his mistress Marion Davis' friends. Marion had a long liaison with Mr. Hearst and though he would have liked to marry her, his wife would not accept a divorce and lived in New York.

Our apartment, reserved for special guests, was called the Doge's Suite. The living room was paneled with blue brocade from the Doge's Palace in Venice. The bed had belonged to Richelieu. All these items were lavishly bought in Europe at enormous prices. The lady who met us, asked if we would like to go horse back riding or to play tennis. When we told her that we had not brought the necessary clothing, in no time she brought us several sizes of riding breeches and boots.

We were also informed that life at San Simeon followed a strict routine. Breakfast was served in the main dining room until 10 o'clock. Mr. Hearst and Miss Davies appeared at 1 o'clock when lunch was served. Everyone had to be in the dining room five minutes early as the doors were closed after the hosts arrived. Cocktails were served at 6 o'clock with a large bowl of fresh caviar flown in from New York. Mr. Hearst and Miss Davies, led by her dachshund, would appear through a door disguised into the paneled woodwork. The dining room was like a cathedral. A long table, originally from an old Spanish monastery, could seat as many as 120 people. According to a seating ritual, Mr. Hearst sat in the middle of the table facing Miss Davies. The guests of honor were on each one's right. Some guests who overstayed were discretely moved one seat at time further away until they reached the end of the table.

We stayed three days and somehow Janet Peck had done something special in introducing us. At each meal we always sat in the same place at the right of Mr. Hearst and Miss Davies. The businessmen who came to see Mr. Hearst, seldom overstayed beyond a day or two after their transactions were concluded. One morning I met the owner of a newspaper that Mr. Hearst wanted to buy. This man was kept at the end of the table without being told what Mr. Hearst wanted to do.

The day of our arrival, Mr. Hearst came to me in the living room, shook hands with us and said that he was very glad that we had come to see him. The next day his private secretary invited me to see Mr. Hearst in his study. On the way, I asked the secretary if the subject of Mme. Lupescu would anger Mr. Hearst? The secretary said: "Go to it! Go to it! We have our own Mme. Lupescu here." I told Mr. Hearst that the fact that his newspapers were carrying front-page articles about Mme. Lupescu was upsetting to Romanians who would prefer if nothing was written about the woman.

Zézé at the San Simeon Castle 'Dodge Suite' as guest of William Randolph Hearst

He answered that her name was very precious to Romania. He said we would have to pay millions of dollars to obtain the publicity that his newspapers were providing for free. "Who knows the King of Bulgaria or the King of Greece?," he asked and then added. "At least every one in America knows that Romania has a King Carol II thanks to his lady friend." Mr. Hearst ended the conversations telling me that anytime I had something to say or to complain about articles in his newspapers to see Mr. Nolan, his lawyer in San Francisco who would be instructed to give me satisfaction. I could not have asked him more.

William Randolph and Marion Davies

Rumors of this special encounter soon spread to Romania. A Romanian magazine *Clopotul* published an article alleging that Mr. Dimancescu had a mistress in California, Marion Davies. This fortunately never reached Mr. Hearst. At the same time, a Romanian politician questioned our Minister of Foreign Affairs on the use of having a Consul in San Francisco.

My principal functions were to certify the origin of movies made in Hollywood and to manage the purchase of oil well equipment from the Hughes Tool Company. There were in fact were very few Romanians in the seven States I represented who needed the presence of a Consul. Occasionally a few citizens would write to request the legalization of some document or to request a passport. In San Francisco there may have been about 30 Romanian families. There were quite a few Jewish Romanians, but most of them had become American citizens and had lost contact with Romania.

MEXICO

Authorities in Bucharest asked that I visit Mexico to study the question of nationalization of natural resources. Romania was considering nationalizing parts of the oil industry and Mexican own efforts were of interest. We were dominated by foreign oil companies that provided 75 per cent of the national budget. When the companies encountered difficulties they would cut some of our revenues all the while influencing changes in the government.

We turned this task into a opportunity to see more of North America. We left on February 26, 1932, from San Francisco with our new Ford car stopping on the way in San Simeon. From there we journeyed to Los Angeles, El Centro, Phoenix, Arizona, then El Paso, Del Rio and San Antonio, Texas, from where we turned southward into Mexico at Laredo.

I had the impression that we were going back two or three centuries. The sharp difference between the United States and Mexico was unexpected especially in rural areas. Adding difficulty to our driving was that road maps were not good. In Monterey I went to the tourist office where I was advised to send the car to Mexico City by train, as a portion of the highway was still under construction. However, I saw what looked like a good alternate route on the map they had given me. We discovered that over half the route did not exist.

Our Ford car on Mexican roads

After spending a night in Saltillo we went on to Vanegas, a small village with only a few houses in a deserted landscape. As there was no hotel I was happy to accept an offer to spend the night at the house of a local inhabitant. The room he offered only had a wooden bed and no linens. We spread some newspapers on the bed and did not even undress. To protect our car from other locals, our host offered to spend the night in it. It was only when we reached Mexico City that I found out that the inhabitants of the village were a notorious team of bandits who had attacked trains between Laredo and Mexico. They were all caught and executed.

We continued along the road, which was little more than a furrow created by other vehicles. For a while we were driving parallel to the railroad tracks and decided that if we ran into car trouble we could take our suitcases and hail the train heading for Mexico City. At a certain point our road turned away from the railroad and became more of goat path, leading towards the top of the Sierra Madre Mountains through a forest of cacti. At the top we came to a clearing where vultures were eating from the carcass of a dead animal.

We continued southward on bad roads eventually came to remote villages. There we were told that we were heading toward San Luiz Potosi where we stayed one night, then Querretarro before reaching Mexico City. Our good fortune was that 1932 Ford Coupe had not let us down after 2800 miles of difficult driving.

We spent the first night at the Imperial Hotel and then moved to the Guardiola Hotel which had been recommended to us by the Brown family. It was a seven storied art-deco-styled building. As-soon-as we arrived some reporters came to interview me probably alerted by the desk clerk who saw my diplomatic passport. Articles appeared the next day and I soon had visits from the leaders of the small Romanian colony in Mexico City who came to welcome us and to say that they were happy to have a representative of Romania.

They invited us to a lunch on Lake Xochimilco. The lake lies in the crater of a volcano and upon it were built floating islands covered with beautiful trees and flowers. A long table and a barge had been arranged in the colors of the Romanian flag and Romanian dishes were served while three guitarists played Romania folk songs. I few years before I had met Mr. Roberto Haberman, now right hand man to Mexico's President Plutarco Elias Calles, and managed to meet him one evening. Roberto had been an active leftist starting in 1917 and risen to be trusted socialist by labor leaders. Much later I heard that he was said to have secretly shared information with the US Department of Justice and the FBI. For now, however, he had gotten the American Federation of Labor to allow export of 'labor-produced' machinery to Mexico.

We discussed the nationalization program in Mexico. "Foreign companies were furious," he told me, "but slowly they calmed down once it became an accomplished fact." On a personal level, I mentioned my interest in visiting Puebla and its unusual churches that I had read about. Apparently there was one church for every day of the year. His intercession led to special invitation from the Governor of the State of Morelos in Cuernavaca not too far from Puebla. It was engraved for "Monsieur and Madame Dimancescu" and delivered by an officer in uniform.

We left on the day that we were to be the Governor's guests at lunch in the Borda Gardens, the Governor's home. All the way there, the road was guarded by soldiers with guns. We were among the first arrivals in a shaded part of the estate's gardens where an orchestra played softly. Nearby, a table was set for about 60 guests on a long porch. Zézé and I went to look at the seating arrangements. I found my card at the right of the governor, but there was no card for Zézé. A Mexican officer told me that according to Mexican tradition wives are invited but are not expected to attend. I asked if it would not be better for us to return to Mexico City. Not at all, he said, a small table would be set for Zézé in a small room overlooking the porch.

When all the guests arrived and took their seats, the Governor said something in Spanish and to my surprise each guest removed a revolver from his pocket and laid it on the table. I was told later that this too was a Mexican tradition and was a sign of friendship toward the host. I gathered that lunch was a meeting for the political associates of the Governor. Nobody took any notice of Zézé or me during the three hours. While the meal was served, there were a series of political speeches. When it all ended, the Governor went into the small room to bid us good-bye. An officer escorted us to the car and a guard presented arms. We were taken to the Governor's administrative building in Cuernavaca to see one of Diego Rivera's best frescoes.

When we left there were horseback patrols every four or five miles along the 100 kilometer distance to Puebla. There were no other vehicles on the road. Haberman later told me that the fact the road was guarded showed that we were under the protection of the President of Mexico. Puebla gave the impression of a dead city lying below the 4,500 meter-high Matlalcueitl Volcano. Except for a crazy man who kept following us and calling me "Papa! Papa!" there was no other living soul. Some of the churches I had read about were in ruin and many closed.

We added a visit to the four massive Teotihuacan Pyramids before completing an enchanting visit. For the return trip to the U.S., on my crude map there was a northward line for the main road with a dotted line for a section that was under construction. But in Mexico City I was again advised to send the car by train to Laredo. Believing in my skills I took the risk of driving. We arrived at a mountainous point where the paving ended and the gravel surface narrowed to the width of the car. Soon we were along the side of a vertical 1000 meter wall on one side and an equally high meter precipice on the other. We traveled at a crawl with my hands frozen to the steering-wheel. I prayed for an end to the ordeal. Applying the brakes was out of question because wheels would not grip on the unstable gravel.

When night came we started downward having covered only about 100 kilometers. In the dark I could not see the precipice any more, just the white gravel ahead illuminated by the car's lights. We both said nothing. Several times we thought we saw lights in the valley below but they turned out to be the lights of fire flies. Finally we came to the village of Tamazun-chale. It was Easter eve and people were leaving church with lighted candles. We pulled up at the largest house which happened to be an inn. We were immediately invited to join the twelve other guests who were having a meal at a long table set under an alcove with climbing plants. It was here that we comfortably spent one of our last nights in Mexico. We went to sleep lulled by the music of a guitarist.

The years we spent in California and the trip to Mexico were among the best adventures of our life.

Traveling was a lengthy process, especially from California back to Romania. In 1932 we drove across the United States, reached New York, sailed to France on April 16 with the car on board and reached Paris, crossed the channel to England on May 5th, crossed back to the Continent on May 9th and reached Bruxelles a day later with our same sturdy Ford car. Berlin the 14th, Prague the 15th. Budapest the 18th. And Rucăr the 1st of June. This was a six-week journey followed by an unexpected invitation a few days later.

The Royal Palace asked that we join the King in helping welcome one of the United States' richest families, the Fleischmann's of Cincinnati, Ohio. In 1836 at age 30, Charles Fleischmann, a Jewish businessman who had run a distillery in Vienna, emigrated with his brother to the United States. To-gether they established a yeast business that altered the baking industry in America and rapidly evolved into a huge enterprise producing not just yeast but vinegar and then gin. Now almost 100 years later, his son, Julius, was embarked on a round-the-world voyage on his yacht, the *Camargo*, then the largest private vessel in the U.S. On board were his wife and two children. Their sailing included a planned visit to Romania and a landing at Tulcea on the Danube River the second week of June. The King along with his young son Voievodul Mihai, then only 12 years-old, offered to welcome them. Queen Marie would come aboard the *Camargo* as well as dignitaries including Foreign Minister Titulescu. Zézé and I were asked to be their hosts during the visit. We took short trips to the Danube Delta to see sturgeon fishermen and to Queen Marie's home in Balcic. From this visit developed a strong family friendship that endured for the rest of our lives.[38] After their departure, Zézé and I spent the rest of the summer months in Bucharest and Rucăr. We departed again for the United States by boat from Constanta with our faithful Ford car.

Left to right: Crown Prince's personal secretary, Julius Fleischmann, Dumitru Danielopol, Dorette Fleischmann, Dr. Rensdall (family doctor), Crown Prince Mihai, DDD.

Once back in California the most important personal events were the birth of our first child, a girl Sandra, born in 1933, and son Dimitri Jr., born in 1934. According to our Romania tradition we decided to christen our daughter in the Greek Orthodox religion. We asked the priest of a small Russian church in San Francisco to perform the christening in Los Altos at Janet Peck's ranch. It took place in October when the weather was like summer. Janet arranged a long buffet table, covered with brocade, outside.

---

[38] When times became extremely difficult, the Fleischmann's would support us fifteen years later in making the escape from Communism to exiled life during which we found ourselves penniless and all material property lost to the War and Communist expropriation.

At one end there was a large bowl of non-alcoholic fruit punch and at the other a large bowl of real punch with brandy, champagne, etc. The godparents were John Farrow and Maureen O'Sullivan. The priest came with the traditional christening food, icons and candles. He set up the altar under a huge oak tree where he performed the baptism. The ceremony was in English, but the guests were taken aback when Sandra was dipped into the font three times. Out of the holy water her little hands reached out and grabbed the priest's beard.

We invited about two-hundred guests among whom was the Mrs. Fremont Older, the wife of the owner of the *San Francisco Bulletin* and President of the San Francisco Temperance Society. She missed the non-alcoholic punch bowl and had a few drinks from the alcoholic bowl and soon had to be helped to her table. Her husband had brought along one of his reporters to cover the christening. The next day an article ran for several columns with the names of the guests, the dresses the ladies wore, a description of the surroundings, the buffet and the table arrangements. It also included a biography of Maureen O'Sullivan and ended with John Farrow's life. Using poor judgment the reporter mentioned Farrow's elopement and court-martial. I hoped that because of its length many people would not read it all the way to the end.

A year and half later our second child, Dimitri, was christened with the same priest officiating. Neither the Fremont Olders nor any reporters were invited.

Without warning Minister Carol 'Citta' Davila, my chief from Washington, arrived in March 1934. It was embarrassing that I did not know his plans. I went to see him at the Mark Hopkins Hotel where he was staying and found him giving an interview to a reporter. This lasted about an hour and a half. He invited me to lunch with him while he anxiously waited for the afternoon paper to arrive. Around three o'clock it came, with two small paragraphs in the middle section and nothing about his long discourse. He had sent a wire to San Simeon asking for an interview with Mr. Hearst, who did not reply. He was to leave for Los Angeles next and allowed me to drive him there for the long journey down the coast. Before he left, a friend of ours invited him to lunch with about forty people at the exclusive Hillsborough Club. The table was beautifully arranged with a large floral arrangement of red, yellow and blue flowers, the color of the Romanian flag. This event and others made him realize how valuable my relations in California had become.

But again when he reached Los Angeles, without asking for my help, he tried to yet in touch with noted personalities high up in the movie world. Finally he asked for my help and I scheduled an invitation to the Paramount Studios where he was received by Maureen O'Sullivan, John Farrow's fiancée. John did not want to see him knowing that he had prohibited me from helping him with his emigration problems. However, I managed to persuade the Los Angeles press to take more notice of him than San Francisco did. Then he left, to my great relief.

ɩɩɩ

All the time that I stayed in California, whenever I had a free moment, I spent it working on one of the most important avocations of my life. Before leaving Romania for the first time in 1919, I visited the Romanian Academy and tried to find out if there was any area of Romanian history that had not been well researched. I found a brief report remarking that few Romanians had taken on the task of cartography. In fact most of the maps of our provinces, Moldavia, Wallachia and Transylvania, were made by non-Romanians. And until the early 1800s, these regions were depicted as under the control or influence of either of either the Austro-Hungarian or Turkish Empires.

The first two Romanians who made maps of the provinces were Dimitrie Cantemir, who published a map of Moldavia in 1700, and Constantin Cantacuzino, who published a very detailed map of Wallachia entitled *Indice Topographicus*. Cantemir's map was well known and one could find quite a few copies. Not so for Cantacuzino's map. It was published in Padua, Italy, and though its existence was known there were no known copies. I decided that as long as I was abroad I would search all the best libraries and collect material on Romanian maps.

During my early travels, I went to the Vienna Library, to the Bibliothéque Nationale in Paris, to the British Museum in London and to the Library of Congress in Washington. Whenever I found a map showing the Romanian provinces, I made a photocopy of it. While I was in California I had an almost complete collection of these photocopies so I decided to assemble them into an atlas. It started with the year 150 A.D. and ended in 1895.

But then came a most unusual circumstance. When I arrived in San Francisco I started touring all the bookstores asking if by any chance they had old maps or atlases. I found a large book department at the Emporium Department Store. When I asked Mr. Newman, the book department manager, if he had any old maps or atlases, he answered as if troubled by my question, that his department was up to date with cartographic material and nothing was older than two years. He did not even appear to know that such things as old maps existed. He told me to give him some time and he would try to fill in this gap. Without telling me, he instructed his European buyers to buy anything involving old cartography.

After many weeks, he invited me to come and see him. On the top floor of the store there was a storage room full of cases and packages. They all contained old maps acquired in Europe. Newman suggested that I fix the prices for the material and in exchange I could choose anything I wanted and pay only fifty cents per map. Of course I accepted this offer, but it took me about three months to sort the material. I was able to find most of the items that were missing from my collection and purchased for what was an extremely low price.

A short time after, Newman organized a sale that he advertised for a month as "Old Map Week." On the first floor of the Emporium there were tables scattered around various departments on which there were antique maps priced from 50 cents to $500 a piece. On opening day he invited me to give a lecture explaining old maps and their value. The one-week sale turned into a great success. All the maps were sold.

Some of those at 50 cents were bought by school children. Mrs. Richard Bennett, the wife of the well-known Shakespearean actor bought several hundred. But she committed the 'crime' of using the maps to paper the walls of her study! In fact even Mr. Newman, without consulting me, committed a similar offense by cutting pages from atlases and selling the maps item by item. He got the idea from an enterprising man who bought a rare volume of Hartman Schedel published in Germany in 1493. The pages were sold individually at $20 to $100 because he was not able to get his asking price of $1000 for the whole volume.

Of my collection of facsimiles, I found a young man who helped me make the three copies on a machine that he only had access to after working hours. It took me from 1933 to 1935 to finish the tedious and detailed work. The title of the atlas was *Monumenta Cartographica Moldaviae, Vallachiae et Transilvaniae*. One went to King Carol, one to the Minister of Foreign Affairs, and I kept the third.[39]

All along, I started to search for and collect antique maps. This became an almost complete collection of rare ancient maps referencing Romania's provinces in all their prior political incarnations. I eventually took it to Romanian to our house. This quite sadly was bombed during World War II by an American plane on a Ploieşti oil fields bombing mission. Unable to reach their destinations due to overcast skies, the pilots released their

---

[39] One of the two found its way into the collection of the Romanian Academy and thus well protected for others to use as a reference.

bombs randomly over Bucharest. One of these bombs fell on our house on Aleia Zoe next to Parcul Filipescu.

Besides the maps I had all the notes that I had made at the various well known libraries and which I was going to use for a history of Romanian cartography. Gone were my old atlases among which were Mercators, Ortelius's and Blaeos and an almost complete collection of English books that mentioned Romanians and their land. Also lost were three large Chinese portraits bought in a San Francisco antique shop where I was told they were from the Imperial Palace in Peking. Burned too was a smaller portrait of a ten-year-old boy with a skull cap and pony tail. I had seen it in a Japanese antique shop but the owner liked it and said it was't for sale. Each time we went to the store I had admired the portrait. Before leaving San Francisco I stopped in to say good-bye to my Japanese friend and asked for one more look at the painting. He was moved by my request and let me admire it. Later, I was surprised to receive a package with the portrait inside. A letter from my friend explained that he was certain that I appreciated it even more than he did. In return we sent him a Romanian hand-embroidered set that Zézé had treasured.

At the time I was in San Francisco, King Carol II went to London to attend King George V's funeral on January 28, 1936. The British communist-influence *The Daily Worker* published an outrageous article saying that the King had been drinking before the funeral. The article claimed that Carol was accompanied by a 'masseur' who had to hold him steady, during the funeral procession and had to go to a Turkish bath to be revived. Indeed near King Carol was a man dressed in a black vest from under which a white shirt hung over some black pants. This were promptly misrepresented as the clothes of a 'masseur.' In England, the "drunken King" article was not quoted in any other newspaper but did appear in the American Hearst newspapers under the byline of their London correspondent. It also appeared in *Time* magazine, which had the habit of copying articles from other publications without quoting the sources.

I immediately realized that damage this story was story was doing. I telegraphed to London asking for copies of the photograph and details of the procession. There was no question that King Carol was in the same group with the King of Denmark and the President of France. There was another picture showing the end of the procession where there was a group representing the Romanian army and the civilian as described by *The Daily Worker*.

I called Mr. Hearst's lawyer, Mr. Nolan, and described the mistaken information. Mr. Nolan contacted Mr. Hearst who said that if I had definite proof, that I be given any satisfaction that I wanted. I suggested that a denial be mentioned over Mr. Hearst's radio stations on the 9 o'clock evening news and that a letter be published on the matter. The letter was written by Zézé's mother who was visiting us at the time and was indeed published much to my satisfaction.

I tried to obtain the same denial from *Time* magazine and they said that it was against their policy to deny information that they had already printed, but they proposed that I write a letter to the editor. This was also signed by Zézé's mother and was published. All this came to the attention the Dean of the University of Washington's School of Journalism, Vernon McKenzie, who became interested in the way the false story of the "drunken King" had been published widely and he made it the subject of one of his journalism courses. He went to London and then to Bucharest where he interviewed participants in the story and later wrote a book *Through Turbulent Years*, in which the details of the story were explained.[40]

Without compunction a Communist writer faked the story about Carol He reported that the king had felt so "seedy" that he had called in a masseur from a Turkish bath to get His Majesty into shape to march in the long and tiring procession. When the time came to march Carol was reported still wobbly and dragged the attendant along in his car... Next day several of the Fleet Street wits (journalists) gathered at the Temple Bar chophouse... A well-known author who was present offered to elucidate the mystery. He said he knew the man and that he was employed at the Ritz as a masseur. As he elaborated his story others at the luncheon table laughed and thought it a great joke. [A reporter from] *The Daily Worker* overheard the conversation ... and so the story grew.

The American public swallowed the story, hook line, and sinker. From the Atlantic to the Pacific millions must have been amused by the affair. *March of Time* was informed, before the drama went on the air, that the whole yarn was faked in London, but thought it too good a story to miss, or perhaps the information reached the radio studio too late to stop the broadcast... The facts are that Carol was marching in a forward part of the procession nearly half a mile away from ... the alleged masseur. [He] was in reality Rumania's number one war hero, Constantin Cotolan. He was sent to London with the Rumanian army delegation to represent the peasant-soldiers of his country. He holds

---

[40] Vernon McKenzie, *Through Turbulent Years*, Geoffrey Bles, London, 1938, pg.138-144.

185

the award "Order of Michael the Brave," equivalent to the Congressional Medal or the Victoria Cross. The photographs published, both real and doctored, showed the shirt outside the trousers, projecting a few inches below the coat. This shirt-tail was said by newspapers to be a "masseur's apron." They were misled. Except for the hat it is the Sunday formal costume of peasants in the Rumanian district of Muscel.

It was now 1936 and I had been in San Francisco for almost five years when I was invited to lecture at the prestigious Commonwealth Club where the previous speaker had been Anthony Eden, British Minister of Foreign Affairs. Following such an illustrous speaker was going to be difficult. I prepared my subject for a month and when I had it ready I sent a copy to Bucharest asking it to be approved by the Minister of Foreign Affairs. Mr. Titulescu approved it without a change. The title was *We Who Are About to Die*.

It reflected on news from Europe that was quickly turning more-and-more alarming. I stressed the critical situation in which Romania found itself surrounded by countries that were arming themselves. I neither mentioned the names of any of these countries nor any of their leaders. The lecture greeted with loud applause led to further invitations to offer the lecture at various other clubs. As a consequence of my speech I was also honored with a Ph.D, Honoris Causa, from the University of Southern California at a graduation ceremony by Rufus von Kleinsmith, President of the University.

During the Commonwealth Club talk, and unknown to me, someone had taken stenographic notes and a newspaper had misquoted my title as *We Who Are Surrounded by an 'Iron Belt'*. And within 48 hours the German and Italian consuls had wired the speech to Berlin and Rome. In Bucharest 15,000 kilometers away, Herr Wilhelm Fabricius and Signor Ugo Solla, the German and Italian ministers, filed protests that I had insulted Adolf Hitler and Benito Mussolini. They requested that I be punished and recalled to Romania. Titulescu showed the protests to the King. The King instructed Titulescu to promote me and send me to London.

Thus ended my Consular duties in California in 1936.

PART V ⸱ CLOUDS

Storm clouds gathered over Europe during the early 1930s. Hitler was now entrenched. The Soviet Union was going through its own Stalinist terror and turmoil. England and France wavered in what measures to take in building alliances that might respond to the Nazi movement enveloping Germany. The smaller countries - Czechoslovakia, Romania, Yugoslavia, Greece - sought refuge in their own international intrigues. Fascist movements were breeding their own power-bases encouraged in no small part by orders and support from Berlin. These became known as Hitler's 'Fifth Columns,' groups active in subverting by force or subterfuge legitimate government institutions.

Excerpts from *King Carol, Hitler and Lupescu* by A.L. Easterman, 1942

In answer to questions posed to him by the British journalist, A. L. Easterman, King Carol would state:
"If I may say so, I do not think you quite understand the inwardness of the political situation in Roumania. There has been an alliance between the Iron Guard and the National Peasant Party. Do you realise what that means? The Iron Guard is not only extreme nationalist, it is a terror organisation. It has the support and the aid of a foreign power, you know whom I mean. The National Peasant Party does not realise that, sooner-or-later, it will be exploited by the Iron Guard and then swamped. What follows? The nation will be in the grip of an insurrectionary, terrorist, extreme nationalist organisation of fanatics in the pay of foreign enemies of Roumania.
"What do you think I should have done? Call them to power in the name of democracy?"

***

"Commenting on the Roumanian King's mission [to England in 1938], one British newspaper put the position succinctly:
   'Roumania today stands at a difficult crossroads, seeking to maintain both her territorial integrity and her independence, both her markets and her friends. She has resisted attempts to drive her into the new German orbit, she has stood fast against the pressure of her ally, Poland, to force her into a so-called neutral bloc. With oil fields which are the most important in Europe and a wheat belt which makes her Europe's granary, she contains minorities which render any provocative foreign policy hazardous. Britain, which has often been too indifferent to Roumania's political importance and too dilatory in seeking

economic intercourse, has lately shown herself a customer upon a large scale for Roumania's wheat and could seize the opportunity for finding fresh markets for British goods which may otherwise be lost for a generation. . . .'

"Britain did not seize the opportunity. Carol made one more effort to retrieve the position, one final attempt to arm himself with the material support and collaboration of the Western democracies, in preparation for his meeting with Hitler, to which neither the King nor any of his entourage looked forward with any zest or confidence. At the same time, this last move was, in itself, hazardous as well as bold, for, it carried with it the prospect of a further incitement to the anger of the Fuehrer, already violently displeased with the [King's] 'provocative' visit to London...

"If Carol ever had any illusions about the close association between the Iron Guard and Nazi Germany and Codreanu's role as the appointed agent of Hitler's plans for the disruption of Roumania, these were now dispelled. Hitler had given him the first brutal intimation that Roumania was within his 'sphere of influence' and that he felt himself in a position to assert his authority in it. [Hitler's] demand for the release of Codreanu, coupled with the criticism of Carol's actions with regard to him, were a direct challenge to the King's status as a sovereign ruler, to the authority of his Government, and to the independence of his country. Any suggestion of weakness on Carol's part in so critical a situation would mean surrender and the collapse of his authority. It would mean acceptance of Roumanian vassalage to the overlordship of Hitler. Carol resolved, therefore, to accept the challenge, summarily to reject the pretensions of the Nazi leader and to assert his status as the monarch of a sovereign and independent state.

"Showing little sign of impatience and none of perturbation, he rose from his chair and looking squarely in the irate, flushed face of Hitler, said calmly: 'Herr Reichskanzler, I am the King of Roumania. I shall know how to deal with this matter.'

"Hitler paled with ill-concealed rage. He uttered not a single word in response to this curt rejection of the all-powerful Fuehrer's 'request', he merely held out his hand in signal that the meeting was at an end. He followed Carol to the door of the audience chamber. Goering escorted the King and his son [now 17 years-old] to the door of the Berghof and bowed politely as they entered their motor car.

"It was related in Bucharest afterwards that, when Goering returned to the presence of his Fuehrer, he found Hitler in an almost uncontrollable fury."

"Dimancescu, Press Attaché of the Roumanian Legation in London, had been brought back recently to Bucharest by King Carol, to undertake, as Director General of Propaganda, the task of counteracting the growingly intensive and obnoxious German propaganda which had aroused the King's distaste and alarm.

"Dimancescu had never concealed his passionate friendship for Britain; his record as one of the foremost protagonists of Anglo-Roumanian collaboration was his chief qualification for the post ... in Bucharest which Carol created specially to secure his services in Romania. Dimancescu became suspicious of Frau Kohler's activities. His doubts were intensified by the fact that this elegant "Investigator of the German Department of Agriculture" allowed it to be known, with becoming modesty, that she was a cousin of Heinrich Himmler, Chief of the Nazi Gestapo. Dimancescu's inquiries revealed that Frau Kohler was, in fact, a Gestapo agent and that her credentials as an agricultural expert were "cover" for simple espionage. When she became aware that Dimancescu was taking a special interest in her, Frau Kohler boldly essayed to seek his acquaintance. He not only declined to meet her, but pointedly snubbed her, when chance or design brought them together in the salons of Bucharest. Dimancescu also took measures to block her further advance into influential social and political circles. So effective were these measures that Frau Kohler soon found herself suspect and so embarrassed that she was obliged to leave Bucharest as unobtrusively as she had entered. She returned to Berlin.

"Her departure was quickly followed by marks of German displeasure with the author of her discomfiture. A few days after Frau Kohler left Roumania, Herr Fabricius and the Italian Minister in Bucharest put pressure on the Roumanian Government to dismiss Dimancescu on the ground that he was an enemy of The Axis. In support of this, the German Minister produced to M. Petrescu-Comnen, the Foreign Minister, the text of a speech made by Dimancescu to a private gathering in San Francisco in 1936, when be had criticised Nazi complaints of "encirclement" by the Euro-democracies. Fabricius and his Italian colleague stated, on behalf of their governments, that if Dimancescu were not removed from his office, Berlin and Rome would regard this refusal as unfriendly act. At the same time, German and Italian journalists were instructed to add emphasis to this diplomatic démarche by ostentatiously absenting themselves from any press gatherings at which Dimancescu was present.

"Carol, who bad personally appointed Dimancescu, described, in private, the demands for his nominee's dismissal as "impertinent diplomatic action", but he felt unwilling to make an international issue of a comparatively minor matter. His reply was to send him back to London, but to express his displeasure at the "impertinence Carol gave Dimancescu the appointment of Chief of Press Services at the Roumanian Legation. This was a new and important post and technically carried the rank of Minister. Dimancescu's dismissal in Bucharest by promotion in London was duly noted in the Wilhelmstrasse and the Germans, with the Italians, continued to exert pressure for proper punishment; they insisted on the removal of this "enemy of Germany" from so responsible a political post. Carol again made a pretence of yielding; he transferred Dimancescu to the diplomatic service with the rank of Counsellor in Charge of Press Services, in which capacity he carried on his work in London. The Nazis thereupon gave up the pursuit."

Excerpts from *A Plea for Roumania* by D. Dem Dimancescu (1941)

"Since 1938, we have offered ourselves as potential allies to those whom we thought might have been willing to withstand Hitler's lust for world conquest. Unfortunately our efforts were treated with little consideration. I remember, in 1939, going myself from door to door with an article which appeared in the Deutscher Volksvirt boasting that if the Germans were once to set foot in Roumania it would be an easy matter for them to get hold of the Suez Canal, and then master Asia and Africa.

"We Roumanians were then saying to certain people here in England, 'You have foolishly allowed the Czechoslovak stronghold to fall into German hands. Let us now be your advance bastion of the Suez Canal. We have a good army of some two million men. Let us buy from you, with our oil and wheat, the tools we need to do the job of fighting for our liberty and independence. We will also fight indirectly for that Suez, which is the lifeline of your Empire. By no means do not on any consideration allow the Germans to come and take from us the wheat and the oil which you will some day need'.

"Unfortunately those who were then in a position to accept our offer spoke different languages from ours: they were interested in unpaid commercial debts, clearing arrangements, higher exchange rates for the pound sterling, and especially in the rates of interest on a prospective loan. They told us that oil could be bought cheaper across the Atlantic, and that our wheat was of a lower grade than that available elsewhere. (The Germans never raised such objections.)"

1939-1940

"On 13 April 1939, France and the United Kingdom had pledged to guarantee the independence of the Kingdom of Romania. Negotiations with the Soviet Union concerning a similar guarantee collapsed when Romania refused to allow the Red Army to cross its frontiers.

"On 23 August 1939, Germany and the Soviet Union signed the Molotov-Ribbentrop Pact. Among other things, this pact recognized the Soviet "interest" in Bessarabia (which had been ruled by the Russian Empire from 1812–1918).

"Following the outbreak of World War II on 1 September 1939, the Kingdom of Romania under King Carol II officially adopted a position of neutrality. However, the rapidly changing situation in Europe during 1940, as well as domestic political upheaval, undermined this stance. Fascist political forces such as the Iron Guard rose in popularity and power, urging an alliance with Nazi Germany and its allies. As the military fortunes of Romania's two main guarantors of territorial integrity - France and Britain - crumbled in the Fall of France, the government of Romania turned to Germany in hopes of a similar guarantee, unaware that the then dominant European power had already granted its consent to Soviet territorial claims in a secret protocol of the Molotov-Ribbentrop Pact, signed in 1939.

"*In the summer 1940, a series of territorial disputes were resolved unfavorably to Romania, resulting in the loss of most of the territory gained in the wake of World War I. This caused the popularity of Romania's government to plummet, further reinforcing the fascist and military factions, who eventually staged a coup [in September of 1940 that forced King to abdicate in favor of his son, Michael] that turned the country into a fascist dictatorship under Marshal Ion Antonescu. The new regime firmly set the country on a course towards the Axis camp, officially joining the Axis powers on 23 November 1940.*

"*As a member of the Axis, Romania joined the invasion of the Soviet Union on 22 June 1941, providing equipment and oil to Nazi Germany as well as committing [600,000 soldiers] more troops to the Eastern Front than all the other allies of Germany combined.*"[41]

---

[41] Excerpts from < en.wikipedia.org / wiki / Greater_Romania >

CHAPTER ELEVEN

LONDON

My stay in England could be divided into two periods: the first when I served as a diplomat and the second after King Carol's abdication late in 1940, when I resigned my position as a diplomat and became an ordinary person. During these two periods I encountered different people: those associated with my diplomatic life and those in industry and business.

It was exactly December 31, 1936, when we arrived in London. Until we came to England we had thought that the English lived in the most comfortable houses, but we discovered that things were not quite so. Most of the bigger houses we saw had only one bathroom, no heating in the bedrooms and poorly maintained kitchens. What counted a lot in England was to have a country house and an apartment in London. Our real estate agent thought we were hard to please.

Then at the Legation on Cromwell Place I had a cool reception. At the time almost all the personnel were anti-Carol and my return came with a reputation of being "Carol's man." One was even a secret member of the German Fascist-inspired Iron Guard. He sent copies of all our correspondence to the increasingly Fascist "Green House" Legionnaire's headquarters in Bucharest. I had read Ion Zelea Codreanu's book "*For the Legionnaires.*" Though patriotic in his admonitions, when needed he resorted to killing those in opposition, a method introduced by a fellow Legionnaire, Horia Sima. They talked about democratic rule but imposed authority through violence.

Next two pages: *Romanian Legation diplomats in formal attire - London, 1940 (Photo from the archives of Nicholas Ratiu)*
Front: *Admiral G. Dumitrescu, Prince M. Ghyka, Minister V. Tilea, R. Florescu, D. Dimancescu*
Back: *B. Vardala, G. Iliescu, V. Styrcea, A. Bianu*

from left to
right:

Bottom Row:
Admiral C-dr St.
Dimitrescu
Prince
Matila Ghyka
V.V. Tilea
Radu Florescu
D.Dem.Dimăncescu

Row 2nd la
St. En. Ilieșcu
Victor Stoyecea
Alex Diann

1940
The Diplomats
at the
Romanian
Legation
London

1940

Such activities reflected poorly on Romania's reputation. In my capacity as Press Counselor I could not deny reports of factually correct reports sent by British correspondents. However, I was very lucky to find Miss Davies an exceptional secretary, an English woman who had been secretary to Nicolae Titulescu when he was with the League of Nations in London. She had also been secretary to U.S. General Pershing at the end of World War I. We first met in 1925 when Titulescu came to Washington to discuss our war debts. Miss Davies could take stenographic notes in English, French and German and could type them out in perfect form. Sadly, Titulescu had treated her with a total lack of delicacy. And though her previous salary had reached 250 pounds per month, I did not barter with her and fortunately had enough budget to pay the same amount. All the while, Vasile Grigorcea, the Romanian Minister in London did not speak English and he could not see why he needed to hire an English secretary.

I did not want to get involved with other sections of the Legation and gave her a free hand to organize the press department of the Legation. The diplomatic section was full of secrecy and intrigue among its counselors and secretaries. The commercial section, however, was led by a capable man, Alecu Bianu, the son of the secretary of the Romanian Academy. Like me, Bianu avoided mixing with the other diplomats.

And there was the military attaché's section, whose chief was Commodore G. Dumitrescu, later Admiral. His aide was Captain George Iliescu, who did not prove to be a hard worker. However, both of them had access to substantial funds for information gathering and remained very secretive. Any news they transmitted was by coded telegram, disguised as a transcript of a newspaper article. Commodore Dumitrescu was in charge of buying material for our army and was in touch with various business merchants. He was obsessed by the thought of being accused of not being honest.

The change from San Francisco to London meant a complete readjustment to social life in England. The English, unlike Americans, had no interest in Embassy or Legation personnel. Their society was more stratified. The elite, mostly carrying aristocratic titles, lived in closed circles hardly accessible to foreigners. Most of the country's leaders were drawn from this elite and resisted being influenced by outsiders. They tended to gather in various clubs where foreigners were seldom admitted. "White's Club," established in 1693, was the most exclusive because the Prince of Wales, heir to the throne, was a member. The only major club that accepted foreigners was the "Atheneum" but membership was based on carefully scrutinized background references and some people were refused. It was thanks to Miss Davies that I was able to enter certain circles by telling me who were the right people to meet.

~~~

During the late 1930s, politics at home were in great flux. The two major Romanian political parties, the National Peasant Party and the Liberal Party, competed for political power. Each accused the other of dishonesty. The National Peasants called the Liberals "rats" and spread slanderous remarks. The Liberals in turn were anti-Carlists and were circulating as much negative news as they could about Carol even before he became King. The Octavian Goga government's anti-semitism[42] created another set of international headlines.

This turmoil made it difficult to draw attention or to feed positive headlines. At work my goal was to make Romania and its leaders known in England. This meant overcoming attitudes in Bucharest. The Romanian Foreign Ministry and the government press bureau in Bucharest bombarded the Romanian Legation in London with long communiqués. A speech by the Prime Minister or a member of the cabinet would be telegraphed in full with instructions to circulate it to the British press. Quite obviously these carried little or no interest to the British public and were promptly ignored by the press. Busy with their own priorities, the editors of the large papers like the *London Times* or the *Daily Telegraph* were not interested in meeting foreign press attachés.

Each newspaper had its own diplomatic correspondent who would stop in at the legations occasionally where they received official versions of various events. It was here that I focused by slowly cultivating their friendship. I never gave them prepared written handouts. I answered all their questions even when the questions were embarrassing. Thus I gradually gained the reputation that they could get "true" news through me rather than "prearranged" news. I made it a habit to pass out confidential news that they could not get from any other source.

Most of the London newspapers had declined in quality and featured sensational stories that sold well to the general public. Only the *London Times*, *Daily Telegraph* and *Manchester Guardian* chose not to feature scandal-

---

[42] Octavian Goga became Prime Minister of Romania and served from 28 December 1937 to 10 February 1938. He had been appointed by King Carol, in his attempt to enforce his own personal dictatorship. During his short period in government, Goga was mostly known for the first anti-Semitic laws which were passed. On 12 January 1938 his government stripped 270,000 Moldavian-Romanian Jews of their citizenship [though 500,000 others were not so affected]. Besides being an anti-Semite himself, Goga attempted to outflank the Iron Guard's popular support. The regime instituted by Goga and Cuza gave itself a paramilitary wing of Fascist "Lance-bearers". They borrowed heavily from the Iron Guard, and started competing with it for public attention. Mainly, they were involved in violence against the Jews. *Source: Wikipedia*

ous headlines. I encouraged their newsmen to go Romania to see the situation for themselves, so too, with several talented British authors.

Because there was censorship in most of Europe, especially in the Eastern and Southeastern countries, correspondents were prevented from sending what was termed "false" news, i.e., embarrassing information whether true or not. The result was that a center was created in Vienna from where correspondents could telephone or telegraph any news they wished. To avoid censorship, news was sent to Vienna from Romania by messenger. Correspondents in Vienna depended on "legmen" in Bucharest who were usually paid £1 or £2 for a news item. The Liberals even hired their own legmen to send their own packaged news from Vienna to Paris. All this propaganda echoed in London. And once it was published, it was hard to deny. The socialist *Daily Worker* chose to publish an article that Carol was suffering from syphilis and was mad.

When I went to the Foreign Office to ask how one could stop false news, I was told that no one could stop the British press from printing what it wanted to print and that the Foreign Office could neither dictate nor stop news. In London, I arranged to have a long conversation about this with Lord Vansittart who was then Permanent Secretary of the Foreign Office. He told me confidentially that the only way to stop the erroneous stories was to buy advertisements in the papers. He explained that generally the papers followed the preferences of their paying clients. When I calculated how much money would be needed, it came to thousands of pounds, which the Romanian government would not have provided.

News articles generally chose to cover the King's personal behavior but mentioned nothing about how he was leading the country. On the subject of stories spread about him and Magda Lupescu, Matila Ghyka suggested a partial solution. He proposed that she should hire a lawyer in London to defend her interests. When an incorrect story about her would appear, the lawyer would threaten a libel suit. Following his advice, we hired a lawyer who was also the lawyer for the Duke of Kent, who was himself having a bad time in the press. The lawyer had a trick. In London, most of the morning newspapers had an early edition that went on sale in Piccadilly Circus at midnight. Mr. Trower, the lawyer, would buy the first edition every night and if he found something unpleasant for his client, he would call the editor of the newspaper. By the next edition the item would be gone. Through his energetic activity very little negative news subsequently appeared about Mme. Lupescu or Romania.

Constantin Argetoianu, his wife, Zézé and DDD - Bucharest, June 1938

NOTE: *Constantin Argetoianu - Romanian politician, a well-known personality of interwar Greater Romania, who served as the Prime Minister between September 28 and November 23, 1939.*

"Two years after a Communist regime was imposed on Romania, on the morning of May 6, 1950, he was arrested by the Securitate; while being taken away, he was heard saying: "Man, you sure are tough, you communists, if you are afraid of a farting old man such as myself." He died in the infamous Sighet prison five years later, never having been put on trial. In 1999, attorney and civil rights activist Monica Macovei, representing Argetoianu's two granddaughters - Yvonne Oroveanu Niculescu and Constantina "Dina" Oroveanu - in court proceedings cleared Argetoianu of all charges, with the prosecutor admitting that Argetoianu's detention had been an abuse." [43]

---

[43]   *Source: wikipedia*

THE KING'S VISIT
NOVEMBER 1938

W hile Carol was in exile with Mme. Lupescu in Paris, Press Chief Eugen Titeanu hired a photographer to picture them together in a nightclub. A story was then published - and believed - that the former heir to the throne was spending all his time in nightclubs. He was widely viewed in England as being an alcoholic and a playboy. Given these attitudes, I thought it would be a good idea if Carol came to London unofficially and stayed long enough for newspaper reporters to follow his behavior. I had no idea whether he would accept the suggestion.

The first obstacle to the proposal was Queen Mary of England who opposed a royal visit to England. I obtained an audience with Queen Mary who retracted her opposition and told me with a feint laugh:

"I will see for myself this Clark Gable of Royalty."

Informed of this, Carol announced plans to be in London for a week staying at the Dorchester Hotel. When the press and the reporters heard, their sole question was in knowing whether Mme. Lupescu would be with him. He had other ideas in mind. He told me confidentially that he hoped that his son Crown Prince Mihai still young boy might at some point marry Princess Margaret of England born only in 1930. On this sensitive subject he instructed me to find out the Court's attitudes to such a marriage. The English Royal Family was on very good terms with Helen, Mihai's mother who often came to London and complained about Carol. Among other things she had told her relative, Marina, wife of the Duke of Kent, that King Carol had taken many of her valuables. However, the Queen Mother, as I found out, liked Mihai who was nine years older than Margaret and suggested that he should come to London alone, which he did with Carol's approval. When he came all the Royal Family kept an eye on him and allowed it to be said that he was a "nice boy."

During his stay I accompanied him and I arranged for him to be invited by Lord Somers, chief of the Boy Scouts. We went to Lord Somers' castle where Lord and Lady Baden-Powell were also guests. One afternoon Lord Baden-Powell took me aside and told me that King Carol was committing a great error by changing the name of the Romanian "Boy Scouts'" ("Cercetasii") to Guards ("Strajeria").[44]

"Tell King Carol," Baden-Powell said, "that through the Boy Scouts he has ties throughout the world which means important support for Romania. Nobody knows the "Strajeria" and you will lose the support of the international scouting movement."

In turn, Carol came to London and contrary to some forecasts of reporters, he was accompanied only by his aide from the royal guard, Ernest Urdăreanu, and a royal guard adjutant, Lt. Ilie Radu. They stayed at the Dorchester Hotel on Park Lane where Carol mostly took his meals in his suite. About twenty reporters installed themselves in the lobby of the hotel where they tried to pry information from the hotel personnel: What was he eating? What was he drinking? Though they represented the major world agencies like Associated Press, Reuters, International Press and Havas, they were not allowed to disturb him or to go to his floor.

Carol was not a drinker and only drank a glass of wine with his evening meal. To divert the press I had given instructions that every evening at 10 o'clock a quart of milk should be sent to his suite. During his stay in London, I also stayed at the Dorchester to be on hand. When he went for walks, he would take me with him, leaving Urdăreanu at the hotel, but taking Lt. Radu who walked a few steps behind as a bodyguard.

Sometimes I would lunch with him. We were always followed by newsmen who would come into the restaurants and watch what the King was drinking and how much. Actually people in restaurants never stared at him. He was left to eat in peace. I toured London shops with him where he mostly bought socks and ties for Mihai. He also bought classical music records. Hardly would we leave a store than the reporters would go in to find out what he had bought. Finally, at the insistence of the reporters, Carol accepted to meet a single reporter, acting as a representative for the others. They chose the correspondent of American International News. He stayed with Carol for about an hour and a half answering all the questions put to him.

---

[44] Carol also sought to build up his own personality cult against the growing influence of the Iron Guard, for instance by setting up a paramilitary youth organization known as *Straja Tarii* in 1935. Its members were known as *străjeri* ("sentinels"), and used a form of the Roman salute as greeting. When the National Legionary State government replaced Carol's regime [1940], after the crisis provoked by the Second Vienna Award (the cession of Northern Transylvania to Hungary), the organization was disbanded and all its assets were taken over by the Iron Guard – which replaced official education with its own version of Fascism.
Source: en.wikipedia.org/wiki/Straja_Tarii

Dimitri Dimancescu and King Carol in London

That evening we dined at the *Quaglino's Restaurant*,[45] which was frequented by London's social élite. The late diners were offered a copy of the *Daily Mail* at midnight. When we looked at it we saw an article about the interview on the first page. It started like this: "The King received me very politely and shook my hand while his hand was covered with rings and a thick gold bracelet." Besides this frivolous detail, the story was otherwise well written. The King did not mind the introduction because it was partly true. Actually he was wearing two rings, one with the coat of arms of Romania. The gold bracelet was an identification bracelet that was fashionable for men to wear.

King Carol left England quietly and I accompanied him as far as Calais ferry boat, where his personal train was attached to the Orient Express. During his stay in London, I used to part from him in the evenings by saying "Good night, Majesty!" One evening after I had taken leave from him Urdăreanu came to me and said I should say "Long Live Your Majesty." Until the King left, I continued to say "Good night Majesty!" or "Good appetite Majesty!"

General Constantin Ilasievici, head of the Royal Military Household, had brought Urdăreanu into the Palace Guard hoping he would marry his daughter. Urdăreanu had the reputation at his regiment of being a very good housekeeper. Everything shined in his unit. In the stables, paint was applied often and the horse's harnesses were kept spick-and-span. When he was brought to the Palace he started by cleaning up the basement, which was cluttered with all kinds of cases piled up in dark rooms. He got rid of everything that did not belong to the Royal Household. All the rooms and halls were whitewashed. He got involved in the affairs of the kitchen that had previously operated as separate unit, checking on all the cook's purchases and eliminating anything that was not strictly needed for the

---

[45] *Quaglino's* still operates at 16 Bury Street St James's, London.

King or the palace personnel. Every day he made a list of all expenses, not only for the kitchen, but for the entire royal household. He took the list to the King for approval. His efficiency impressed the King who appointed him Minister of the Royal Household, a post I had been offered years earlier but refused because I did not like the idea of being superintendent of the Palace. Urdăreanu took his job seriously and established a protocol and a set of rules for the Royal House. Slowly he became indispensable and assumed discretional powers. He started making decisions in the name of the King and eventually everything had to go through him. Even cabinet ministers had to discuss issues with him before they saw the King.

In 1938, I was appointed Minister of Press and Propaganda in Bucharest, a position responsible for the press, radio, cinema and tourism. During this period, King Carol asked me to help organize his official visit with the King and Queen of England in 1938. It was all carefully coordinated. On the first night of his visit there was an official dinner given by the British Foreign Office in honor of King George VI and King Carol II. During dinner there was not much occasion for conversation, but the Foreign Office had planned to have about two hours of discussions after the dinner. The King sat in a seat of honor but the Romanian Minister of Foreign Affairs, Nicolae Petrescu-Comnen, remained inconspicuous as, so too, our Minister in London, Basil Grigorcea, who did not speak English.[46] Urdăreanu was furious that neither Petrescu-Comnen nor Grigorcea were talking to anyone. At one moment he openly berated Petrescu-Comnen saying: "Why are you standing around like a stick?" Then he went to Grigorcea and said, "Who brought you to London? I shall change this situation." It was embarrassing to see their behavior.

The dinner that King Carol gave at the Romanian Legation in Honor King George VI was a success and the King was pleased with the way it had been orchestrated. But it was an example of the less visible difficulties. King Carol had brought from Romania all the needed silverware and china with the Royal initials. He also brought butlers from the Royal Palace to serve the dinner. They wore the same uniforms that they wore in Bucharest.

Of his visit, I gathered hundreds of clippings not only from the major London newspapers but also from many small provincial ones. Summaries

---

[46] The following is a list of the Legation personnel in London who participated in the events honoring King Carol: H.E. Basil Grigorescu, Romanian Minister H.E. Matila Ghica, Minister Plenipotentiary Mr. Radu Florescu, Counsellor of Legation Commodore G. Dumitrescu, Military and Naval Attaché Commander C. Nicolau, Air Attaché, Mr. D. Dem. Dimancescu, Counsellor on Special Assignment, Mr. Alexandru Bianu, Commercial Attaché, Captain G. Iliescu, Assistant Military Attaché, Mr. Victor Starcea, Second Secretary of Legation, Mr. Ion Vardala, Third Secretary of Legation

were telegraphed to Bucharest that had no other way to gauge the reaction to the Royal visit. Of the many that appeared, I selected the best ones and decided to publish them in a book that I would be offered to members of the British and Romanian press. It was published in 1939 with the title *King Carol II and the British Press*[47] with an introduction written by D. J. Hall and the preface by me. E.T. Heron, the owner of the publishing house, took extra care with the production and supervised the selection of type and editing. This book reflected my attempt to create a more correct image, not to simply get favorable publicity. The view of Romania in England was described by Donald Hall in the Introduction:

"While it is rare and acceptable, it is no easy task to introduce a work that has been compiled out of love for, and dedication to the honour of a living king. I say this neither from false modesty not in flattery, for, on my first meeting with King Carol, I learned that he was as quick to perceive pretence in others as he was uninterested in eulogy of himself. We the people of Great Britain and the Empire, are attached to the idea of Kingship. We revere our Kings, while we acknowledge their faults; thus, while we criticize them, we find it hard not be indignant when such criticism is found on foreign lips. It is for us then in particular, to understand the regard held by the people of Roumania for their king, and to sympathise with their distress when thoughtless and unknowing strangers have disparaged him. With all our separateness from them, both in distance and tradition, we have in common with them an ideal of personal freedom which seeks social unity under the Crown. Though their forms may be different, we have, both of us, that peculiar but strong co-partnership of democracy with monarchy."

In my own Preface I made reference to the press.

"The power of the press to create and influence public opinion is an acknowledged fact. It is also true that newspaper editors are obliged to rely on the good faith, judgment and accuracy of the correspondents who supply the material for their newspapers. Once a distorted fact enters the huge machinery of editorial offices it cannot be easily dislodged. Newspaper routine implies continuous consultation of the files and reference libraries; thus a wrong statement once entered in the journalistic sanctums is perpetuated without end, creating a legend which outside efforts cannot destroy."

In this manner an exaggerated one-sided persona had been created about the King of Romania. Vernon McKenzie, the distinguished Dean of the School of Journalism of the University of Washington, once wrote that

---

[47] *King Carol II and the British Press*, E.T. Heron & Co. Ltd., London., 1939.

"of all the Sovereigns of Europe, King Carol of Romania was the most unjustly maligned." Even R.H. Bruce Lockhart in his own book, *Guns and Butter*, declared that the British picture of King Carol was 'out of focus'.

King Carol's official visit to England helped to alter this image. His visit, though planned long before, took place at one of the most critical periods in Europe as Nazism grew more threatening by the day. One day, he called me to Buckingham Palace where he was staying and told me to find Frederick Leith-Ross, chief economic advisor to the government, and to make an appointment with him. The guest arrived the following morning at 8:00 am, an unusually early time for a meeting with a King. They were together for over an hour After they left the King called me from an adjoining room where I was waiting and said.

"I am no longer the King of Romania. Leith-Ross decides what to do in our country. He told me that I must give more concessions to the oil companies, especially the British ones. If this happens, our income will be reduced severely." A major part of the national revenues was dependent on oil.

I had never seen Carol as agitated as he was that morning. The oil question had been a problem that Romania could not resolve. Most of the oil production was controlled by foreigners and when World War II started, the British press accused us of favoring the Nazis by giving them the biggest oil quota. This was quite untrue. The sale of oil was done independently by the foreign oil companies themselves and the German quota was smaller than the British one. The false information was circulated by the British government. Though the true situation was known by the British press, they continued to badger us and claimed that if German planes bombed England they would be using Romanian fuel. My efforts to convince them of the contrary were ineffective. The Romanian government sent to London the Director of the National Bank, Muitza Constantinescu, to explain the situation regarding oil. His visit was in vain. He was followed by Grigore Gafencu our Minister of Foreign Affairs. His outcome was the same.

❧

Members of the Romanian Legation (June 1941) lft to rt: I. Murgu
Press Attaché, D. Dimancescu Counselor, Mircea Eliade[48] Cultural
Attaché, Gh. Munteanu Press Attaché

---

[48] After leaving London [Mircea Iliade] was assigned the office of Counsel and Press Officer (later Cultural Attaché) to the Romanian Embassy in Portugal, where he was kept on as diplomat by the National Legionary State (the Iron Guard government) and, ultimately, by Ion Antonescu's regime. His office involved disseminating propaganda in favor of the Romanian state. *Source: en.wikipedia.org/wiki/Mircea_Eliade*

CHAPTER THIRTEEN

ENGLAND

L ong before the war started, I guessed that war would break out between Germany and Britain. One could already foresee aerial bombing and that London would be the Luftwaffe's main target. And indeed, when the air bombing started, German planes dropped bombs randomly all over southern England. Some even fell near where we were staying. I decided to look for a larger house for my wife our two children and their nurse, a butler and cook who came from Romania. I searched near London so I could come home every evening. I finally found and rented a big house in Maidenhead, west of the city and near the Thames River. We moved there in 1940.

Since the house was big enough, we also lodged the Romanian assistant Military Attaché, George Emil Iliescu, his wife and their maid. The house, "Cheniston," was located at the edged of the Maidenhead Thicket. From our garden we could step right onto the Thicket paths. Later some of the garden was sacrificed to potato growing. Here too we had some nearby bombs. During the first six months of the war, there was almost no fighting activity but many believed that the Germans were preparing a big offensive and would cross the channel and invade England. Such an invasion would have had London as its first objective. I was wondering what to do: to wait for the Nazi occupation or to leave for Portugal and then travel from there to Canada or the United States? I discussed this with my wife and we both decided to stay put.

Life at Cheniston continued normally. In September 1940, the bombing intensified but no one seemed scared. When a bomb fell no one screamed or panicked. Many people had dug shelters near their homes. In our house there was a wine cellar built with concrete walls that could serve as a shelter. In March 1940, our third child was born, a son, Mihai-Dinu. In June 1940, he was christened in London at the St. Sophia Cathedral with a Greek Orthodox service. His godfather was King Mihai, who being in Romania, had authorized his Assistant Military Attaché to stand in for him. A reception followed at the Romanian Legation. Fortunately there was no bombing on that day.

By September the bombing intensified and we would promptly go to our shelter as soon the air raid warning were sounded. We crowded in this small cubicle until we heard the all-clear signal. After a few times of this discomfort, we decided to stay in our beds. We took the three children in our bedroom with us, thinking that if the house would be hit we might as well die together. When our fourth child, Peter Dan, was born three years later in March of 1943, the bombing was heavy.

During this time the Germans invented the flying rocket, the V-I, which was a bomb with two small wings and a jet motor. The bomb flew until the motor ran out of fuel. It then fell vertically, but could not be aimed accurately at a target. We, the supposed victims, would see the them coming and would hear the motorcycle-like roar of their motors. All one could do was lie flat on the ground when the motor stopped. The British devised an anti-V-1 defense system in which planes would touch the V-1's wing lightly causing it to lose its balance and fall. This took place over the English Channel and the area between the coast and London. British reconnaissance planes discovered a site on the Baltic Sea coast where the Germans were setting up launch pads for the V-2. These came silently, producing loud explosions and damaging large areas. It was almost impossible to count the dead when a V-2 fell. These weapons soon terrorized London and the West of England. To live day and night with the danger of death, no matter how indifferent one might appear, each person felt inwardly insecure. My family and myself, even though we pretended indifference, lived with the uncertainty of what the next day might bring.

'Cheniston', Maidenhead, England

❧❧

BOOKS, AUTHORS, AND MAPS

During the two World Wars, there was always a tug-of-war between good and bad news regarding Romania. It was surprising, however, how much had been written and popularized when it came to books about personalities, politics and day-to-day culture. During the 1930s, especially when working at the Legation in London, I was able to befriend many contemporary academics, journalists, and worldly travelers who took the subject of Romania to heart.

Marie, the second Queen of Romania, granddaughter of Queen Victoria, wrote several books and lengthy diaries in English, her maternal language. She was an untiring writer always insisting on having her work printed as elegantly as possible. Published in England, these books were popular and had a larger circulation. *The Country I Love* made her well known. *The Story of My Life* in three volumes went through five editions in the first year of its publication.[49]

Portrait of Queen Marie as a young girl painted at Windsor Castle by Sir J. E. Millais

---

[49] *The Story of My Life*, Cassell & Co., Ltd., London, 1934.

"Let it be Roumania and I, or I and Roumania," she wrote, "it comes to the same thing, and I have patience with me if many thoughts, many inferences and conclusions are woven in among facts I have to relate, for life has always been long enough and events plentiful enough to have taught me many a lesson, and to have made of me something of a philosopher in my own small way."

The most important work of the inter-War years, and remains so to this day, was *A History of the Roumanians* by Robert William "R.W." Seton-Watson[50] whom I was fortunate to first meet when he was a professor at London University and to become good friends.

"To some, Roumanian history may seem obscure and often inglorious," he stated in the Preface, "but there is a certain dynamic force in its vicissitudes, and Europe cannot show any more striking example of the corroding effects of foreign rule, of the failure of a policy of systematic assimilation and of the gradual triumph of national sentiment over unfavourable circumstances."

While he was a student at Oxford University, Seton-Watson and a colleague Henry Wickham Steed traveled in Central Europe and the Balkans in the first years of the Twentieth Century. He recognized the great injustice imposed by the Austro-Hungarian Empire on ethnic minorities such as the Czechoslovaks and the Romanians in Transylvania. In 1915, Seton-Watson published *Roumania and the Great War* defending the cause of Romanians living under then Hungarian controlled Transylvania. From that time on both men never ceased writing and denouncing these injustices. Seton-Watson foresaw the solution of dismembering the Austro-Hungarian Empire into a federation of independent people. Especially devoted to the Romanians, he learned our language and could read documents and books. During the Second World War, R.W. Seton-Watson ensured the operation of my Romanian Section at the Secret Political and Economic Welfare under the overall control of Bruce Lockhart, who too was his friend. R.W. and I met almost daily to discuss future possibilities for Romania - of which more later.

There were serious works such as *The Agrarian Revolution of Roumania* by Ifor L. Evans and *The Land and the Peasant in Roumania* by Dr. David Mitrany, an Englishman of Romanian origin. Contemporary affairs commentaries appeared by the American academic Vernon Mackenzie who, in two of his books[51] *Through Turbulent Years* in 1935 and *Here Lies Goebbels* in 1940,

---

[50] *A History of the Roumanians*, University of Cambridge Press, 1934.

[51] *Through Turbulent Years* Geoffrey Bles, London, 1935; and *Here Lies Goebbels,* Michael Joseph Limited, London,1940.

wrote entire chapters on Romanian issues. Charles Upson Clark, a professor at Columbia University, well traveled in the country contributed his own work under the title *United Roumania*[52] following prior published works by him on Greater Romania and the Bessarabian territorial question. Explaining his interest in the subject, he remarked "Our ignorance of Roumania is so great ... her part in the war has been so maligned."

In 1928, Cambridge University published the pioneering archaeological work *Dacia: An Outline of the Early Civilization of the Carpatho-Danubian Countries* by Vasile Pârvan[53] first in English then translated nine years later into Romanian. It quickly found its way onto the shelves of all the large academic libraries.

There was an engaging account by Donald Hall of rural travels in *Roumanian Furrow*, a book that remained popular for decades to follow its publication in the 1930s. On his own initiative Archibald Forman authored *Rumania Through a Windscreen*[54]. He traveled by car to Romania and without being influenced by anyone. Back in England he lectured with his own projected slides and played recordings of folk songs registered by him. Also on her own initiative, Elizabeth Burgoyne, wrote a biography of Carmen Sylva.[55] She was a great admirer of Carol I's wife and came to Romania to research her life. So, too, the Scottish writer, Elisabeth Kyle in a popular book *Mirrors of Versailles*[56] also devoted a whole chapter on her visit to Romania when she was also our guest at Rucăr.

Another friend of Romania was Sylvia Pankhurst the daughter of the famous suffragette of the same name. She published *Poems of Mihail Eminescu* translated directly from Romanian with the help of I.O. Stefanovici and an introduction by Nicolae Iorga. It was prefaced by Bernard Shaw but Shaw had refused to write the introduction declaring that he was not qualified to introduce a Romanian poet and especially one that was dead. Sylvia Pankhurst published a facsimile of Shaw's letter which produced a

---

[52] *United Roumania*, Dodd, Mead & Co.,, New York, 1932.

[53] Vasile Pârvan studied history in Bucharest, with Nicolae Iorga as one of his professors. He continued his studies in Germany. His Ph.D. thesis, written in 1909, was titled *The nationality of merchants in the Roman Empire*. Subsequently, he became professor at the University of Bucharest, and was elected member of the Romanian Academy. His main interests were in prehistoric archaeology and classical antiquity. He organized several archaeological excavations, the most important one being at Histria, from 1914 to 1927.

[54] *Rumania Through a Windscreen*, S. Low, Marston & Co. London, 1939.

[55] Pauline Elisabeth Ottilie Luise zu Wied (1843 – 1916) was the Queen consort of Romania as the wife of King Carol I of Romania, widely known by her literary name of *Carmen Sylva*.

[56] *Mirrors of Versailles*, Constable & Co. Ltd, London,1939.

great sensation in England and helped the "dead poet" Eminescu become well known.

The British "Le Play Society," named after the Frédéric Le Play, carried out sociological and geographical studies. In 1939 it published a two-volume study *Eastern Carpathian Studies* focused on Romania edited by professors H.J. Fleure and R.A. Pelham. The two volumes were very well illustrated with photographs and maps. Given the Society wide respect, the books were well received in intellectual circles.

Many times during my stay in England, I was asked to furnish information about Romania. I did this with pleasure as part of my job as Counselor of the Legation. One "subscriber" to my information, was the English writer, Bernard Newman. In one of his books, *Balkan Background* published by Robert Halle, Ltd., London, 1940,[57] almost an entire chapter on Romania was written by me.

Derek Patmore wrote *Invitation to Roumania*[58] and Sacheverell Sitwell *Roumanian Journey.*[59] The latter is one I felt closest to. Sitwell had two brothers and a sister who together were considered leaders in the intellectual community of England. Having met him, I convinced him to come to Romania. He arrived with his beautiful Canadian wife, Georgia, the writer and painter Richard Wyndham and A. Costa, a photographer. I covered all their expenses and promptly sent two tickets for the Orient Express 2nd-Class thinking he and his wife would share a cabin. He sent them back with a note saying that they never traveled in 2nd-class. Thereafter everything had to be 1st-Class. After being our guests, we toured the whole country together and when finally published his book became a bestseller. I was happy to see his mention of days spent with us in Rucăr.

Another friendship developed with John Peel, a history teacher at a high school in Leicester. It was a Saturday when he appeared one day at the Romanian Legation looking for information and I was the only one there. He had come by bicycle from Leicester, about 80 miles away. During our conversation, Peel who told me that he had very little money and always traveled by bicycle. He was headed for Romania - by bicycle - and wanted to know which was the best route through the Carpathian Mountains to Bucharest! I advised him to travel through Brașov, then Bran and to stop in Rucăr to visit us. He was thin and I did not believe he had the strength for a trip across the whole of Europe. He said that he only took only two shirts with him one of which he would wash every evening. But we parted ami-

---

[57] *Balkan Background*, Robert Halle, Ltd., London, 1940.

[58] *Invitation to Roumania,* McMillan & Co., London, 1938.

[59] *Roumanian Journey,* B.T. Batsford Ltd., London, 1938.

cably with the words "see you in Rucăr" as I was going to Romania in a few days to vacation with my family in Rucăr. I never thought that I would see him again.

But that summer we were all in Rucăr waiting for dinner one evening when we heard the dogs barking, a signal that a stranger had arrived in the village. The barking started in the distance and became louder until it reached our gate. A servant went to see what was happening and came back saying that there was Englishman on a bicycle. It was John Peel, who had crossed the steep mountain road south of Bran and had followed my instructions to our house. I was both amazed and impressed.

John Peel had named his bicycle "Lady Marshmallow." We welcomed him warmly and immediately invited him to dinner with us. He made himself right at home just as if he was a member of the family feeling well enough at home to stay for three weeks. He told us how he lived in a 'council house' for poor people in Leicester. His front room, he mentioned, was full of books piled from floor to ceiling with hardly enough space for his desk. There was hardly a subject in which he was not conversant. He was an admirer of Martha Bibescu, whose book *Izvor* had been translated into English as the *Country of Willows* in 1924 by William Heinemann.

He had also read *Smaranda* by C.B. Thompson who had been attached to the British Legation in Bucharest during the First World War. During the winter of 1916-17, under the command of Col. John Norton-Griffiths ordered to Romania by British Intelligence, he joined in the sabotage of the oil wells around Ploiești where I participated with him in the destruction of the wells helped by my Romanian company of retreating soldiers. When Thompson returned to London he was knighted, becoming Lord Thompson of Cardington. Thanks to his recommendations I received the British Military Cross for my war efforts, an honor then rarely awarded to foreign combatants. While he was in Romania, Thompson fell in love with Princess Martha Bibescu. They remained friends until his death that occurred on his way to India.

Peel was aware of these details and wanted to meet Martha Bibescu. One day while Peel was still with us, a social reporter from Bucharest called to find out whom we were hosting in Rucăr. In jest, I told her that our guests were "Lord and Lady Marshmallow." These fictional names were used by Peel's brother Gilly Potter in a weekly comical sketch ridiculing British nobility on London radio. The reporter took this seriously and promptly reported the news in a social column. A while later, Martha Bibescu called to say that she would like to meet Lord and Lady Marshmallow. I took John Peel in my car, with his bicycle tied on top, and left him in front of "Posada," Martha Bibescu's palatial mountain estate in Campina. I continued on to Bucharest. That evening, he came to see me in Bucharest and told me about his meeting. He left his bicycle at the front door to the castle and was ushered by a butler into the living room where Martha Bibescu was waiting in a long robe copied from those that Queen Marie used to wear. She greeted him in a friendly manner and asked where Lady Marshmallow was. He answered that he had left her by the front door, explaining the "she" was his bicycle. He did not tell me if he was thrown out but for years afterwards Martha Bibescu refused to speak to me.

Peel returned to England with Lady Marshmallow and remained a good friend. During the War he frequently came to spend a weekend with us at our house near London. We enjoyed his visits but he had the habit always of coming empty-handed. Food was rationed during war and guests were supposed to bring their own ration of butter and jam with them. We did not realize then that Peel's wife and children in Leicester were going hungry.

Peel wrote a booklet that gave a brief history of the Romanian people. It had appeared as an article in a magazine published by Cambridge University Press. At my own expense I had several thousand printed and sent them to people who were requesting information about Romania. Eventually Peel turned prolific in writing many letters to the editors of the *Times* and the *Telegraph* to correct wrong information about Romania. John Peel always signed his letters on behalf of Romania under the pseudonym "John Capel." He continually fought our detractors.

He never accepted financial help from me. The only gratitude I could show was to invite him to all the social events and dinners at the Romanian Legation. He was touched by this honor and was known in Leicester as a person who had access to the diplomatic world. In all the bulletins released by the Legation listing details about our receptions, I always made sure that John Peel's name appeared among our list of guests. Many years later, his last letter to me before his death in 1969 said that he was expecting a letter from me with news about the situation in Romania.

More eccentric was another friend, Philip Thornton, who traveled in Romania on foot. He walked from village to village dressed in a peasant costume enjoying meeting with locals. On a second trip he made his way by train and car to communities along the Bessarabian and Russian border. Two of his books[60] on these experiences were published. One outcome of this trip and thanks to Philip Thornton, a Romanian group from Bucovina was invited to London for their first trip outside the country. They were a huge success and won the first prize in a folk festival sponsored by the "Le Play Society."

---

[60] *Dead Puppets Dance* (1937) and *Ikons and Oxen* (1939) by Collins, London.

During my stay in London, many persons came to me with problems regarding Romania.

At the *News of the World*, I met a young newspaperman named Ernest H.G. Barwell who was very impressed with what I told him about the oil situation in Romania. In less than three weeks he managed to author a manuscript entitled *Betrayed for Oil: The Story of a Country Sacrificed for Her Black Oil*. He toured all the large publishing houses but none accepted to publish his book. Barwell, thinking I was rich, came to ask me it I would finance its publication. The book described British complicity in oil transactions involving countries that the Germans had occupied.

"The total production of the Rumanian oilfields for [1941] was 6,154,000 tons," he wrote, "and 80 per cent was in the hands of British, Dutch, French, American, Belgian and Italian shareholders." And he asked: "Did any of them sell oil to the Germans after September 3rd, 1939? If so, until what date did they continue to sell? Some companies," he wrote without mentioning names, "thought it was better to get hard cash from the Germans than to have the oil blasted by bombs." This said he added his belief that oil companies were pressuring Carol to reduce the royalty rates by saying its oil was of low grade and too difficult to transport. Working with the approval of the British and other governments this had the effect of allowing the Nazi regime to be the sole buyer.

To these observations he added that for Romanians "the biggest shock and disappointment was when the last Briton departed and the oilfields stood intact."

It was evident that Barwell's book contained details obtained from official sources in Romania. To finance this book would have offended the British. However, Barwell had made several copies of his manuscript and distributed them to publishers and newspaper editors. In this manner its contents were fairly well known though not to the general public.

An odd visitor was John Toyne, who came to see me complaining that he was being persecuted by the British government. Could I help him? John had been for a while the head of British espionage in Romania during the early years of World War II. He had been pretending that he was German as he could speak perfect German that he had learned from his first wife, whom he had married in the Ukraine when he was spying there. The Germans found him out and gave orders to arrest him. His agents in Romania warned him that a trap had been set for him and he fled, taking with him a woman from Banat who was of Hungarian origin and also a spy. They both reached Istanbul and then traveled by ship to England.

Toyne had spent millions of lei in Romania. This money belonging to British companies in Romania had been put at his disposal by the British Secret Service. He was living extravagantly and one of his excesses had been to buy eleven cars, one of which had previously belonged to King Carol II. He entertained lavishly at the Athénée Palace Hotel and often hosted high-ranking German officers who did not know he was in the British Secret Service. He told me that all his activity had been focused on the Germans and he had tried to help the Romanian cause in every way. But once back in England, he was informed without explanation that he was dismissed.

After the War Toyne wrote a book, *Win Time for Us,*[61] published in Canada. In it he described his adventure in Romania where he had organized a scheme to sink some barges in the Danube to block river traffic. He was going to send a chain of barges pulled by a tugboat as far as the Iron Gates where they would be sunk with explosives. While they were waiting for instructions the sailors were waiting at the Romanian town of Giurgiu. One evening they had a big party and one of the sailors got so drunk he loudly gave away the secret. Toyne had asked me to write the preface for his book which I did. The younger generation, I wrote, "should know that men have - against their own principles and morality - committed unprincipled acts to serve the lofty cause of their own country."

To this I added: "A great statesman has said that he was ready to shake hands with the devil for the sake of preserving the integrity of the British Empire. Mr. Toyne shook hands with many devils, and million of gallant men have shed their blood and given their lives to save the Empire. This was the basic motive of their actions and sacrifices."

Many acquaintances came from diplomatic circles. One was the Counselor of the Czechoslovak Legation, Ian Kraus. He had a good relationship with the Soviet Embassy and insisted that I should develop good rapport with the Soviet Ambassador Ivan Maisky.[62] This contradicted the warning that Bruce Lockhart had given me to avoid any contact with the Russians. One day Kraus invited me to the Dorchester Restaurant for lunch where he had reserved a table in the middle of the room in full view of everyone. According to Slavic tradition there were small bottles of red and white wine and vodka at each setting. Kraus whispered to me that it would be of great benefit to Romania if King Carol would go an official visit to Moscow to visit Stalin. He then said that Stalin loved Romanians but hated Hungarians. Later Kraus was appointed Minister of Czechoslovakia then to Romania. When Zézé went to Romania in 1946, he was very courteous to

---

[61] *Win Time for Us*, Longmans, Toronto, Canada, 1962.

[62] Throughout his career Ivan Maisky succeeded in walking a tightrope between maintaining his integrity as a professional diplomat and surviving the vagaries of Stalin's regime. For almost a decade he served as Ambassador in London from 1934 to 1943.
Source: www.tau.ac.il/~russia/projects/maiskyprj.html

her and immediately gave her a transit visa for Czechoslovakia that she needed at the last moment.

Re-appearing in our London lives was John Farrow on a special personal mission. He was being accused by his friends in the movie world of pretending to have noble ancestry because he signed his signed his name 'John Villiers Farrow' claiming descent from an English Duke named Villiers. He had come to London to search genealogical records so he could prove that he was a descendant of the Villiers family. With help from A.T. Butler at the Windsor Herald of the College of Genealogy, an institute that kept records of British nobility, Farrow found out that he was indeed a descendent of the Villiers family. He was happy to return to Hollywood with the proper proof, certified by the "College of Arms." Through John, I became acquainted with Butler.

At-that-time British newspaper editors were inquiring about the genealogy of the Romanian Royal family. Inquiries were referred to the Hohenzollern family. I asked Butler to try to trace the genealogy of King Carol's mother who was the daughter of the Duke of Edinburgh. It took several months to compile the genealogical tree that went back to William the Conqueror and his wife Matilda, the daughter of Baldwin V, Count of Flanders. I sent Butler's beautifully illustrated chart to King Carol in March 1940. In return, I received a 'personal-confidential' letter from one of the King's aides, saying the King wanted the name of Jeanne Dumitrescu, who had married Prince Nicolae, erased from the family tree. King Carol had refused to recognize the marriage and had deprived the Prince of his Royal rights.

Mr. Butler insisted on creating a coat of arms for me, even though it is not customary for Romanians to have one. Even Romanians who were descended from nobility were not allowed by law to carry titles. One of Butler's draftsmen designed my coat of arms that was registered in the "College of Arms." Later this coat of arms was used when Prince Francois de Bourbon conferred a Knighthood on me in the Order of St. Lazarus of Jerusalem, one of the four original orders of the Knights of Malta. I had to ask the King's permission to use the coat of arms. I expected him to refuse, but he was impressed that a Romanian had become a member of the Order. One outcome was that he asked if he too could be admitted to the Order. I started to negotiate with the Order for his admittance. As a result a Romanian branch of the order was created with King Carol as Great Master and myself as Master. My wife and I received various insignias and medals from the order, which the King authorized me to wear. At Queen Marie of

Romania's funeral in 1938, the members of the funeral procession were arranged according to their status. As a Knight of the Order of St. Lazarus, I walked in the procession directly after the members of the Romanian Royal Family.

One of my accomplishments during my stay in England was to discover the map that Constantin Cantacuzino had commissioned in Padua, Italy, in 1700. It was a very complete map of Moldavia and few researchers knew about it as no one had succeeded in finding an original. Nicolae Iorga would frequently mention the map during his lectures, but would always point out that it had completely disappeared. In London I went occasionally to the British Museum to visit its map room. There I spent many hours searching the card index for references to maps of the Romanian principalities. Besides Cantemir's map that was cataloged under the title "Moldova." I found nothing else because the Romanian principalities were usually depicted within maps of the Turkish or Austro-Hungarian empires. The only solution was to ask for and then check each map separately.

Patiently I went through thousands of maps until, one day, I found Cantacuzino's map under its unlikely title of *Indice Topograficus*. It was a beauty. It contained almost all the localities then known in Wallachia and Oltenia. I made a photostatic copy of the map and on my first opportunity to return to Bucharest I took it to Iorga. He was most enthusiastic and congratulated me for the find. I expected him to make an announcement of the discovery before the Romanian Academy. He made the announcement in a small note at the bottom of a page in bulletin that he published. In very small letters the note said: "The map was discovered by Mr. D. Dimancescu of the Romanian Legation in London."

PART VI - WORLD WAR II

"On 13 April 1939, France and the United Kingdom pledged to guarantee the independence of the Kingdom of Romania. Negotiations with the Soviet Union concerning a similar guarantee collapsed when Romania refused to allow the Red Army to cross its frontiers.

"On 23 August 1939 Germany and the Soviet Union signed the Molotov-Ribbentrop Pact. Among other things, this pact recognized Soviet "interest" in Bessarabia which had been under Russian Empire rule from 1812–1918.

"Following the outbreak of World War II on 1 September 1939, the Kingdom of Romania adopted a position of neutrality. However, the rapidly changing situation in Europe during 1940, as well as domestic political upheaval, undermined this stance. Fascist political forces such as the Iron Guard rose in popularity and power, urging an alliance with Nazi Germany and its allies. As the military fortunes of Romania's two main guarantors of territorial integrity — France and Britain — crumbled in the Fall of France, the government of Romania turned to Germany in hopes of a similar guarantee, unaware that the then dominant European power had already granted its consent to Soviet territorial claims in a secret protocol of the Molotov-Ribbentrop Pact, signed back in 1939.

"In summer 1940, a series of territorial disputes were resolved unfavorably to Romania, resulting in the loss of territory gained in the wake of World War I. This caused the popularity of Romania's government to plummet, further reinforcing the fascist and military factions, who eventually staged a coup. In September of 1940 King Carol was forced to abdicate in favor of his son, Michael. He fell under the control of the fascist dictatorship of Marshal Ion Antonescu. The new regime officially joining the Axis powers on 23 November 1940.

"As a member of the Axis, Romania participated in the invasion of the Soviet Union on 22 June 1941, providing equipment and oil to Nazi Germany as well as committing [600,000 soldiers] more troops to the Eastern Front than all the other allies of Germany combined. Romanian forces played a large role during the fighting in Ukraine, Bessarabia, Stalingrad, and elsewhere. Romanian troops were responsible for the persecution and massacre of Jews in Moldavian territory controlled by the Romanian authorities, though most Jews living within Romania survived the harsh conditions."

"Romania was bombed by the Allies from 1943 onwards and invaded by advancing Soviet armies in August of 1944. King Michael of Romania led a coup d'état, which deposed the Antonescu regime and put Romania on the side of the

Allies for the remainder of the war. Romanian armies moved against German forces into Hungary and Czechoslovakia. Approximately 370,000 Romanian soldiers were killed during the conflict. Of those 110,000 died fighting Germany after August 23rd, 1944.

"There was hope for countries like Romania that Allied support would turn the Soviet Tide back, this was not to be. Its fate had been secretly settled in October 1944 by Churchill and Stalin and three months later at the 1945 Yalta Conference with Roosevelt.

"Timeline leading to the final agreement:
October 9, 1944 - First meeting of Churchill/Stalin in Kremlin - establish post-war spheres of influence
January 21, 1945 - Harry Hopkins (USA) flies to London w. doubts about Yalta
February 2, 1945 - Churchill plus British and American chiefs of staff meet in Malta to prepare for Yalta Conference
February 4, 1945 - First Plenary mtg w. Churchill, Roosevelt, and Stalin
February 6, 1945 - Second Plenary mtg
February 9, 1945 - Third Plenary mtg - AGREEMENT"[63]

Events as recollected by Sir Winston Churchill in *Triumph & Tragedy*, Houghton Mifflin, Boston, 1953.
Meeting Stalin:
"We alighted at Moscow on the afternoon of October 9... At ten o'clock that night we held our first important meeting at the Kremlin. There were only Stalin, Molotov, Eden, and I... The moment was apt for business, so I said, "Let us settle about our affairs in the Balkans. Your armies are in Rumania and Bulgaria. We have interests, missions and agents there. Don't let us get at cross-purposes in small ways. So far as Britain and Russia are concerned, how would it do for you to have ninety per cent predominance in Rumania, for us to have ninety per cent of the say in Greece, and go fifty-fifty about Yugoslavia?" While this was being translated I wrote out on a half-sheet of paper:

> *Rumania*
> *--- Russia ---------- 90 %*
> *--- The others ----- 10 %*
> *Greece*
> *--- Great Britain--- 90 % (in accord with U.S.A.)*
> *--- Russia ---------- 10 %*
> *Yugoslavia -------- 50-50 %*
> *Bulgaria*
> *--- Russia ---------- 75 %*

---

[63] Edited excerpts from wikipedia < en.wikipedia.org / wiki / Greater_Romania >

--- The others ----- 25 %

"I pushed this across to Stalin, who had by then heard the translation. There was a slight pause. Then he took his blue pencil and made a large tick upon it, and passed it back to us. It was settled in no more time than it takes to set down...

"After this there was a long silence. The pencilled paper lay in the center of the table. At length I said, " Might it not be thought rather cynical if it seemed we had disposed of these issues, so fateful to millions of people, in such an offhand manner? Let us burn the paper." "No, you keep it," said Stalin."

On the subject of Romania, he wrote to colleagues in London:

"It is seen that quite naturally Soviet Russia has vital interests in the countries bordering on the Black Sea, by one of whom, Rumania, she has been most wantonly attacked with twenty-six divisions... Great Britain feels it right to show particular respect to Russian views about these two countries, and to the Soviet desire to take the lead in a practical way in guiding them in the name of the common cause."

At Yalta:

"At this first meeting [Feb 5] Mr. Roosevelt had made a momentous statement. He said that the United States would take all reasonable steps to preserve peace, but not at the expense of keeping a large army in Europe... The American occupation would therefore be limited to two years...

"The remaining details were settled very quickly [Feb 8]."

FREE ROUMANIAN MOVEMENT
The National Committee

Free Roumania House,
108 Eaton Square,
London, S.W. 1

STATEMENT

THESE present days are grave days for the whole world. But they are graver still for our Nation which is being dragged and pushed down into a pitch dark abyss. Great Britain has declared war on Roumania! For the first time in history Great Britain is at war with our country. The Roumanian Nation, this peace loving people, has been involved in a war she never wanted. But still less did she think of Britain being at war with her; she never dreamed of such a terrible thing. *She*, herself, is *not* at war with Great Britain and never will be.

The vast majority of the Roumanian Nation has always been, and still is, pro-British. The passive resistance and continuous sabotages which have been going on in Roumania since the very beginning of the German military occupation is manifestly showing the people's attitude. This attitude, widely known, is not based only on political convictions and instinct but also on gratitude to the British statesmen who have repeatedly helped Roumania in her long hard struggle for Unity and Freedom. Therefore the war declared on Roumania can be taken as only against the Government and its regime—those alluring Quislings duping a sober, hard working and peace loving Nation into such an unfortunate adventure.

General Antonescu himself, according to a semi-official statement published in all Roumanian papers only a few days ago, on 27th November, 1941, took full responsibility for the new state of affairs by declaring that *'under his regime Roumania's foreign policy has changed fundamentally.'* He and his Quislings, therefore, have to bear the full consequences for the abyss into which this change of foreign policy has brought the Roumanian Nation.

Such being the facts, we are convinced that Britain's great Prime Minister in his idealistical and highly wise policy is now separating in thought, later on in practice, those who helped the Nazis from the bulk of pro-British Roumanian people. In his sound political judgement he will make use of those who are only waiting to have a real opportunity to bring their contribution in this struggle for a better world.

In this hour, the gravest hour for our Nation, we, convinced of the sentiments the vast majority of the Roumanian population has for British people towards whom she is eagerly looking for LIBERATION. we, who stood up a year ago for a FREE ROUMANIA, are determined to continue, on our part, to do the utmost for the victory of RIGHT and JUSTICE, and to fight for the realisation of the war aims of Great Britain and her Allies, outlined in the Atlantic Charter.

11th December, 1941.

CHAPTER FOURTEEN

WAR YEARS

King Carol abdicated in September 1940 pressured out by General Ion Antonescu who transferred the Monarchy into the reluctant hands of Prince Michael. Antonescu took on dictatorial power. Allying Romania with Germany, Antonescu, now self-declaring himself with the title 'Marshal', declared war on Russia in June and sent more than 600,000 soldiers into suffering enormous losses occupying Odessa and then Sebastopol. In December of 1941 he declared war against England.

For us, the members of the Legation, we were given the possibility, if we wanted, to return to Romania through neutral Portugal. Only one, Ion Vardala, Secretary of the Legation accepted the offer. Another Mircea Iliade chose to accept a post representing the Antonescu Government in Lisbon, Portugal. The rest of us chose to remain in England.

King Michael at Center, to left in photo General Antonescu, and next Horia Sima (no hat), leader of the Iron Guards. Source: PIC Magazine (London)

After several meetings we formed the "Free Romanian Movement."[64] There were not many of us and the British knew that the Russians were not happy with the formation of a patriotic Romanian movement in Britain.

Strange as it may appear, the only help we received was from the *New Times and Ethiopian News*, owned and edited by Sylvia Pankhurst, daughter of the famous suffragette. Miss Pankhurst had founded a movement to support the cause of Ethiopia, which had been occupied by Italy. The Emperor, Haile Selassie, had taken refuge in England. Miss Pankhurst wrote long articles in support of the Ethiopian cause. She sent copies of her newspaper to all members of the British parliament and government and to leaders of the Anglican Church. Her voice had a strong echo and the Foreign Office took serious notice her attacks.

Generously she offered us as much space in her paper as we wished and named me a special correspondent. Thus we had an opportunity to voice the complaints of Romanians in England along side those of Ethiopia. Mr. Anthony Eden, British Foreign Minister, declared in Parliament that the Free Romanian Movement neither represented Romanian public opinion nor the opinion of Romanians in England. The Free Romanians were not allowed political activities and were limited to publishing pamphlets that were distributed to famous personalities. I was responsible for these publications. All of our publications were restricted to 10,000 copies as paper was rationed in Britain during the war. Articles appeared under different by-lines. For example, I wrote an article, titled "Free Romanians" for the *New Times and Ethiopian News*. It was published under the pseudonym "Tranmontanus."

Our members started quarreling among themselves about the positions they would have at the end of the War. They were certain that they would be called upon to form the new government. Captain Iliescu, who promoted himself to major, wanted the post of Minister of War. Some of us thought that Admiral Dumitrescu, an older man with much more experience, was entitled to this position. Beza, the most intellectual among us, wanted to become Minister of Education. Constantin Laptev, an old diplomat, wanted to claim the Ministry of Foreign affairs, a post that we thought should go to Matila Ghyka.

---

[64] *Free Romanian Movement* members:
Belitoreanu, Traian; Beza, Marcu; Callimachi, Anne-Marie; Dimancescu, Dimitrie; Draghici, Alexandru; Dumitrescu, Gheorghe (Rear Admiral); Ghyka, Matila; Iliescu, Adiana; Iliescu, George-Emil (Major); Laptev Constantin; Mezincescu, Alexandru; Niculescu, Barbu,; Ratiu, Ion; Smilovici, Otto; Statescu, Sanda; Tilea, Viorel - President; Vargolici, Constantin

Then there was Viorel Tilea, he had been appointed Minister of the Lega-tion and was an ambitious young man. He was sure he would become prime minister. He grew up in the shadow of Alexandru Vaida-Voevod,[65] whom he had accompanied to the Paris Peace Conference in Versailles in 1920. When the National Peasant Party came to power, Tilea had been ap-pointed Under Secretary of State. Now in Britain he represented himself as a spokesman for Iuliu Maniu, the head of the National Peasant Party. Meanwhile, he obtained confidential financial help from Polish and Czechoslovak refugees. From these sums he distributed monthly salaries to the members of the National Committee of the Free Romania Movement. I did not have any desire to become a minister in the government and I re-fused any help from Tilea.

Instead, early in 1941 I accepted a position with the British Political Intelligence Department (P.I.D.) headed by Bruce Lockhart.[66] Most of my work involved broadcasts to German-occupied Romania as though they originated from within the country. Over 900 broadcasts were made from Bletchley Park.[67] Much of the content came as daily reports of everyday news from intercepted sources within Romania or forwarded through neu-tral Portugal and then to London.

Our goal was to craft broadcasts that led the listener to believe that they came from resistance pockets within Romania. It was described as the "Roumanian Freedom Station." The decision was made by PID to support such an effort to be carried out by me and Major Iliescu and agreed to by

---

[65] Alexandru Vaida-Voevod was a Romanian politician who was a supporter and promoter of the union of Transylvania with the Romanian Old Kingdom when it was part of the Austro-Hungarian Empire; he later served three terms as a Prime Minister of Greater Romania. *Source: Wikipedia*

[66] In 1918, Bruce Lockhart and fellow British agent, Sidney Reilly, were dramatically alleged to have plotted to assassinate Bolshevik leader Vladimir Lenin. He was accused of plotting against the Bolshevik regime and, for a time during 1918, was confined in the Kremlin as a prisoner and feared being condemned to death. However, he escaped trial in an exchange of "secret agents" for the Russian diplomat Maksim Maksimovich Litvinov. He later wrote about his experiences in his 1932 autobiographical book, *Memoirs of a British Agent.* During the Sec-ond World War, Lockhart became director-general of the Political Warfare Executive, coordi-nating all British propaganda against the Axis powers.

[67] "During the Second World War, Bletchley Park was the site of the United Kingdom's main decryption establishment, the Government Code and Cypher School (GC&CS), where ciphers and codes of several Axis countries were decrypted, most importantly the ciphers generated by the German Enigma and Lorenz machines. Bletchley Park also housed a secret radio inter-cept station, and also a message sending station." *Source: en.wikipedia.org/wiki/Bletchley_Park*

Ralph Murray[68] with whom I stayed in almost daily contact. Two goals were outline:

"a) To determine the Roumanian People to prosecute vigorously their claims for the restoration of Roumania's Western frontier and eventually stir them up into a fight with Hungary in-order-to re-cover Northern Transylvania.
b) To convince and determine the Roumanian People to breakup the alliance of Ion Antonescu with the Axis and thus restore their friendly relations with Great Britain, the United States, and the U.S.S.R., and their Allies."

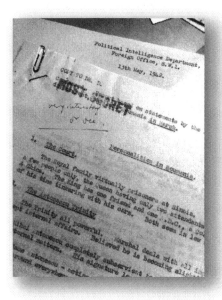

My instructions very precise including travel as noted in letter to me by James D. Stewart: "*To come across from Maidenhead would involve leaving at 6:58 a.m. ... and catch the 11:54 a.m. from Bletchley.*" Broadcasts from the estate were scheduled for three times a day seven days a week. Our travel often consumed six hours to make the round-trip by train and on the platforms of various stations.

For our broadcasts to be effective the information had to be fresh and sourced from within the country. Such details would be forwarded with a "Most Secret" designations. On one occasion, our job was to compare information especially when it came to war casualties of Romanians fighting against Russian armies.

Romanian sources of official losses:
Oct 5. 1941. 15,000 missing of whom 7-8,000 must be presumed dead. 20,000 killed. 76,000 wounded of whom 80% only slightly.
June 22nd, 1942. Casualties since June 1941: Killed, missing and wounded ... 5,998 officers, 2,633 N.C.O.s, 140,941 corporals and pri-

---

[68] Ralph Murray in common with many on the periphery of Special Operations Executive (SOE), knowledge of his wartime service is hazy. He was most closely associated with propaganda, and from 1941 was a member of the Underground Propaganda Committee (UPC) which had been formed to fuel a whispering campaign to undermine any invasion. He was also associated with Bletchley Park, and was involved in supporting resistance activity.

vates. Of these 20% in Bessarabia and Bucovina, 63% between Dniester and Bug, 5% between Bug, Dniester and Sea of Azov and 12% at Kerch, Sebastopol and Donetz.

Compared to B.B.C.'s far larger figures:

After Sebastopol 350,000 casualties of which 200,000 dead.

February 9, 1943. PID suggested what to broadcast based on cumulated information.

Germany's new line of morale propaganda is the promise of total mobilisation for total war. This is nonsense, Germany and Italy have long passed their mobilisation nook. They have no reserves of manpower left. Germany is calling up children, and is afraid to use many more foreign workers because of revolt and sabotage. On the other hand there are still 180 million Russians, and the complete British Empire and United States, whose production is still rapidly increasing, though it has long overtaken that of the Axis. This is the weakest propaganda Germany has yet produced and a sure sign of the Nazis unsurmountable difficulties.

This total mobilisation means though a new despoilment of Roumania, consented to at Hitler's Headquarters by Antonescu. The last reserves of men and food are to be taken. The peasants are to be taken from the land, those that are left, and their place taken by Russian prisoners. They will be used for a last desperate attempt to save Germany. TOTAL MOBILI-SATION means NATIONAL SUICIDE. Because of the lack of fodder there are not enough animals left in the country to work the fields, because the Germans have not won the Caucasian oilfields there will be no oil in the country for tractors, thus if Germany gets the last reserves, to which Antonescu has agreed.... THE COUNTRY WILL STARVE. TO-TAL MOBILISATION MEANS THE RAISING OF A NEW ARMY NOT TO DEFEND THE NATIONAL FR0NTIERS, BUT TO DE-FEND GERMANY. ROUMANIAN DIVISIONS WILL BE SENT TO THE CENTRAL AND NORTHERN SECTORS OF THE FRONT TO DEFEND GERMANY AND HUNGARY....SO THAT THEY WILL BE UNABLE TO WITHDRAW WHEN THE TIME COMES TO THEIR OWN FR0NTIERS AND PEOPLE, left by Hitler 'in voi a sortie.'

Such details would be forwarded with a "Most Secret" designations. This one was noted as used in broadcast No. 849.

March 12, 1943 - Most Secret

THEME:

ROMANIA: PENALTIES FOR PUBLICATION OF OFFICIAL SE-CRETS

Bucharest: The publication without previous censorship of dossiers, notes, or letters of the Rumanian King, State leaders, of members of Government, if they touch upon matters of State interest, will he henceforth punished with five to 10 years forced labour and other additional penalties, according to a Decree issued today. This also pertains to petitions submitted to the King, State leaders and Government members. Only the State Leader may permit such petitions and replies to be published, if it should be deemed advisable in the interest of the country or in the interest of enlightening public opinion. (T.O. 10. 3 A3)

BROADCAST:
Marshal Antonescu and Mihai Antonescu have often told us that their various Ministries are plagued with a flood of letters and petitions; they have threatened that unjustified claims would be penalised by dispatch to the concentration camp. This pair has called on us again and again for fines, compulsory loans - they have increased our taxation to the point of bankruptcy. They have extracted the wealth of the country to fight a war for Germany, and now they come with a decree which they trust will finally silence any complaint from any quarter.

I occasionally tried to mention Tilea's name in my speeches at the secret radio station but the representative of the British Foreign Office told me not to mention his name. I was convinced that Hitler would be defeated and I could not see that those who had had suffered in Romania should not choose their own government. But gradually British policy turned away from favoring Romania and the broadcasts were brought to a halt.

When I left the P.I.D., in August of 1943, I had a long talk with Bruce Lockhart, who was head of the organization (later its name was changed to Political Warfare and Economic Ministry). Lockhart sent me an invitation to meet after I sent him a letter saying that I knew the British had transferred Romania to Soviet influence and that I therefore could no longer collaborate with the British.

During this meeting I told him that as long I had access to many British government secrets, I doubted that I would be allowed to leave England, but that I was prepared to remain and that in-order-to receive food rations I would have to find a job in a war-related activity. Lockhart did not deny my assertion that Romania had been "ceded" to the Soviet Union. He praised my past activities and advised me to find work that was more commensurate with my abilities. However, he had no specific suggestions. We parted on friendly terms.

Then from Romania came news that by 'official decree' some of us in London were stripped of our citizenship.

In ziua de 20 Maiu DEUTSCHES NACHRICHTEN-BÜRO a transmis urmatoarea telegrama de presa:

"Bucharest. More members of the former Roumanian Legation in London have been deprived of Roumanian nationality (citizenship) by a decree of the Council of Ministers. Their names are : the two former Cultural attaches, Marcu Beza and Matila Costiescu-Chyka ; the former Deputy Minister, C.M.Laptew ; former Press counsellor, Dimancescu ; former Assistant of the Military Attache , Capt. George Iliescu ; information officer (!?) M.Grindea ; secretary of the Cultural Attache ,Alexandra Mezincescu ; and architect,Eugen Botez . The Official Gazette points out that these persons , living abroad, were guilty of derliction of duty , concerning themselves with activities which ran counter to the fundamental interests of Roumania."

20 May 1943 - Romanian Government Decree removing our citizenship

FINDING A JOB

Now on my own cut off from any income and with a family to support, I had to find a source of income. I inquired of possibilities from my friend Colonel George Rowlandson Crosfield, who told me that his neighbor was a successful manufacturing industry manager in search of capable people. He telephoned this neighbor and made an appointment for me for the next day. The man I went to see was Mr. Merryfield. Energetic and capable, he was buying companies that were going bankrupt during the war. As-soon-as he acquired a company, Merryfield converted it to the production of war material. In this manner he was able to secure Government support for new equipment and capital. In a short time he had put together an eleven-company conglomerate that was an important contributor to military production.

The only thing lacking Merryfield told me, was the men to lead and inspire the new enterprises. My interview with him was short. He did not ask for references to prove my qualifications. And I did not know what I could do for him. He told me that I should meet one of his vice-presidents, a Mr. Naismith, an expert in hydraulics. Before I met him, I bought and read several books on the various applications of hydraulics. He gave me several gadgets and asked me if I could figure out what they were intended for. It turned out that these items had nothing to do with his work. After I spent a long time trying unsuccessfully to understand these mechanical devices, Mr. Naismith told me to come to work the next day as Mr. Merryfield had told him to consider me hired. He asked me which of the eleven companies I would like to work for. I chose Nichols Compressors Ltd. in Letchworth about 30 miles north of London.

I told Naismith that I would prefer to start as a simple worker to familiarize myself with the work. At Nichols I was lost among the 400 plant workers. Shortly after I started, I heard that there was to be an important meeting for employees. Apparently some of the compressors were not working properly and as a result many planes had serious accidents. While the company manufactured a large variety of hydraulic compressors, it was also making a small compressor that was used in the landing gear of British bomber aircraft.

In a large room at the factory there were on display about 300 compressors recovered from damaged planes. A special team of engineers had been working long hours to find the cause of the malfunctions. For several weeks I listened to their discussions. Then one day I told them I could solve the mystery. At first they were surprised that a plant foreign worker could come up with a suggestion. I told them I was an engineer with a degree from an American university. I asked permission to dismantle all the compressors and analyze them piece-by-piece.

On a wall I drew a huge chart. On the left I wrote the serial number of the compressor and on the right in various columns I wrote comments about the parts. Finally the chart provided the information we were looking for. Only one part in each compressor was bad. This was a tube through which oil passed and which was invariably blocked by dirt. As I discovered, the tubes were assembled in room where the air was dirty. I suggested that the compressors be assembled in a room with perfectly clean air. My suggestion was adopted and overnight I became a 'personality' at the Nichols plant. The plant manager made me his assistant and gave me a free hand.

I chose to make a study of the Nichols compressors and compare them with similar products produced by other factories. This led to a recommendation that Nichols build a larger compressor for other purposes. Mr. Waghorn, the plant director agreed with me. He was a mechanical genius who had invented a tank turret that could rotate 360 degrees. Merryfield had 'stolen' him from another company and promised him a bright future at

Nichols. I spent many nights with Waghorn perfecting a portable compressor activated by an electric motor. We thought might address a problem on the battlegrounds in Europe. As German armies were beaten, air would needed to pump-up the tires of abandoned military vehicles.

It was during this time that sad news arrived from Bucharest. Our home and all our personal belongings had been bombed when American planes dropped excess bomb loads during Ploiești raids. My treasured collection of maps was lost.

Destruction of family home in Bucharest by American bombs in 1944

Delegation to the Paris Peace Conference - 1946

Left to right in Paris: D. Dimancescu, G. Gheorghiu-Dej, ?, ?, G. Tătărescu, G. Maurer, Gnl.
Dămăceanu, L. Pătrăşcanu, ?, R. Franasovici

CHAPTER FIFTEEN

PARIS ~ DIPLOMAT AGAIN

A
s the situation in Romania looked brighter with German armies slowly retrenching on the Eastern fronts, I started to look for a new job. In a Romanian newspaper I read a proposal by Gheorghe Tătărescu[69] that interested me. I wrote to him saying that if he needed my services I would be happy to be at his disposal. Romania was still considered by England to be at war, but relations between the two countries had been resumed with the exchange of representatives who were not recognized as Ministers or Ambassadors. Tătărescu became Minister of Foreign Affairs in a coalition government dominated by members of the Romanian Communist Party. Tătărescu nevertheless succeeded in having his friend, Richard Franasovici, sent as representative to London. During the war, Romanian interests in England were handled by the Swedish government and a Swedish secretary of legation had moved into our offices at Belgrave Square.

Soon after the Soviets invaded in August of 1943, Romania turned sides and joined the allies in fighting the Germans. The new coalition government sent a young communist to London with the title of Counselor of Legation.

I disliked the whole atmosphere at Belgrave Square. But the situation quickly changed with Franasovici's arrival. He had been our ambassador in Paris and Warsaw where he had left good impressions. He settled in at Belgrave Square and put the Legation back in order. With him came a letter from Tătărescu asking for my support and to accept being recalled in the diplomatic service. I accepted his invitation and thus became the number two at Belgrave Square. Franasovici insisted that I have lunch with him every day. He was extremely courteous towards me and working with him

---

[69] Romanian politician who served twice as Prime Minister of Romania (1934–1937; 1939–1940), three times as Minister of Foreign Affairs (*interim* in 1934 and 1938; appointed to the office in 1945-1947), and once as Minister of War (1934). After the start of World War II, Gheorghe Tătârescu initiated a move to rally political forces in opposition to Ion Antonescu's dictatorship, and sought an alliance with the Romanian Communist Party (PCR). In 1946-1947, he headed the Romanian Delegation to the Peace Conference in Paris. Following the Communist takeover, he was arrested and held as a political prisoner, while being called to testify in the trial of Lucretiu Pâtrâscanu. He died soon after his release from prison. *SOURCE: Wikipedia*

was a pleasure. He insisted that everything we did be very well documented. Any report that we sent to Romania was accompanied by all sorts of back-up documents.

Tătărescu proposed to Franasovici to come to Romania to take over the Ministry of Foreign Affairs as he was hoping to become Prime Minister. In his turn Franasovici proposed that I become Under-Secretary of State. Both offers remained in suspense awaiting the course of events but I decided not to accept the position.

Meanwhile the Post-War 1946 Peace Conference in Paris was anticipated to conclude peace with Italy, Romania, Hungary and Bulgaria. In Bucharest, material had been compiled in-the-form-of memoranda for use at the Conference. It dealt with such topics as "The Hungarian-Romanian Frontier," "The Treatment of Minorities," and "The Jewish Question," The Romanian delegation was led by the Communist Gheorghiu-Dej and included among others Franasovici, who asked me to be Secretary of the delegation. The members were mixed group with half being non-Communist and the other half hard-core Communists in the process of maneuvering to take over the Government with Soviet support.

I thus found myself moving from the peaceful life of London to a much more contentious life in Paris. Tătărescu had found at the Legation in Bern several million Swiss francs, which had been accumulated there by the different heads of missions. These funds were used to help finance our delegation in Paris.

PARIS PEACE CONFERENCE (1946) [70]

DELEGATION
- *50 person delegation*
- *Headed by Mr. Gheorghe Tătărescu, Vice President of the Council*
- *Secretariat: Hotel Continental (Paris)*
-

CONTEXT:
Post-War border settlements were one of Romania's principal issues, especially on the Western frontier with Hungary which had been extended into Romania (Transylvania) during the pro-Nazi wartime regime of General Antonescu. Hungary

---

[70] Source: Original files and records of D. Dem Dimancescu, member of the Romanian Delegation at the Conference.

argued for control over several urban zones of major demographic and economic importance to Romania. On this issue Romania benefited from the Soviet Union's disfavor with Hungary's support of the Nazis while Romania, in 1944, had turned its armies against the German/Hungarian western military front and fought on the month-long siege of Budapest and beyond to Czechoslovakia.

SYNOPSIS:

Two major issues faced Romania's delegation in Paris in 1946:

One was to establish the point at which it entered the war. Was it August 24, 1944, when King Michael aligned himself with Romania's natural western allies, or was it as proposed by others on September 12, 1944, at the moment when an armistice was signed in Moscow. It was successfully argued by the Romanian delegation that no less than 15 divisions and up to 18 totaling 385,000 men plus an air corps were engaged against Germany and its Hungarian-Horthyst allies during this interim period. From the 23rd of August to May 10, 1945, a period of 260 days, 12 divisions moved 1000 km into enemy territory. The earlier date was agreed to thus giving Romania vital leverage in making post-war claims.

A second was to argue for its pre-war borders including Bessarabia, Dobrogea and all of Transylvania. The first two were not successfully achieved because of Soviet opposition. But Hungarian territorial claims within Romanian territory were successfully resisted. Those maps prepared by D. Dimancescu were a backdrop to a speech by Mr. G. Tătărescu to the Political and Territorial Commission for Hungary & Romania. His speech was factual, emphatic, and successful in persuading the Commission to deny Hungary those claims.

Hungary initially claimed 22.000 km2 (or about 22% of the total Transylvanian surface of an estimated 103.000 km2) but facing opposition reduced its claim to 4.000 km2. In the words of M. Paul Auer speaking for the Hungarian delegation on August 31, 1946: "Under these conditions, the return to Hungary of this territory, which does not belong to the geography unity of Transylvania and which, in the course of history, did not constitute an integral part, would seem to be a simple frontier adjustment."

In response on September 2, 1946, G. Tătărescu presented the Romanian case before the Political and Territorial Commission for Hungary & Romania (Conference of Paris). Romania's pre WW-II boundaries had been established at the Peace Conference of 1919 and, more than a quarter century later, they were confirmed on May 7, 1946, by the foreign ministers of the Soviet Union, the United States, Great Britain and France.

Presentation by Prime Minister Tătărescu; DDD in lower center.

"But against this decision, Hungary interjects a new appeal. Reappearing in this new appeal are claims that were examined and debated twenty-five years ago.

"The frontier of 1920 is an ethnic frontier. Its path coincides as perfectly as possible with the line of contact between the Romanian element and the Hungarian one.

"If, on the borders, the infiltrations are greater and islets of Hungarian more numerous, it is due to the forcing back of the Romanian element away from the richer plains and into the poorer hills and mountain regions. The integration of these areas into the frontiers of the Romanian State is linked to the strengthening of the Romanian population's economic development, impoverished long ago by design by the Hungarian regime.

"The territory included in the frontiers of 1920 consists of a single economic unit from which one would not know how to extract any one fragment without resulting in serious inconveniences to the whole population. The railroad and the parallel road that originate at the Danube follow the western frontier thereby assuring the sole link between these regions of Transylvania. In addition, the plain regions possess agricultural resources that the adjacent mountain regions could not do without...

"The 4.000 km2 newly claimed by Hungary represent, it is true, 4% of the Transylvania territory. But on this territory of 4% live, not a corresponding percentage of people, but one that is equal to 8.5% of the Transylvanian population which should be enough to suggest the importance of the Hungarian pretensions.

Further, this area small as it appears, contains the three large towns of Arad, Oradea, and Satu Mare. And this, again, contrary to Hungarian affirmations, is of extreme importance for Romania.... To cut out these towns would result in the immediate collapse of the provincial economy.

"A simple look at the physical map of Romania, one of which is executed in relief and on which are marked in white the regions demanded by Hungary and put at the disposal of the Commission, is enough to realize the insurmountable geographic and technical difficulties in the way of constructing a new railroad further east...

"For its frontiers and for its independence, Romania, in the last phase of the war, let loose against Germany and Hungary all its living forces. For this global war of liberation, the Romanian nation mobilized all its reserves of men and its last material resources. Fourteen fully equipped Romanian divisions cooperated in the fight which permitted the world to shake the Nazi yoke and for Transylvania to escape the Horthyst yoke .... 120,000 dead and wounded fell in the hills of Transylvania, in the plains of Budapest and in the valleys of the Tatras. And it is precisely under the walls of Arad, Oradea, and Satu-Mare, of Hungary now dispute our sovereignty, it is under these walls of these towns and for their liberation that our soldiers shed the best of their blood and that our elite divisions were decimated...

"To accept the Hungarian claims would be a defeat for international morality, and would be a fatal error for history."

My job as secretary of the delegation was to take care of administrative matters. The French Government reserved rooms for the Romanian delegation at the elegant Hotel Continental where I always used to stop when I came to Paris and which almost felt like home. On the second floor there were three suites, the so-called 'royal apartments,' where foreign personalities were lodged when they came to Paris. One of these suites, with a view of the Tuileries, had been reserved for the head of the Romanian delegation, Gheorghiu-Dej. There was a fight over who would get the other suites. Mr. Tătărescu chose to stay at the beautiful and mansion-like Romanian Embassy. None of the delegates wanted to stay there.

I had the problem of moving back and forth between the Hotel Continental, the Embassy on Rue Dominique, and the Palais Luxembourg where the conference was taking place. The French Government had put four cars at the disposal of the Romanian delegation but none of our delegates wanted to ride in those cars. They were Citroëns belonging to the French army and were painted light brown. Since Mr. Tătărescu was using the Legation car, which was possibly a Cadillac, a Lincoln or a Hispano-Suiza, they wanted similar cars. These could be rented but there was not enough parking space for them around the hotel. Another problem was lodgings for the Romanian newspapermen who accompanied the delegation. It could have been a simple matter. I had asked the Hotel to reserve a number of rooms for the newspapermen, but these rooms were not as large or luxurious as the ones of the delegates. The reporters held me responsible for not treating them with the consideration they felt entitled to. Most of them were in reality not newspapermen but friends of the delegates. Their complaint was picked up by the delegates and made into a major issue. Finally the hotel agreed to move some of its permanent guests to accommodate the newspapermen.

All the delegates who had a small suite (bedroom and living room) had an artificial palm tree in their living room. One delegate was offended because he did not have a palm. Every time he saw me, he reminded me about the plant and I made the mistake of promising him one. Not finding a florist that had one, I found a funeral director who rented me four artificial palms which were actually nicer than those of the other delegates.

However, I was not forgiven by a delegate who insisted that I should not be allowed to sign any documents in my capacity as Secretary of the delegation. His recommendation was accepted and none of the documents where my name should have appeared has my name. He was a clerk from the Romanian Ministry of Foreign Affairs appointed as treasurer of the delegation. He went to Switzerland frequently to get money that was now under Tătărescu's control and then exchanged the money on the black market. No one checked on him or found out about the profit he made. After the Conference ended, he resigned his position and immigrated to the United States where he bought a large farm that eventually failed and left him broke.

The delegates and newspapermen visited Mr. Tătărescu daily to ask for money for their needs. I found among my papers a list of the amounts approved for one day and even now I am amazed at the waste. All of these details would have been without importance if Romania would have obtained a better treaty. But the treaty had been drafted before the Conference. Russia asked us to give them all our navy ships, plus all commercial freight and passenger ships. The only one who resisted was Tătărescu. On one occasion he made an outstanding speech that I translated into French and English. I was not allowed to distribute the speech or to send copies to Romania. The only ones that reached Romania were taken there personally by him.

Another tragedy was the way our boundaries were drawn. A map of poor quality, lacking detail was used to define the boundary. It contained a thick colored line to show the boundary between Romania and Russia. The line was so thick that it was impossible to tell on which side of the border some towns and Danube River islands were located. Because the boundary was so poorly defined the Russians took any towns that they wanted.

Our big victory, however, was that the boundary between Romania and Hungary remained intact. I heard later from Mr. Molotov, the head of the Soviet delegation, that Stalin was furious at the Hungarians because they had tried with bloody battles to halt the Russian advance on Budapest. The Hungarians were asking for certain boundary changes with Romanian, particularly around Oradea and Arad. I prepared a map of Transylvania that clearly showed the areas requested by Hungary and how the loss of these areas would have meant the economic death of those towns. Tătărescu illustrated his speech (excerpted in the preface to PART VI) with this map. He reminded the audience that Romania had ended the war as an ally of the Great Powers and had lost an enormous number of men and much material fighting on the allied side. He pointed out that Hungary had fought with the Nazi's until the very end.

Two foreign delegates deserve credit for defending Romania. One was the Frenchman, General Catroux who praised Romania and its armies for their generous contribution in the last phase of the war.[71]

DDD with Ian Mazaryk

The other was the Czech delegate, Ian Masaryk, who stood up after Mr. Vyshinsky had spoken unfavorably about Romania. Masaryk said that the Romanians had behaved as one would expect an ally to behave. He said that Romanians had helped Czech citizens escape from Hitler's claws. Actually the Romanians had fought ahead of the Russian army and were first to liberate Prague. Two years later in Prague, Masakyk was pushed to his death on the Castle grounds by Communist goons.

We had another friend in the Czech General Heliodor Pika, who asked that Romania be recognized as a co-belligerent. This request was opposed

---

[71] After the Soviet Union, Britain, and the U.S.A., Romania had the largest number of WW-II casualties fighting against the Germans even though the country turned against them in August 1944. An estimated 167,000 were killed, wounded or missing in action during that eight month period.

by the Russians who later orchestrated his arrest and death by hanging in 1949. The General pointed out that Italy, which had only put six divisions at the disposal of the allies had been recognized as a co-belligerent while Romania had thrown 29 divisions into the battle against Germany. These arguments did not help because the Russians were determined to consider us as enemies. Regrettably the terms of the Peace Treaty had been written before the Conference by the Russians. Their draft was approved without changes. The Russian delegate, with whom Franasovici was on good terms, had deliberately lied in assuring him that the Russians would not touch our boundaries and would leave us our maritime fleet.

During the entire duration of the Conference we were treated as 'enemy delegates' and were checked in a needless humiliation at the entrance of the Luxembourg Palace. Having toured the Palace, I discovered that the main entrances to the Palace yard were over-guarded while the entrances from the Luxembourg Park side were unguarded. This way I found a door by which I could enter at any time of the day or night. Quite to my surprise I could find myself alone at the end of the day with only the night guards who never asked me who I was. I could go into the offices of the other delegations and especially the Russian one and collect papers that were left on desks. These papers were mostly notes and helped show how the other delegates were thinking.

When the Paris Conference ended, there were some unresolved issues that were to be discussed in New York at Lake Success. Mr. Franasovici was sent as a delegate and he took me as his assistant. He was very demanding and wanted to know all kinds of details. He would constantly send me after information. I was on the go all the time, especially when the big four were meeting at the Waldorf Astoria Hotel in Manhattan. With the help of a secretary of the French delegation, I was able to enter the hotel by a service door and then hide in the service elevator among the food trays. Each delegation had its own floor and I would go from one door to another trying to get some news for Franasovici. One time I was unable to enter as there were security guards checking everyone. Luckily the French secretary was willing to help Romania and promised to give me documents drafted during the secret meetings. The service elevator would get me to the floor where the French delegation was lodged. There she gave me a large envelope containing secret documents collected by the French delegation. With this precious package, I went all the way to the basement and from there to a place that made photo copies. I had previously arranged for the young owner of the photocopying business to wait for me. I stayed with him until 4:00 a.m. and then returned breathless to the Waldorf Astoria where the wonderful secretary was waiting for the originals. She sighed from relief when I gave her back the package she had entrusted me with. I brought Franasovici the copies. He had not slept all night either, not knowing whether I had been caught. I had taken a great risk. So had the French secretary. If I had been caught, it would have caused a great scandal and my diplomatic career would have been ruined. Franasovici would have also suffered the consequences. Anyhow Franasovici was shaken by the knowledge that he was being misled by the Allied delegates who were reassuring him that they would help Romania - but now the documents proved otherwise. We found not a kind word said for Romania.

Unfortunately, the copies were sent at Franasovici's insistence to Tătărescu in Bucharest and we had no duplicates. I doubt that they reached Tătărescu but whoever read them could not have known how we got them.

Months following the Conference were increasingly tense. As the Soviet Union tightened the noose on its border states, Romania quickly lost any control over its own affairs. The Western nations had other priorities.

I traveled back to Bucharest with Zézé - leaving the children in England. She left before I did. I managed to get on a flight out a week before the King was forced to abdicate in December of 1947. Romania was now Communist ruled. Little did we know how many thousands would perish from torture, famine, or slave labor in ensuing months and years.

My brother - "Jamborel the Younger" - suffered that fate in 1951 dying in a jail cell.

Ioan 'Jamborel cel Mic' Dimancescu - 1898-1951

PART VII - EXILE

The immediate aftermath of World War II turned tense as the United States now confronted the Soviet Union. East Europe - including Romania - fell into the oppressive Soviet orbit. Winston Churchill declared the drawing of an 'Iron Curtain' across Europe. With threats of a Third World War looming, Europe seemed less and less a refuge from further calamity. Where to turn next? For some it was immigration to the United States or Canada, for others South America. One option was Morocco, close to Europe yet far enough away.

Lord of the Atlas by Gavin Maxwell published in 1966[72] may be the best description of the Berber el Glaoui family of southern Morocco and the intrigues and violent settlement of scores that followed the Arab Alaouite dynasty of northern Morocco who maintained the Sultancy for more than 350 years into the present. The French, controlling the nation as a 'Protectorate', would play a divide and conquer policy pitting Arab and against Berber; one ruler against another. He makes extensive reference to the writing of Walter Harris who authored Morocco That Was.[73]

"The independence movement started as early as 1926 when Moulay Youssef was still Sultan. Like most similar movements, it began as a number of scattered groups, who later became unified under the single name of Istiqlal - independence. The movement did not at first demand the total ejection of the French from Morocco, but merely that France should admit once and for all the distinctions between a Protectorate and the colony that Morocco had become. France replied in 1930 with a transparent move to divide the country against itself - the Berber dahir (imperial decree"), which was not only designed to underline the racial and cultural differences between occupied Berber and occupying Arab, but to exonerate the numerically superior Berbers from the Islamic law-called chraa exercised by His Chereefian Majesty, and to substitute the laws of Berber custom and of French law to all criminal cases. The young Sultan signed this dahir in all good faith... The Berber dahir did more to foster the independence movement and the ultimate downfall of the French regime than any previous action of the Protectorate; it was a signal failure to divide and rule. In the opinion of the present writer its greatest weakness was a failure to recognise that the majority of the Berbers to whom it was intended to appeal were already labouring under the despotic rule of the Great Caids -

---

[72] *Lords of the Atlas* by Gavin Maxwell, E.P Dutton, New York, 1966.

[73] *Morocco that was* by Walter B. Harris, Blackwood, London, 1921.

notably T'hami El Glaoui, Hammou El Glaoui, and El Ayadi of the Rchamma. The dahir, therefore, insulted the Arabs and the spiritual powers vested in the Sultan, without providing practical attraction for the bulk of the Berber population, who were unaffected by it; moreover it gave the Istiqlal potent ammunition for propaganda...

"The [1943 Allied] Casablanca Conference included Roosevelt, Harry Hopkins, Winston Churchill, General de Gaulle, and the Sultan's eldest son Moulay Hassan. Roosevelt and the Sultan made a markedly favourable impression upon each other, and the Sultan saw in America the possible instrument that would liberate him from France. Roosevelt certainly did nothing to discourage this belief, and six months later the Sultan sought a second interview, this time in private and without the presence of any officer of the French Protectorate. This meeting also took place ... and again Winston Churchill was present...

"Roosevelt spontaneously asked the Sultan for his opinion on the French Protectorate, and the Sultan replied at length, saying that it was no Protectorate but an oppressive colonialism, and that his aim was to liberate his country. He described the growth of the independence movement, stating that it had his absolute support in so far as was consistent with his pledged word to the French to support them until they were victorious in the war against Germany. Roosevelt told him in reply that he could have confidence in the independent future of his country, and that meanwhile he should rigorously guard the mineral rights of his country from exploitation by the occupying power. This conversation appeared far from pleasing to Churchill, who did every thing in his power to interrupt it by violent and loud fits of coughing which he punctuated only by reiterated excuses that this was due to a new brand of cigar that he was smoking... This meeting gave more impetus to the independence movement than any other single happening to date, for it convinced the Sultan that President Roosevelt stood solidly behind the concept of an independent Morocco.

"[French] General Nogues, receiving at least as much news of the Sultan's meeting with Roosevelt [knew that the Berber Pasha El Glaoui] could be counted upon to resist the Istiqlal to the limit of his powers.

"As T'hami [el Glaoui's] status and responsibility to the French grew, so did his need for money. Besides the revenue from the great tribal lands he had assimilated, he received ten per cent on the gross sum of the tertib, or agricultural tax, which he levied upon all lands under his command; and this, together with the customary hediya or present in cash or kind from all his subjects on feast-days, constituted the greater part of his unearned income. He had also gone into business in a very large way, an enterprise for which his absolute power over the people gave him unique qualifications. He had cornered the market in all the most important products of southern Morocco, by the simple means of forbidding their sale to any but his own agents, and at prices distinctly advantageous to himself. By these means he had acquired a monopoly in almonds, saffron, dates, mint and olive oil. From the

State he rented for the nominal sum of 25,000 old French francs the vast olive gar-
den of Agdal; some indication of the profit accruing from this single item may be
given by the sale to France of one year's crop (1948) on the branch, for 30,000,000
francs. Crops from the great olive groves of Taliouine and of the Haouz yielded no
less than 300,000,000 francs."

CHAPTER SIXTEEN

MOROCCO

I t was December 1947, as political pressures intensified in Romania and the Communist with Soviet support were verging on absolute control of the government, I went to Morocco to determine whether as a political exile I could make my home there in the event I gave up my residence in England. A good friend, Jean Lerche of Paris, encouraged me to take a look and said that he would gladly accompany me.

Years before I had read the trilogy by the brothers Jerome and Jean Tharaud's: *Rabat or the Moroccan Hours; Fez* or *the Bourgeoisie of the Islam* ; and *Marrakech or the Knights of the Atlas Mountains*.[74] Among our common traits, Zézé and I had an unexplained appeal for certain geographical names. She like the idea of going to Santa Fe, New Mexico; I played with the idea of settling in Marrakech. I imagined it to be a small traditional village at the foot of a high rocky mountains and beyond the Sahara Desert.

I left London by train in a snowstorm for Paris. That night I boarded a night-flight at the Orly airfield which landed in Casablanca before sunrise. Here, 46 hours later, spring-like weather greeted us as our taxi hurried to the railway station along palm tree-lined streets. For four hours I watched Morocco slide by on our way to Marrakech. Well-groomed farms, then only small green patches, then arid uncultivated land. Donkeys and camels abounded.

The city's beauty was most unexpected. Flowering bougainvillea covered the awnings of the small modem railway station where a bus from the acclaimed Mamounia Hotel awaited us. The French quarter with modem stores and beautiful villas were all painted in «light pink" to break a harsh reflection from the sunlight on otherwise white walls. These colors contrasted with the deep blue sky and a dramatic backdrop of the snowy Atlas Mountains ridge-lines rising high only sixty kilometers to the South. This 1,000 year-old city, its medieval ways character almost intact, seemed to be

---

[74] *Rabat ou les Heures marocaines.* Plon, 1921.
Fès ou les Bourgeois de l'Islam, Plon 1920, 1930.
Marrakech ou les Seigneurs de l'Atlas, Plon, 1920.

enveloped in a vast palm tree oasis. Three hundred thousand inhabitants lived within its massive crenellated walls. Outside lived fifteen-thousand Europeans settled there for less than twenty-five years.

The Mamounia lay inside a great entrance to the walled city, its architecture was elegant neo-Moorish with most rooms having balconies overlooking orange and lemon orchards or olive-tree groves. Like an imaginary Garden of Allah, this created a symphonic view of sweetly scented trees full of singing birds extending towards the distant purple-blue skyline of the Atlas Mountains. All this beauty I absorbed in the first moments at the Hotel.

Hotel Mamounia, Marrakech, Morocco

When the desk clerk saw my name on the registration slip he nearly shouted in my face:

"*Son Excellence* the Pasha of Marrakech has been waiting *Votre Excellence* since a week ago. The secretary of *Son Excellence* has been telephoning us three times a day to find out whether *Votre Excellence* has arrived. Shall I get him on the phone for you, Excellence!"

Though I had addressed myself to many high ranking diplomats, especially French and Italian, with the superlative "Your Excellency," I didn't enjoy being called one. I considered the title obsolete and in my case not at all justified .

"Please let me go first to my room," I told the hotel receptionist and I will phone later to the Pasha's secretary."

"But, *Excellence*, he wants to talk to you before you will register."

I was quite puzzled by the urgency. A visit to the Pasha was not part of my program. In fact, by the time I reached my room the telephone was ringing with a persistently.

"*Excellence,*" said a voice coming softly through the earphone, "*Son Excellence* the Pasha was so happy to learn that you have arrived in our city. I am coming with a car to bring you to the Palace. *Son Excellence* wishes you to be his guest."

"I am very honored by His Excellency's invitation", I replied, "but in the first place I already have a room at the Mamounia Hotel. I am also with my business associate Monsieur Jean Lerche of Paris. Please express my thanks for the hospitality he wishes to extend to me and ask His Excellency to let me know when I can call and pay my respects to him."

The voice answered "Just a minute" and a few seconds later returned with the information that the Pasha would be very happy to have my French friend and myself for tea at 6 p.m. and the secretary would come to take us to the Palace.

Jean and I were dumbfounded. What would we wear and what should we talk about with the Pasha. I called the concierge for advice and was reassured that anything would do, but he thought it would be best to wear a white shirt and plain dark color ties. These, he added, could be found in the French-section of Marrakech.

We were enveloped in a most unbelievable situation. But now, my colleague and I went in search of shirts and ties. The shops in the French town outside the walled Medina had everything from Lanvin perfumes to Sulka ties. But we soon discovered that the window displays did not match what was in stock. It concluded with my friend wearing a shirt one size too large and myself one size too small.

When the concierge phoned to our suite that the Pasha's car was waiting for us, we both started with the self-conscious feeling of having too-tight and too-wide collars. We were met by a middle-aged man wearing a perfectly cut European suit who introduced himself as the Pasha's private secretary. This was Ichoua Corcos who spoke French and English and later we learned that he was also the president of the Jewish community of Marrakech. He led us to a Rolls-Royce with a chauffeur and a guard wearing traditional Moroccan *djellabas*. From the guard's shoulder hung a silver sheathed dagger tied to a red silk cord. Within minutes we were in the Medina where streets narrowed to the size of alleys. These were crowded with pushcarts, donkeys, and men in long robes and women wrapped in white their faces veiled up to the eyes. We reached a large closed gate on the sides of which a crowd of people was huddled. Large wooden gates opened and the Rolls-Royce entered.

"This Is His Excellency's Palace," whispered the secretary. Inside, along the way were more men squatting by the side of the tall walls. We passed two more doorless gates to suddenly enter a small park dominated by majestic cypress trees.

Exterior to the Pasha El Glaoui's Palace - Marrakech, Morocco

The car stopped in front of a simple but dignified three-story high building. At the main door was a crowd of Moroccans of all ages and dressed almost alike with a black-gray-and-white striped djellabas in predominance. Some were wearing dark red *fez* hats, others white turbans, and a few had a sort of caped hood on their heads. The secretary rushed out of the car and to help us out. I gave him my overcoat to an older man who came toward us and bowed gently saying something we could not understand.

They showed us in and with the two men leading us we walked slowly to the third floor, through a corridor its walls covered with beautiful green tiles. Here, with a graceful gesture of the right hand, the old man invited us to enter a very large drawing room furnished in Moorish style: huge divans covered with velvet brocades, a profusion of pillows encased in the same material, from wall to wall a carpet repeating the designs of the brocades. Large hassocks were grouped around small low tables. The ceiling, in the shape of an inverted ship bottom, was painted in a pattern reminiscent of the frames surrounding Persian miniatures. The predominant color of the entire decoration was a Veronese green.

The room was empty. Our two escorts handed our coats to a guard who was standing by the door. The old man went to a divan and signaled us to come and seat by his side. The younger man sat on a hassock some distance away from us. Then silence followed. My friend passed his right hand around the collar of his shirt, and I pulled the end of my necktie trying to breathe more freely. We were wondering when the Pasha was going to come in, when the younger man said to us in French :

"Son Excellence the Pasha, my respected father, wishes me to welcome you to our city." Saying this he bowed toward the old man and then toward us.

I nearly shrank in embarrassment. The man to whom I had given my overcoat, mistaking him for a servant, was His Excellency Hadj Thami El Glaoui, the Pasha of Marrakech , and one of the last legendary Berber *Lords of the Atlas Mountains*.[75] And the young man was Si Brahim El Glaoui , the Caid of Telouet and Pasha's oldest son. The only symbol of the exalted father and son ranks were gold daggers hanging very long white silk cords.

Pasha Hadj Thami El Glaoui

The silence was broken by the Pasha - speaking in his native Berber language with his son acting as an interpreter - who told me that more than a week ago he had received a cable from a mutual London friend announcing my visit and asking the Pasha to do for me more than his best. He had an apartment in his Palace waiting for me and as many friends I may wish to bring along. That apartment or two or three more apartments were still there ready for me, a car, two or three would be at my disposal, his private golf course was at my disposal and that of my friends. During my stay in Marrakech, his son Si Sadeq would help in any way needed.

All this came so unexpectedly and especially to me, an exile without a country and a home, shorn of diplomatic titles and my material possessions by war and the Communist regime. What had the cable from London said? The Pasha said a few words to his son, who clapped his hands softly. An attendant walked in followed by two servants carrying two large silver trays. On one were four demitasse cups and on the other a silver tea set. After bowing first to the Pasha, then to us the guests and last to the son, they placed the cups on small tables which were brought to our sides. Mint tea was poured in them.

---

[75] Gavin Maxwell, *Lord of the Atlas*, Pan Books, London, 1970.

Again the Pasha made a gesture toward our cups which we understood to mean "Please help yourselves." He asked whether we have had before mint tea and added that the tradition required to drink at least three cups, but if we did not like it, we could have any other kind of drink we may wish to have at this hour.

That moment the button of my shirt popped up and the collar opened widely. I felt that this was the moment to break the ice. I told our hosts the shirt story. The Pasha smiled and told us that there was no formality in his house.

"You have seen me and my son leaving our babouches at the door when we entered the house. This is part or our tradition, but we never ask our friends to take off their shoes.".

I had not noticed when this was done and only now I observed that our hosts were in their socks. More at ease, I told the Pasha that we had come to Marrakech just for a brief look at this city which Winston Churchill had fallen in love with during the 1930s and again when he came here with President Franklin D. Roosevelt in 1943 just a few years before, for a brief rest from their war worries.[76]

"Monsieur Churchill," interrupted the Pasha, "is a very good friend of mine. He is a great man. On your return to London, please, go and see him and take my warmest greetings to him." And in the same breadth he added "You and your friend should not leave our city so soon. I want to have you both for dinner. Please stay at least one more day and be my guests tomorrow night."

There was no question of refusing and we accepted with grateful thanks. The Pasha then stood up and extended his right hand to us. It was a fine hand with long fingers. He remained there standing as Si Brahim led us out of the room and went with us down to the Rolls-Boyce. The same crowd of courtiers and attendants at the door bowing. Mr. Corcos accom-

---

[76] Roosevelt and Churchill's *North African Desert Excursion* by Robert Lanzone, Taj mahal Review, June 2004.

"You can't come all this way to North Africa without seeing Marrakech--an oasis in the North African desert," Churchill said. "Why don't we spend two days there?"

"This is a time of war," Roosevelt said. "I don't think it would be appropriate for us to be vacationing in the midst of it."

"Nonsense. You must see the sunset on the snows of the Atlas Mountains. It's a breathtaking sight."

"But where will we stay?" Roosevelt asked.

"Vice-consul Pendar has a villa there, La Saadia, that will accommodate us."

"Very well then, Marrakech it is."

Thousands of American troops were assembled and lined the one hundred fifty-mile route [from Casablanca] to Marrakech. The planes of the Army Air Corp protected it from the skies.

panied us to the Mamounia. It was quite cold, the sky was clear and studded with stars.

At the Mamounia the magic of the honorific "*Excellency*" followed me at every step. I would have accepted it if it would have not been the fear that this exalted title would be reflected in the hotel bill. Then too, I was traveling with a French friend a member of the resistance movement in France who in his country was best known from Boulogne to Marseille and Biarritz to Lyon as one of the subtle food and wine connoisseurs. He was known to the French staff of the Mamounia, from the Managing Director to the waiters in the dining room who during the closed summer Marrakech period, worked in the leading hotels and restaurants of France. Thanks to him we were given a suite of rooms at the Mamounia, though it was in peak winter season with people being turned away.

While waiters were hovering around our table, my friend and I still worried about our inadequate clothes. On the back of the menu we scribbled a message to the concierge and by the time we reached our rooms a shirt maker was there waiting for us. At nine o'clock in the morning we had each one not one but three shirts each with a perfect fit and made out of the best Manchester poplin.

At our request, Mr. Corcos came to brief us on the etiquette of a Moroccan dinner. A *diffa*, as dinners for guests of honor are called, consist of about fourteen courses, beginning with a *pastilla* of breast of pigeon mixed with almonds and covered in *mille-feuilles*, followed by *mechoui*, an entire barbecued lamb, and a succession of *tagines*, mutton cooked with various vegetables, then chicken with olives, lemons, and almonds, to end with the native main course of *cous-cous*, a boiled home made semolina shaped into a conical shape in which are choice morsels of lamb and chicken and all doused with a fine spiced broth. With the mechoui come small plates of cumin as a fine powder. It is delicious with lamb. There would also be plenty of fresh orange juice and cold milk. Before and after the dinner, he continued to explain, mint tea is served, and during the meal a never to be forgotten milk of almonds. There are no forks or knives. European guests are given spoons for the cous-cous. Only the right hand is used in taking food. The left, which is considered by Moslems as the "unclean hand," rests on the left knee. Before and after the meal, servants would bring in basins and water pitchers for the guests and hosts to wash their hands. Later, at lunch time in the Hotel, we asked for a discrete table behind a pillar and practiced eating with the right hand.

At a quarter to eight, the concierge phoned to say that His Excellency Si Sadeq, the second son of the 'Pasha was downstairs waiting for us. Very informally introduced himself to us:

"I am Sadeq El Glaoui and I came to take you to my father's house."

This time we entered the big gate, and stopped at a side entrance leading to the private apartments of the Pasha. Following Si Sadeq, we walked through long corridors, lined with attendants who bowed to us. After a long walk, turning right or left, we suddenly entered a riad, an enclosed patio-garden looking like a setting of an "Arabian Tale." Candle lanterns lined a tile-paved lane leading to a small elongated room, beautifully decorated with mosaics from floor to ceiling. The Pasha came to the door with stretched hand, Si Sadeq translated his greeting:

"I am happy again to welcome you in my home."

After servings of mint tea, he stood up and asked us to follow him to a larger and even more beautiful room with a high cathedral-like ceilings. Three Murano glass chandeliers cast a glittery light over the entire interior. Around the walls were long divans and pillows covered in brocaded velvet. The Pasha sat at the end of a U-shaped divan gesturing me to his right and Jean on his left and Si Sadeq to a hassock facing his father.

Following a hand washing ritual with lukewarm and orange scented water, the diffa began. A low round table was placed in the center and covered with what looked to be fine Venetian lace. In whispers Si Sadeq passed orders to a servant. A large tray, the size of the round table, appeared with a conical velvet covering that was immediately removed disclosing a pastilla. The Pasha made the first move, by breaking the delicate crust and picking out a choice morsel which he placed on the edge of the tray in front or me, then a second morsel for my friend. He hardly ate anything. He fed us or encouraged us to eat more. This he did to the end of the meal. All the while Si Sadeq explained the dishes while also giving us choice morsels. The cous-cous came as an anticlimax. It was a whole meal in itself, the *plat de resistance* of a diffa. It was light and so tasty that we honored it with a good helping. Then trays with fruit were brought in. I took the moment to say to the Pasha that I was coming from London were we still lived on war rations. A family could have lived for a month on the food served to us.

After the table was removed, again we went to the ritual of washing our hands, which by this time badly needed a thorough cleaning. Once more we moved to another room equally large and just as breathtaking as the one in which we had the diffa. After we were asked whether we wished to have coffee, an offer we declined, mint tea was served, we were offered cigars and cigarettes, though knowing that smoking was not approved by Moslems. It was now almost ten o'clock and we thought that we not tire our gracious host. We were at a loss to know who should make the first move. For a few minutes we were silent. The Pasha broke this quiet spell by saying how happy he was to receive us. His house was always ready for his friends. He wished to honor me as a Romanian having learned of my country from a time when Queen Marie had been his guest. As to my arrival in

Marrakech was there anything he could do now or later? This was not a question I had anticipated nor had an immediate answer for.

My trip was in fact a search for a place where, as a political exile from Communist rule, I could bring my wife and children, forget the past and start life anew. Instead of a quite remote place I had imagined, what I found was a thriving city, the capital of southern Morocco with a prosperous modern European quarter. And because of the Mamounia Hotel's reputation, it was a gathering point for the rich and famous from the four corners of the world. And within days I was called an 'Excellency" and known, at least to the Mamounia, as a friend of the Pasha. But now I had to find an answer to my host's question.

"Votre Excellence, my friend and I wish to thank you for the honor you have extended to us by having both as guests in your palace," I said cordially. "We are deeply grateful for the opportunity given to us to me Votre Excellence and your two sons. I was very much touched by you referring to me as Romanian and the sympathy you expressed for the sad fate of my country."

Si Sadeq started translating when the Pasha signaled him that he understood my French.

"May I confess." I continued, "that I came to Marrakech to see whether I could establish a new home. In return, Votre Excellence, allow me to reverse your question." I improvised, what might I do for your people, for Marrakech, for your country?"

The Pasha closed his eyes and bent his head down. He put his hands together as in a silent prayer. Then I heard the Pasha's voice like a whisper echoed in French by Si Sadeq:

"So kind, very kind of you to offer to do something for our people and our country." And after a long pause, "Many other distinguished men, some great soldiers and great statesmen, whom I had the honor to receive in this house, have asked what they could do for us. I told them, as I am telling you now we are thirsty. Please give us water, water, more water."

I turned questioningly towards Si Sadeq, "I do not understand the meaning of what his Excellency your father said." The Pasha answered my question immediately and this time in French.

"Oui, j'ai dit de l'eau, de l'eau, et encore de l'eau."

In answer to what have still seemed like puzzlement, an explanation followed.

"From times immemorial, this part of our country has been plagued by droughts recurring in four year cycled. How could a toiler of the earth live for four years on the lost crop of one year? The soil is rich and fertile. When it rains in the spring, the barren lands you have seen around our city turn into green fields with flowers to the edge of the desert. But when the rain stops, in two weeks the sun burns everything."

He followed with a long and eloquent discourse. "When our ancestors came from other side of the Atlas Mountains to lay the foundation of our ancient city, it was bare and dry. Not a single blade of grass, nor a single tree grew on a cursed land from which men and even beasts rushed away. One of our greatest engineers - we had them long before you - conceived a mammoth water adduction plan. He had thousand and thousand of men and women dig over three thousand tunnels from the springs of the Atlas to this barren site. One man standing on an other's shoulder could not reach the top of each tunnel. At regular intervals there were aeration vents. Thousand of young palm trees were brought from Mauretania and the countries beyond. For centuries and centuries thousand of men and women cared for these tunnels, so water could flow freely to the growing city of Marrakech and its oasis of palm trees, now the largest in North Africa. All this was done at the price of thousands and thousands of human lives. Men died so their children may have water to drink, water to wash their bodies and their clothing, water for their olive groves and the small gardens within the walls of the city."

He stopped for a minute before adding, "One of the American generals who have visited me when our lands were in bloom said that the Haouz plain between the Djebilet and the Atlas Mountains was a second California. He said what we needed was irrigation, he promised to come back and build dams and give us water but we are still waiting. We the Berbers have lived in the Atlas Mountains for thousands and thousands of years by building small dams to provide water for our patches of good soil brought from the bottom of the valleys on the back of donkeys or our own shoulders. There is plenty of water when the winter snows melt. But all goes rushes in torrents rushing to the not too far sea. When it overflows the river beds, it washes away houses, drowning men, women and children, and their few animals and fowl. Only big dams can tame that water. But we do not have the means to undertake such gigantic work.

"Our great friends, the French have the technicians and the machines to build the dams but French investors are not interested in irrigation projects. The French bankers paid to build Casablanca into as a modern commercial city. Do you know anyone among your friends in England or America who would come to help in this great challenge?"

Pondering my own answer, I knew that I could approach certain friends who might help Hadj Thami El Glaoui in his quest. But he, the ruler of the Berbers, in all probability had many more friends. France itself owed a debt of gratitude to the Pasha in his help pacifying Morocco and the establishment of the French protectorate. Would English or American bankers take more interest in irrigation ventures than the French financiers?

In answer I said, "As a child, Your Excellency, my father would not allow me to answer a question calling for action with a no. He wished me to say: "I am not sure whether I can do something, but I could surely do my best to find a way to it. So, I am going to answer your question the same way. Yes, I could find among my friends one who would be so bold as to tackle the water problem of southern Morocco but I would take great pride in finding a heart responsive to your touching appeal. I will pray God to help me come back to you with good tidings."

It was past midnight, when my friend and I returned to the hotel, in our rooms we found each two huge Moroccan baskets full of oranges and tangerines. Attached was a visiting card engraved "Hadj Thami El Glaoui" and below in smaller characters "Pasha of Marrakech."

I sat down at a small desk and wrote down word for word as much as the conversation with the Pasha. This was a page of history for a man, labeled a feudal lord, a trying to get water for his thirsty land. Unable to sleep, I read from documents provided by Si Sadeq after the dinner that one or two large dams could store enough water to irrigate about 240,000 acres. Immediately I wrote a letter to a friend in far away California outlining the southern Moroccan water needs. It was daylight when I handed the letter to the night concierge with instructions to have it sent by Air Mail on the first plane to Casablanca.

On returning to Paris, Jean and I lost no time. We made plans on the vague hope that my California message would yield a positive answer. The challenge proposed by the Pasha captivated me. I wanted to act.

Finally back in England, I was welcome by the same bone chilling winter I had left behind and our new home at "Dane Court" in the small village of Loxwood, south of London. My wife and the children greeted me with Joy. It was warm inside with a large log burning in the living room's huge fireplace. The house built in 1454 and its sturdy oak furniture had been in continuous use since the Elizabethan days. From Morocco, I managed to bring two baskets of luscious fruit. As I told my Marrakech tales, my two small sons born during wartime in England tasted tangerines for the first time. At one point I asked Zézé whether I had any mail. She answered casually that there were a-lot-of uninteresting letters.

"Any cables?" I asked.

"Oh yes, there is one from Jerome Politzer from San Francisco. It's badly garbled."

Too nervous to open it, I put the cable in my pocket my heart beating with a sudden emotion of fear and failure. Why would I want to leave the comfort of this ancient country house? Or England? I pulled the blue telegram paper from my pocket, unfolded it, and by the light of a candle read the message:

GREATLY INTERESTED MOROCCAN PROPOSITION STOP EVENTUALLY CAN RAISE UP TO THIRTY MILLION DOLLARS REPEAT THIRTY MILLION DOLLARS STOP AIR MAIL LETTER FOLLOWS.[77]

Family pose at "Dane Court" in Loxwood, England

---

[77] A 1950 dollar would be equivalent to ten dollars in 2010. The telegram suggested raising an amount equivalent to $300 million.

CHAPTER SEVENTEEN

MARRAKECH

With this telegram a most unpredictable next eight years would unfold in Morocco. Soon after, we left England to settle as a family in Marrakech. When I arrived in Marrakech we first stayed at the famed Mamounia Hotel.

All our possessions and my library of books accumulated in England came in wooden crates came with us.

We could not have come to a more extreme setting. In the Medina one would still encounter lepers, blind-men one following another arms resting one each other shoulders. The main square called the Djemaa-el-Fna was a gathering place for acrobats, snake charmers, food and water vendors, story-tellers, barbers. Berber villagers selling their own products catered to city-dwellers. All this carried its own special allure in the colors, vistas of the Atlas Mountains, and lively merchant culture in the souks.

During a visit with the Pasha, I mentioned that I was looking for a home for my family. The response was more than stunning. He offered us one his palaces which was empty. It was called 'Palais Menebhi'. To reach it, one had to either walk through the merchant 'souk' or with our small Austin car shipped from England through narrow, crowded alleys. We occupied the palace but had to install a modern bathroom as none existed in what was a warren of dark steam-bath rooms. Enormous mosaic-lined rooms opened onto a vast patio, which had three marble fountains, orange trees and several fountains on a sidewall. There were no outside windows as was true of all houses in the Medina. We furnished the palace in Moroccan style with low divans and small round tables. A modern adaptation was a long dining room table. All this was crafted by the best local carpenters.

It was from here that I planned to coordinate the 'water' project.

Life gradually fell into place. Zézé organized the "Palace" into a working home. Our children were soon enrolled in French schools in the Guéliz. Our daughter, Sandra and 5-year-old son Dan, at a Catholic school run by nuns. Our sons, Dimitri and Mihai, at public schools where Dan was sent too a year later. Our British nanny who had come with us, unable to adapt to the dust and dirt of the Medina, soon returned to England. Over the years to come all was not easy. The children got all the diseases one might catch in the daily routine of dusty streets, unsafe water, and mosquitos: malaria, jaundice, trachoma, typhoid, and even a scorpion sting. Zézé and I somehow escaped these health scares.

Around Marrakech there were several French families with large properties. They had come as settlers and were called 'colons'. They had orange and olive groves and beautiful houses built in the French style. We met many of them and started exchanging invitations. They had little to do with the Moroccans except the Pasha and his sons. We also met other Moroccans.

Family at our home in the "Palais Menebhi"
(Present-day it is known as the official Museum of Marrakech)

Marrakech had its own charms as a magnet for exiles, worldly travelers, artists, and movie personalities attracted by its natural beauty, medieval ways, and sophistication. Not the least to have given fame to Marrakech was Churchill who had found a painter's heaven there during the 1930s, returned during World War II, and was now planning another visit.

All the high ranking civil servants, officers, 'colons' and their wives moved in a closed, polite and formal circle towered over by the aristocratic de Breteuils, who were more exclusive and selective in their list of guests. They were the only ones to have, from October to May, a stream of distinguished outside guests staying at their 'Villa La Saadia'. Roosevelt and Churchill had stayed there in 1943 during the midst of World War II. After our arrival, we shared with them the honor of entertaining unusual visitors, though our list showed a greater variety, ranging from American G.I.'s to British admirals. Having lived for so many years in England and the United States, it was normal to have many friends in these countries. A few came to see us. They were followed by their friends and their friends' friends.

The Marrakech locals were just as puzzled as the French as to who we were. Some thought I was the American consul. Others believed I was the British consul. A few mistook me for the *toubib*, a doctor. Some called me a *malem*, which in Arabic means a foreman or supervisor. Whenever an American or British tourist would get in trouble, the native guide would bring him, or the entire group, to our house. We made friends out of strangers by helping such stranded tourists in need of advice. The postman was the first to call me a 'malem.' There was no other house in the Medina receiving so much foreign mail as we did, plus heavy rolls of magazines and newspapers. The local customs officer took great delight in going through our packages that came from abroad. Each Christmas, when we received dates from Jacqueline Cochran, a friend in California, he made the same remark: "Coals to Newcastle, Monsieur? We have plenty of dates. Why get these from America? Ours are fresh from the tree." Another friend kept sending orange marmalade from Florida.

As a result of friendships and acquaintances we made in Hollywood in the 1930's, we met movie stars on film projects while we were in Morocco. Among them were Tyrone Power and his wife Linda Christian. They were stars in a film called the "Black Rose," which was being filmed in Marrakech even though the scenes were supposed to be in China. We were invited to have box lunches with Power and Christian watching as Moroccan extras dressed as Chinese warriors battled along the high walls surrounding the city.

Jimmy Stewart and Doris Day, who came to Marrakech for the filming of Alfred Hitchcock's "The Man Who Knew Too Much," visited our home along with a photographer from *Life Magazine*. A photo showed them in our house, which the caption wrongly identified as "the home of a Romanian baron." Gladys Robinson, the wife of Edward G. Robinson came to paint and visit us while she was in Marrakech.

Si Sadeq El Glaoui (lft), DDD, and Tyrone Power (rt)

Alfred Hitchcock and an image from his film "The Man Who Knew Too Much"

There was a small colony of painters, the leading one being Louis Majorelle, who was known outside Morocco. Once or twice a year he would have an exhibition where he would sell his paintings at a high price. For years Majorelle had done life-size paintings of Moroccans. His hobby was keeping cacti of which he had hundreds of varieties. There was another painter, Max Moreau, the son of a Belgian painter by the same name. Besides his paintings of Moroccan villages, he was an excellent portraitist. He painted a water color of our daughter as a gift for my birthday. Another artist who lived in Morocco at-that-time, was a Dutch sculptor who had made two huge statues to be set in front of the Marrakech town hall. They had been brought in sections, but remained unassembled, at least during the eight years we stayed in Marrakech.

An English writer of Viennese origin, Rom Landau, had fallen in love with Marrakech and Morocco. He was quite politically objective in his writings. However, the French authorities accused him of not been favorable to them and refused him any help he might have needed. Landau, had asked through French intermediaries for an audience with the heir to the throne, Prince Moulay Hassan, but it was refused. But he did manage by other intermediaries to interview him. They became friends and the friendship continued when Hassan became King of Morocco in 1961. The Moroccan government provided Landau with free lodgings when he came to the country in subsequent years to complete several books on Moroccan subjects. This was all thanks to King Hassan.

The following is an excerpt from his book, *Moroccan Journal*.[78]

"D. Dimancescu's company is a perpetual delight however often one may share it. His wide humanity sets him far above the common run of Marrakech society, or indeed of society at large. I had met Dimmy - as all his friends call him - during my previous visit to Marrakech, thanks to an introduction from our mutual friend, Sir Cyril Cane, British Consul General at Rabat. As-soon-as I had arrived for the first time in the 'Capital of the South' or, as Mr. Churchill calls it, 'the Paris of the Sahara', Dimmy presented himself at my hotel, and I soon fell under the spell of the vital little man - little only in the matter of inches - overflowing with kindness and generosity. What would I like to see in Marrakech, he enquired; whom did I wish to meet, to which sights might he take me in his car.

"Dimmy is that typical symbol of modem civilization, a refugee with no country, no position, no rank... The Iron Curtain shut off Rumania from the western world, and with it his home, his job, and his possessions. With what he was able to save from the debacle he decided to try his luck in Marrakech. Though diplomats are supposed to have one-track minds, Dimmy soon forgot his diplomatic past, and turned his attention to one of Morocco's most vital matters, namely irrigation of the sun-parched regions of the South. He worked out schemes for transforming those regions into fertile land, and succeeded in interesting American financiers in his project. But a protectorate that is ever suspicious of any form of foreign intervention does not easily lend a sympathetic ear to schemes devised by non-Frenchmen; and so far as I know, after years of hard work, Dimmy and his American friends are still waiting to put his plans into effect, and his dwindling savings have been his main standby.

"Yet nothing can curb his generosity, and no personal disappointment has ever dimmed his enthusiasm for helping others. Naturally I was only one of many foreigners to drift into Marrakech with an introduction to him. Yet for every casual guest he would do as much as he did for me, going to endless trouble to render the stranger's visit infinitely more profitable and

[78] Rom Landau, *Moroccan Journal*, Robert Hale Ltd., London, 1952, pgs. 143 - 146.

agreeable than it would have been without his assistance. You may possible visualize Dimmy as a member of that pseudo- religious fraternity ever conscious of it humanitarian mission in life, and seldom missing an opportunity of referring to it. If you do, you are greatly mistaken. Whatever, religious views he may hold he does not disclose them, for he would rather discuss literature and art, people and politics, all the while bubbling with an irrepressible vitality, as though quick-silver were running through his veins, and as though life were one long sequence of untroubled days. Never a word of complaint about his personal tragedy, never a bitter inflection in his voice, nor the slightest sign of discouragement. If anyone deserves to have a share in the good things life has to offer it is Dimmy. In a town in which European social life easily assumes a snobbish, ostentatious, or colonial character, Dimmy and his wife have created a home that is far more than a mere background for parties; a home, moreover, in which the things of the mind are cultivated for their own sake and not as props for social graces or as landmarks in intellectual fashions."

❧❧

CHAPTER EIGHTEEN

CHURCHILL

I t was the baldness and pluck of Walter Graebner which secured for *Life* the priority rights for the publication of Winston Churchill's Second World War memoirs. Walter, at-that-time Chief of *Time* and *Life* London bureau, was authorized by Harry Luce to meet all the wishes of Churchill, who had the shrewd foresight to include in the terms of his agreement that the publisher should pay all his expenses whilst he wrote each volume of the memoirs at some secluded and agreeable place of his choice.

To write his fifth volume, Churchill selected Marrakech where he arrived by plane in December of 1950 taking quarters in one wing of the Mamounia Hotel. With him were Mrs. Churchill, his daughter then still Mrs. Diana Duncan Sandys, Lord Cherwell, Lieutenant-General Sir Henry Pownall, Colonel and Mrs. F.W. Deakin, Denis Kelly, two personal secretaries Miss Sturdee and Miss Gemmel, the crew of the plane, and the always present watch dog provided by Scotland Yard.

How my connections to the Churchills came-to-be goes back to John Farrow and our meeting in Hollywood twenty years earlier. When we were in London, we had met and gotten to know Diana through a mutual friend of John's. Seeing her and inviting her to our house in Marrakech was not an infringement on her father's privacy. This also applied to Colonel Bill Deakin's wife Livia (Stela) who was the daughter of a great Romanian journalist and a good friend. In 1943 he had been parachuted into Yugoslavia to support Tito's partisans and eventually helped Churchill draft his memoirs

Eagerly anticipating the visit, the local Marrakech élite - one of unusual distinction and character so soon after the War years - was stunned to learn that Winston Churchill was dead-set on not wasting his time attending social affairs. From the moment he entered the Mamounia Hotel, he and his entourage were sheltered by an impregnable "Chinese Wall." Phone calls were cut short at the Hotel's switchboard and those who managed by trickery to reach Miss Sturdee were met with a gentle but stern "I am sorry."

The most persistent caller was Pierre Lyautey, the nephew of the famed French Maréchal Hubert Lyautey, architect of the French protectorate system imposed on Morocco in 1912. Following his death, Pierre lived on the glory of his uncle's name. There was no official function at which he would not be present and make a speech. He had a small but charming house in the Medina, the native quarter of Marrakech, and he and his wife, ex-Madame de Pourtales, graciously entertained distinguished visitors of this city. Pierre, however, was very much a snob in the selection of his guests. To be invited to his house one had to have a title of *noblesse* or be a high ranking official or diplomat or movie star, great artist or writer of confirmed repute, or if American - a millionaire. It goes without saying that I was not on a list of distinguished guests though we had met on occasions at various luncheons and dinners hosted by mutual friends. Our conversation would begin and end with a formal greeting "Comment-allez vous Monsieur le Ministre?" and my reply "Trés bien Monsieur Lyautey."

Thus it came to me as a great surprise when a few days after Mr. Churchill's arrival - he was not yet Sir Winston - Monsieur Lyautey phoned me asking whether I could receive him immediately as he had something very important to discuss. In no time after his call he was at our traditional Moroccan house on Derb Dabachi to which we had moved also in the Medina. In true continental style, he began by praising the interior. "Quelle maison, adorable. Et votre bibliothèque!" This was certainly so as I now had a beautiful house our stay at the 'Menebhi Palace' stay having run its course. I had arranged to live in wing of the 'Madani' Glaoui's Palace which had fallen into ruin. My luck was to get one small section including its three story watch tower. This my wife and I turned into a more welcoming family "home."

"I am in despair," Monsieur Lyautey announced unabashedly. "I cannot reach Monsieur Churchill. You should help me get to him. I want to give a dinner for him and Madame Churchill. His secretaries would not transmit my invitation to him. I sent them flowers and they have not been acknowledged," he lamented. "And what is worse *Madame la Maréchale* is also at the Mamounia and wants to see the Churchills." Madame was the aging widow of the illustrious Lyautey whom her nephew had invited to Marrakech to preside over the proposed gala dinner.

Though I replied that I had no entrance to Churchill's *sacro-sanctum* at the Mamounia, Pierre Lyautey knew better. He had learned from one of the hotel's managers who in turn kept track of all phone call that I was the only Marrakech inhabitant whose calls were allowed to be put through to some members of Winston's closed group. The taboos applied only to the "Old Man." But I did tell him that Diana, Churchill's daughter, and the members of his staff were free to do as they wished. This last bit of Information cheered Pierre Lyautey though he left my house disappointed at my categorical refusal to convey any message from him or *Mme. la Maréchale*. It was quite evident that a more devious scheme might be working in his mind.

A few days later he reached me again by phone.

"My wife and I would like to have you and Madame Dimancescu for lunch tomorrow. Our guest of honor is going to be Monsieur le General Pownall. There will be also Monsieur Kelly and Mademoiselle Sturdee.

"Monsieur Lyautey," I responded, "I thank you and Madame Lyautey for your kind invitation but I cannot say that we can come until I ask my to see whether my wife has not made other arrangements for tomorrow."

"But, Monsieur le Ministre, you cannot let us down. Arranging this lunch we counted on you as you speak English and our guests do not speak French. Even if Madame Dimancescu has accepted another invitation for lunch please, please cancel it."

Pierre had no idea that my wife had a mind of her own and that she would not care to lunch with the Lyauteys because they were *the* Lyauteys. The very idea of being invited to act as interpreter-guests would have made her furious as indeed I was. This was a delicate situation and I won her agreement to accept the invitation by arguing that we should protect Sir Henry, Denis Kelly and Miss Sturdee against Pierre's insincere hospitality. The lunch went smoothly, the food was excellent as were the wines. The English guests to Pierre's surprise spoke fairly good French. The only time I was called to act as an interpreter came at the end of the lunch when the host raised a glass of champagne with the toast: "Le President" followed by a confused silence.

Sir Henry whispered to me across the table: "Which President?" I turned to Pierre Lyautey for an explanation. Did he follow the English tradition of drinking first to the Head of State, meaning the President of the French Republic?

"Non, non, non I give my toast to *Le President* Churchill" not knowing what correct title to use.

On leaving the Lyautey's house, Pierre took my wife aside and said to her in most unequivocal terms:

"Chère Madame, we have invited you to this lunch because we want you to invite us when you will give a dinner for Monsieur and Madame Churchill."

The most he got from us was a letter of thanks for the lunch written in English, as he had addressed our invitation in English. This affair was just the beginning of the more troubles to come on the presumption that I could help others rub elbows with Mr. Churchill. My wife, Zézé, and I suddenly became very popular. More invitations to lunches and dinners with our friends appeared than we could accept or cared to accept.

Soon another man took notice of my presence in Marrakech. He was Oscar Nemon,[79] a Yugoslav sculptor who became an English citizen. Nemon had a narrow head like Mephistopholes with a small mustache and short pointed beard. Besides being a sculptor, he was also a psychoanalyst and a friend of Sigmund Freud for whom he had a created a life size statue. This had been a well received work of art in the manner of Auguste Rodin. Now in Marrakech, he had come to the city to sculpt the head of the daughter of Antenor Patino, inheritor of the Bolivian 'Tin King." Nemon was staying at the Mamounia where Senor Patino was footing his bills. He had full access to the hotel's dining room where Churchill had his meals. And by tipping the Head Waiter generously, he managed to have a table facing the Old Man and instead of eating he kept sketching, all the while annoying the restaurant's most distinguished guest with his stares. I learned from Miss Sturdee that Churchill was greatly annoyed by the looks of Nemon and that the management of the Mamounia has been asked to have him seated at some other table. By now Nemon was fixed on the idea of meeting Winston Churchill and to do his bust if not a monumental statue. His efforts to that end remained fruitless.

Then one day, he appeared at our house and I had to receive him. Nemon, whom I'd never met, had not bothered to announce himself. He brought with him photos of his work which I immediately admired for its artistic qualities. My wife and I invited him for dinner and till late at night we talked art and psychoanalysis. He was a master of both subjects and I enjoyed listening to him. I was quickly convinced that he should do a statue of Churchill. I then took the idea went one step further. The Pasha El Glaoui, friend of Churchill, should commission this work and have the statue erected in one of the city squares of Marrakech.

In-spite-of-the-fact that my wife hurt Nemon's feelings by vaguely making fun of his high sounding psychoanalytical ideas, and more so by saying that many psychoanalysts take advantage of week minded people, he and I became friends. I wasted no time and went the next day to see the Glaoui. In less than five minutes he agreed to pay the expenses for a statue of Churchill. He did not even look at sketches Nemon proposed. However, there was one condition. The Pasha asked that French authorities be consulted and give their approval.

Nemon and I searched for a place where the statue might be placed. We agreed that the site of an existing large water fountain not far from the city's casino was perfect. From there, the bronze statue would have an unobstructed view of the Atlas Mountains to the south.

---

[79] Background on Oscar Nemon's work at: www.oscarnemon.org.uk

All the while I did not have the courage to ask Churchill to sit for Nemon. And Nemon-the-artist would not produce a statue without seeing his subject in three dimensions. We had reached an impasse and I was now growing sorry to have involved myself. But Nemon, like Lyautey, was persistent. He would appear at my house at any odd hours much to the displeasure of Zézé.

One evening, thinking of a way to get rid of him, I said "Look here, I have an idea. Why not try to make a clay model from a small bust I have of Churchill in my study." He immediately wanted it. What he took with him had seen better days. It had fallen one day, and the head had broken away from the shoulders. With some fish glue and soldering metal, I had re-attached them. Moving his fingers over the bust he said: "My hands are itching to work. I want to do something tonight." Grumbling as he left that it was a much younger looking Churchill, he took it back to the Mamounia.

He produced a clay model twelve inches high. And somehow without any of my doing he got it through the "Chinese Wall" and into Mrs. Clementine Churchill's hands. She loved it and said that it was a perfect image of her husband. She wanted to have a bronze copy as-soon-as possible. When Queen Elizabeth saw it sometime later, she wanted a copy. Oscar Nemon became a favorite of the Churchills and crafted varied large and small statues of the "Old Man" that became famed across England including one that dominates a hall in the House of Commons in London.

His success in Marrakech did not help us to carry out our more ambitious project for a larger statue adorning the city. The French authorities would not hear of having a monument to Churchill before having one of the great Maréchal Lyautey. Pierre had gotten even with the man who did not come to his house for a dinner presided by *Mme la Maréchale*.

Our doings and un-doings never reached the ears of the great "Old Man." Winston stuck hard to his writing desk, ate hearty meals, smoked big cigars, drank good French wines, and for relaxation painted with the zest of a young Beaux Arts student. During the day a large sedan car stood ready by the door of the Mamounia ready at the last minute to take Winston to whatever place would be the subject of his next canvas. Always ready in the car for use was his painting paraphernalia: a small portable chair, two large white parasols to protect him against the sun, a small table for his large box of oil colors, and an assortment of easels and fresh canvases or painting boards.

Except the chauffeur and the Scotland Yard detective, no one else would go with him. He wanted to be alone and once settled in one corner of the Medina, the Pasha's private guards would discretely keep the curious away from him.

The detective kept an eye on professional or amateur photographers. No one was allowed to take pictures of Churchill at work with the exception of a local Swiss photographer who would take snapshots of houses or streets with people for Winston to have. While painting, he wore a Texas sombrero and a loose white smock. He was very quick in sketching the outline of his subject with charcoal. He was bothered only by the Moroccan blue sky which he could not find in his palette.

Churchill had met Jacques Majorelle, a highly respected French painter living in Marrakech, who more than any other artist had found the secret of rendering in his landscapes the incomparably vivid Moroccan blue sky. When I told Jacques of Churchill's trouble, he gave me a small bottle. "Here is my mysterious powder. I make it myself out of some stones which I can find only in one special place in the Atlas Mountains. Take it to him but ask him to keep our secret." I hurried back to the Mamounia where I found the Old Man in the garden painting a palm tree the trunk covered with a huge cluster of flowering Bougainvillia.

"I brought you, Mr.Churchill, a present from Majorelle."

"What is it," he growled without looking me.

"The Moroccan blue you cannot get with your paints."

He turned, snatched the bottle from my hands, emptied it on his palette, mixed it with oil and with a large brush smeared the lot on the top of his canvas. He was happy.

"Go back to Jacques Majorelle, thank him and ask him to give me a large bottle of his powder. Its marvelous," he growled. "I will need a lot on the sky of his canvas. I am going to clean all the skies I painted and do them over."

I had on my lips the words "use it sparingly" but Churchill's next words had made me speechless. He did not want a little more, he wanted *all* the blue powder Majorelle had. The painter could hardly resist the request and spent the rest of the day crushing Atlas Mountains blue rocks in a white marble mortar.

A most persistent nuisance was the representative of an American light refreshment company who wished me to have a bottle of that drink placed by Churchill while he was painting outdoors. A photographer could then get a shot with a telescopic lens. He offered to pay me a very large sum for making this happen. Though I told the man that this proposition was an insult to me, he kept on coming back with larger bait. What annoyed him was that Churchill kept an unlabeled bottle full, not with brandy as some suspected, but with turpentine for cleaning his brushes.

There were also requests for me to get Churchill to autograph books written by him. I did not ask such an honor even for the favorite items in my Churchilliana collection, a small poster posted everywhere during the Battle of Britain with his immortal "We shall Not Flag Or Fail" and "We Shall Go On To The End." Luckily, though, my very good friend Emeric Mandl, the Swiss "King of Selected Grains," who was sending his Christmas vacation with his family at the Mamounia, sent me a copy of the *Gathering Storm* which Churchill had graciously signed without anyone's intercession.

The most dangerous stalkers were the journalists. Their quarry was still a man who still held news-making political potential and their editors wanted exclusive stories. Some were predicting his return to 10 Downing Street as Prime Minister. Besides the local reporters, there was a large number of foreign correspondents and legmen of American newspapers. While all these pundits respected their subject's outward privacy, their real targets were 'inside': the Head Concierge, the Maitre d'Hotel, the bellboys or chambermaids. What Mr. Churchill drank or ate was reported, as were his comings and goings. Great attention was paid to the people who came to see him as he remained in touch with the rest of his world. Rumors flew when Sir Kenneth Anderson, the Governor of Gibraltar arrived with Lady Anderson at the Mamounia to spend Christmas vacation. Word spread of a secret conference with Churchill. Some of the more resourceful journalists did not fail to notice that Sir Kenneth and Lady Anderson came one afternoon to our house for tea. They noticed too that His Majesty's Consul General at Rabat, Sir Cyril Cane, who managed Mr. Churchill's Parliamentary correspondence by sending it to London by the diplomatic pouch, resided with us rather than at the Mamounia. Press fervor grew with the arrival of Time-Life's Walter and Connie Graebner. This was fueled by the couple's immediate entry into the Churchillian inner sanctum. They too, friends from our years in London, visited our home. Some reporters could not see why callers on Mr. Churchill were also our guests. Something important had to be in the works. We rather enjoyed the idea of leaving the question unanswered.

Behind his "Chinese Wall" Churchill moved freely but when outside he was in sight of everyone. All the Hotel's guests politely avoided staring at the great statesman though many undoubtedly wished for that moment when a handshake might be possible. Among them was Dr. Rene Laforgue, the French psychoanalyst with a world reputation, who was itching for his own contact with the outstanding man of our times. Dr. Laforgue had post-humously psychoanalyzed Charles Maurice Talleyrand, the diplomatic gen-ius under Napoleon and subsequent French rulers of the first half of the 19th Century.

One day, as Dr. Laforgue and I conversed in the Mamounia garden, Churchill walked out for his usual stroll. He was alone, the Scotland Yard detective having remained discreetly by the restaurant's door. Not far from where we were sitting, Churchill engaged animatedly with the Mamounia's chief gardner, a retired French officer.

"I hate these olive trees," he said gruffly. "They block the view from my balcony. I want to see the Atlas Mountains, not olive tree leaves. You should trim them down."

He tried flattery.

"You are an artist with your flowers. You should be an artist with your trees."

Then there was a more direct order.

"That cypress should not been planted there!"

"Monsieur Shure-shill," the gardner answered obligingly, "the olive trees will be trimmed this afternoon as you wish. But I am sorry, Monsieur," he added assertively. "I cannot have that cypress cut down. It has been there for the last three hundred years."

"Then if you cannot cut it down move it away, tell your manager not to charge double rates for the apartments behind it."

Evidently, Churchill knew the rates of the rooms facing the splendid southern facing view of the snow covered High Atlas Mountains rising to heights of 4000 meters. In no time a small army of workers were up in the olive trees cutting branches down to ugly stumps. The chief gardner imme-diately saw the advantage of pleasing the maker of history at the loss of a few-crops of olives. Three years later the branches had grown taller than before and the olive crop that much larger. What Mr. Churchill did not know was that the shrewd Manager of the Mamounia was getting a good profit by selling annual the annual crop of olives to local merchants all the while guests were charged for a "view" hidden by a curtain of trees.

But Churchill had one more desire that of crossing Atlas Mountains to complete a few more paintings. Churchill's arrived in Tinherir a traditional oasis village on the edges of the Sahara Desert known for its serene beauty and remoteness. A squad of *meharis* awaited - camel mounted patrolmen wearing the garb of the Sahara touaregs. Churchill passed them in review hat in hand, then he drove to the Gîtes d'Étape, a modern French hostelry situated on a hill overlooking the village and its palm tree oasis. It was an ideal place and some fifteen miles away the dramatic Todra River gorges became his favorite place during his brief-stay in the heart of the Saharan-side of the Atlas Mountains. Here he painted a canvas which up to that time he considered his best.

One late evening, while he was there, the phone rang in my study. The French operator informed me that it was a long distance call from "Monsieur Shure-shill." It was not the Old Man but Miss Sturdee, his secretary.

"Mister Dimancescu?"

"Yes, speaking."

"I cannot hear you. May I speak to Mister Dimancescu. I have a message from Mr. Churchill for him."

"I can hear you very well. I am he?"

The line went dead. The operator intervened with an assurance that she would get me a better line. Phone communications in Morocco were often bad; across the Atlas Mountains they where torture. I clung to the receiver and could hear the Marrakech operator talking to the Ait Ourir one; Ait Ourir to Telouet; Telouet to Ouarzazate; and Ouarzazate to Tinherir. There where whistles, shouts, and repeated calls of:

"Donnez moi une ligne pour Monsieur Shure-shill, priorité, priorité je vous prie."

The line was to be cleared for the great Churchill but obviously everybody wanted to listen to his voice. I was sorry for Miss Sturdee. After an hour we got a clear line.

"Mr. and Mrs. Churchill would like to know whether you and Madame Dimancescu can have dinner with them at the Mamounia on the nineteenth of January. Black tie. They ask your kind advice whether it would be in-order-to invite for that evening Si Sadeq El Glaoui, the Pasha's son."

"Please, Miss Sturdee, thank Mr. and Mrs. Churchill for their most kind invitation which my wife and I accept as a great honor. As to Si Sadeq, if he is invited, the oldest son of the Pasha, Si Brahim, would have to be Invited too. This I will explain to you when you will return here. Many thanks again and good night."

After the Tinherir phone call the Dimancescu's reputation normally in the background reached a record high. Any phone conversation in Marrakech was like a public announcement in a public square. Before I even had the chance to tell my wife of the message I received from Miss Sturdee, top French officials and their wives knew about it. This was to be Churchill's farewell dinner as on the 20th of January arrangements had been made for his flight back to London.

I could not tell Miss Sturdee over the phone when hundred ears may have been listening - a few understanding English - why Brahim El Glaoui had to come along with his younger half-brother Sadeq. The old Pasha had four legal wives. Their children lived in good harmony but the mothers were very sensitive as which one of their sons was entitled to social priority. If the Pasha was not able to attend a party, automatically the invitation was passed to his eldest son. If he could not go, the next in age replaced him and so down the line to the youngest, Sadeq. He was the most brilliant of the Pasha's sons but the fifth in rank. Though this protocol applied to formal or official functions and the Churchill dinner was a very private affair, the mother of Brahim would have suspected political implications. A great storm in the Palace would have been created. Yet, Sadeq's invitation was in thanks for hosting Diana and a few members of the Churchill entourage with a lavish "diffa."

Soon after, the newspapermen's luck in the search for an as yet elusive headlining story was about to change. Information filtered out of the Mamounia kitchen that an important farewell dinner was planned. It was learned by the press that this affair would take-place not in the Hotel's dining room but in the more private *Salon de Lecture*. There was to be a long table but the number of guests and the menu remained a well-guarded secret closely managed by Mrs. Churchill.

For the most stubborn stalkers, one solution would be to find a comfortable seat in the lobby and watch guests arrive for the dinner. But even this was not a sure way as there were four separate approaches to the *Salon*.

❦

My son Dimitri facing Churchill at a Mamounia Hotel event

***

DINNER

Only those who have had the privilege of meeting Clementine Churchill, can understand why she was the wife of the greatest man of our century. Graceful and still beautiful in her old age, she was unassuming and self-effacing. Some of the people who have worked with Churchill have said that he is a difficult man to deal with. It is natural that a man, who has carried on his shoulders the burden and troubles wished upon him, should be difficult. He was responsible to the British people, not his detractors. While prime minister he had to face daily, not one, but thousands of problems.

For his ability to stand the strain of his many duties, Clementine Churchill should receive her share of credit. Her voice was soft and soothing. Evidently she knew how to care for her husband, who often enjoyed acting like a naughty boy. Her first thought on greeting us was to say that she was sorry that we had not brought along our daughter Sandra, and insisted that we should phone her at home and ask her to join us after dinner.

My wife and I had managed to get into the hotel unnoticed. In the *Salon* where we found Mrs. Churchill, her aunt Mrs. Henley, Walter and Connie Graebner, Sir Cyril Cane and his daughter Joan; and the two private secretaries, Miss Sturdee and Miss Gemmel. The honor of greeting Si Sadeq and Si Brahim that evening, fell on me. I escorted them to the *Salon*, where Diana Sandys who already knew Sadeq, introduced the El Glaoui sons to her mother and the other guests. At eight thirty sharp, the Old Man came in. One felt his presence immediately as all eyes turned toward him. With a quick glance he a made a tour of the room trying to see who was there with one look.

After the two brothers were introduced to him, he came to us with his hand stretched out and said:

"I am so glad you could come."

Then without further introduction, he added in almost the same breath:

"I tried so hard to save your country from the clutch of the communists. I am sorry I could not do more for Romania, but I saved Greece at a terrible price. Thirty-thousand men had to be killed."

My wife and I could not say a single word, completely stunned by Churchill's apology. At that moment we could not see what compelled him to offer the apology it to us. That was not an off-hand remark. He must have worked it in his mind before coming down to dinner. I made a desperate effort to say something. This was not an occasion to wish upon my great host the pain in my heart.

"It was a great tragedy for the Romanian people, that you failed in your efforts, Sir."

"I know," he replied and then went to greet the other guests.

We were told before that Zézé my wife was going to sit on Churchill's right, and that she should not mind if, during the dinner, he would not speak to her as this being his last chance to have a good French dinner, he most probably would pay more attention to the food. And knowing that my wife had a mind of her own, and a few questions to ask, I had begged her to be more than careful not to incur the strong words from the host by bringing up a controversial subject. The table seating would have been problem for any experienced hostess, but not for Mrs. Churchill. Though this was not a formal dinner, it became one because of the presence of the Pasha's two sons. Sadeq spoke French and English. Brahim spoke only French.

A genial hostess, like Clementine Churchill, thought first of seating her guests so they could converse during the meal and not stare in silence at their neighbors. We were fifteen in all, nine ladies and six men, including the hosts. Each member of the Churchill party only had to talk with the persons on his or her right. The hostess to Si Brahim El Glaoui; Diana Sandys to Si Sadeq; Mrs. Deakin to Walter Graebner; Mrs. Henley to me; and the host to my wife. No one said that one should not also talk to the people on the left, but the arrangement became evident during the dinner. The centerpiece flowers, on Mrs. Churchill's instructions to the Maitre d'Hotel, were short-stemmed so as not to obstruct the views across the table. The menu was simple: soup, fish, roast lamb, fried potatoes, green peas, chicory salad, ice-cream with fresh strawberries and assorted pastries. It was printed in French, which did justice to the care with which the meal had been prepared:

Petite Marmite Henri IV
Delices de Sole Marguery
Barron d'Agneau de Lait Roti
Pommes Mousseline
Petit Pois Frais au Beurre
Salade d'Endives
Fraises de la Targa Melba
Corbeille de Friandises

Though the lamb was supposed to be the main course, the soup was the real piece de resistance. This particular one was a favorite of Churchill's. It consisted of spring chicken and lamb boiled in beef stock together with vegetables and spices. It is the only soup that requires the use of a knife and fork in addition to a spoon. No wonder that there was complete silence around the table during the first course. When Churchill finished his second helping of Marmite Henri IV, he turned to my wife and asked her:

"How would you like us to talk this evening? In French or English?"

"It is the same to me," answered my wife, "but as you give me a choice, I would rather speak in English."

But when I heard Churchill saying: "What should we talk about?" and my wife replying: "I would like to ask your advice on a personal matter," I asked for a third glass of Champagne. "I am worried about our children's education. Though the schools are not too bad, I would like to send them back to England. With so much talk about the Russians starting a new war, they may be safer there."

"I venture to say, Madam, that you and your children would be better off right here in Marrakech. Who would be foolish enough to waste a bomb on this city? These days, a bomb, any bomb, is an expensive thing and Marrakech is not worth bombing. If the Russians would move further into the heart of Europe, they would be blasted out of the continent and pushed beyond the Urals. The Americans have, I am sure, more than a thousand atomic bombs. They would press the Russians back to Asia where they came from."

"But, Mr. Churchill," interjected my wife, "pushing the Russians out of Europe and into Asia would mean bringing together two hundred million Russians with over four hundred million Chinese. Wouldn't this huge block of humanity be a greater danger to all of us in the years to come?"

"The Chinese?" almost bellowed Churchill looking at my wife quizzically. "Can the Chinese fly? Can they swim? Can they make the one thousand and one things which a nation, any great nation, needs to wage war on a global scale?"

And hitting the table with his fist, he answered his own question with a loud "No, Madam!"

From that moment on, I could not hear what turn the conversation between Churchill and my wife subsequently took. No one at the table seemed to be perturbed, but me. I turned to Mrs. Henley, and said to her:

"I am afraid that my wife has upset Mr. Churchill with her remarks about the Chinese."

"Oh, no, by-all-means do not think so. On the contrary," she reassured me. "Most obviously he is enjoying his conversation with Madame Dimancescu." At the end of the dinner we all moved to the small drawing room, the ladies gathering around Clementine Churchill, and the men going to the opposite corner. Churchill came to me and said:

"You have a clever wife; she knows what she is talking about. Bring the Pasha's sons and let's sit at that table. Help me talk to them."

Coffee *en demie tasse* was brought in. Churchill took the cups himself and placed them in front of Brahim and Sadeq. Then a waiter came with a large silver tray on which were bottles of French liqueurs and an assortment of Scotch whiskey. Another waiter brought a tray on which were English, American and French cigarettes and a large box with Churchill's famous cigars. Pointing to the trays, he asked the Pasha's sons:

"Would you, please, have something to drink, and try one of my cigars. They are very mild."

"Je vous remercie beaucoup," answered Brahim. "Je ne bois pas. Je ne fume pas non plus."

"Like my brother," replied Sadeq in English, "I do not smoke or drink. It is against our Moslem religion."

After Churchill helped himself to a glass of whiskey and took a cigar, he invited me to do the same. There was no further conversation. To break the silence, Churchill addressing Sadeq, asked him to tell his father that he had enjoyed his stay in Marrakech and that he was sorry to leave the city he had enjoyed so much. We all four then walked to Mrs. Churchill, and Brahim thanked her "Pour l'honneur de nous avoir invité a ce diner." To which Sadeq added: "Et qui sera pour nous, Madame, inoubliable."

By this time our son and daughter had arrived, she with her our guest book, a conversation piece in itself, which I had bought from a London antique dealer. It had as many pages as the days of the year, each with the date printed above a pattern of flowers. Since it came into our possession, we had asked our friends to sign their names on the page with the day of their birth. My daughter wanted the Churchills to do the same. Mrs. Churchill was gracious enough to ask all the guests present to add their names, which each of them did after turning the pages to find the correct day. When Churchill's turn came, he just opened the book randomly. He wrote his signature carefully on the July 1 - a day which quite coincidently happened to be my father's birthday.

"Come along with me," Churchill said, showing me the way to the door, "we will go upstairs and look at my paintings." We made a quiet exit and walked slowly toward the elevator. The corridor was full of people clapping their hands. There were a few "Vive Shure-shill! Vive Shure-shill!" Smiling, he bowed graciously to the left and right and made the victory sign with his fingers. One large room in his suite had been turned into a painter's studio. One wall, from floor to ceiling, was covered with the paintings he did during his Marrakech stay. Four projector lamps cast light on the paintings. Churchill sat down on a folding chair in front of an unfinished canvas and invited me to sit in an arm chair at his side. We both still had our cigars. For a while neither of us said a word. We just looked at the paintings.

"Which one do you like best?" he suddenly asked me. Pointing with my finger I declared "That one, which looks to me like a corner of the Dades Valley."

"You picked the right one. That's my favorite too. It is the best I have done. Which one should I give the Pasha?"

"Well, Sir, I think you should give the Pasha a painting which he could easily recognize. I think that the one, there in the center of the wall showing the ramparts and the green tiles of the Pasha's palace should please him."

"Yes, yes! You are right." he replied. "That one has everything in it. His house. The Koutoubia. The palm trees. And the Atlas Mountains. Yes, I am going to give that one to him."

"Now, I should let you go home. Your wife must be waiting for you downstairs. Please say goodnight to her for me."

"I am not taking leave from you, Sir, as tomorrow morning, my wife and I will come with our children to the airfield to see you off."

"Will see you all tomorrow then. Goodnight!"

Back home, I wanted to hear from my wife all about her dinner conversation with Churchill. We spent the evening reconstructing the conversation word by word which she recorded it in her diary. Missing only were the sound effects, especially the loud thump of his fist hitting the table shaking the glasses, silver and plates.

At five in the morning, I was up and went to the native market where I bought a large Moroccan basket for each member of the Churchill party. We filled each with freshly picked oranges and tangerines. To each basket we attached a farewell message signed by "The Dimancescu's of Marrakech."

An hour later we were all at the airfield. It was a cold January day. The sun had just risen casting a red glow on the snow-capped peaks of the Atlas Mountains - a fitting backdrop for the great Old Man's departure from his beloved Marrakech.

Those who came to see the Churchill's off, formed a thin line almost in military fashion. The line was broken into two distinct groups separated by a space. It looked as if someone had said: "French on the right; the others on the left." At the head of the French group stood Colonel d'Hauteville and his wife, then the commander of the air base, the director of the Hotel Mamounia, and six journalists. In the group of the "others" were the Canes, father and daughter, and the six Dimancescus.

The Churchills, Winston, Clementine and Diana, arrived with British punctuality, just five minutes before the scheduled departure of the plane. They alighted from the limousine and Churchill, a big cigar in his mouth, walked straight to Colonel d'Hauteville, the highest ranking of those present, and then shook hands with the rest of the French group. The he went over and exchanged a few words with Sir Cyril Cane, Her Majesty's Consul General.

Winston Churchill, my daughter Sandra saying goodbye to Mrs Churchill

By this time my undisciplined family had broken ranks and surrounded Mrs. Churchill and Diana. Churchill walked into our midst and made a point of saying a kind word to each one of us. At the door of the airplane, a cigar still in his mouth, he waved to us and made his famous V sign. We watched the plane disappear into the blue Moroccan sky.

CHAPTER NINETEEN

TURMOIL

My idea, that the Pasha had encouraged and supported, was to build several dams in the valleys along the Atlas Mountains to store water for the Haouz Plain. I had hired a team of French engineers and technicians and produced a well-documented report. It was a simple plan that only involved building the dams and a canal. We all saw the project coming to fruition.

In ways unforeseen by us, the French would not allow foreigners to irrigate the Haouz plains under the control of the Pasha El Glaoui, and especially Americans who were supporting the Sultan in his efforts to achieve independence from France. They tried everything to stop me from pursuing the project. I went to Rabat, the capital of Morocco, with influential colleagues and from there we went to Ministry of Finance in Paris. Both in Rabat and in Paris we received the same courteous refusal. Every time I saw the Governor of Morocco, General Alphonse Juin, he gave me the impression that I had won my case, but then I would receive a letter from him saying that he was still considering the project but not giving a final decision. All these negotiations lasted for four years and led nowhere. Although the Pasha was all for the project, he could not do anything either. It came to end as did our residence in the Menebhi Palace. We moved to our new home in the Medina which we modernized with plumbing, electricity and other comforts and later to yet another. In each case my library followed in wooden cases loaded onto two-wheel push carts that could maneuver through the narrow alleys.

In 1951, word reached me that my brother died a prisoner in a Communist jail cell. These were the terrible times in Romania. Tens of thousands had been imprisoned - many friends and colleagues. Others were forced into hard labor. Those with larger homes were pushed into single rooms and multiple families co-located with them. Zézé's mother and grandmother, living in Rucăr away from events in Bucharest, had their home burned by soldiers. They were then forced to live in a single unheated room without plumbing. Only by the hidden friendship and courage of local peasant families did they survive.

My oldest son, Dimitri born in the San Francisco and thus a U.S. citizen, now aged eighteen enlisted in the U.S. Navy. I drove to Port Lyautey on the Atlantic coast where there was an American naval base. A few days later he came home dressed in a Navy uniform to say good-bye to us as he was about to leave for the United States and transferred as a naval clerk at the Pentagon in Washington. He never went to sea and because he served during the Korean War, the G.I. Bill helped him pay for his college education after he enrolled at Tufts University in Medford, Massachusetts.

The most important event for us in Morocco was our only daughter's marriage to an American employed on one of the air-base projects. His father had a small printing house in New York and his grand father had been an engraver for Tiffany in New York. The civil wedding was performed a few months before the religious ceremony. One of the witnesses at the wedding was Si Sadeq El Glaoui. The church was on a narrow street in the Arab town. We had a small reception at hour house and two months later they left for their United States to live in New Jersey.

Meanwhile, the situation in Europe was such that some people feared a Russian aggressiveness. Nuclear war became a threat. The situation led the U.S. to build five military bases in Morocco which, in this case, were approved by the French and the Moroccan authorities. Though the plan was for five bases, only three were finished. The largest was at Nouasseur, near Casablanca with a runway three-miles long that could accommodate the largest new B-52 and B-47 jet bombers. The runway needed a very strong foundation as it was being built on sandy soil and many structural changes had to be made to perfect it.

Two companies were created for the construction of the bases, one for the engineering studies and the other for the actual construction. The first company was 'PUSOM' and the second, 'ATLAS', both under the control of the U.S. Army Corps of Engineers. I went to see the commanding general of the Corps of Engineers in Morocco to suggest ways in which my engineering skills might be put to use. I was immediately hired with the title of staff industrial engineer. It was a position that fitted me like a glove and made use of much of what I had learned an a 'Taylorist' at Carnegie Tech. The chief of the management branch was also my chief. He gave me all the freedom to function as organization and methods examiner.

The two companies had an overflow of personnel, brought in a rush from the U.S. Many had not even had their qualifications checked. I assumed the responsibility for a survey of PUSOM and ATLAS. I analyzed their organization charts and interviewed almost every employee to determine if his job was really necessary. Much of the $450 million budget for the construction project went to high salaries for people who had very little supervision. As a result of my survey, a number of employees were fired. This did not improve my popularity among many who thought that I would get them fired too. However, this won the appreciation of the Corps of Engineers' commander who befriended me.

But these were the early 1950s and more alarming events started to take hold. On December 26, 1953, Nationalists set off a bomb in a Casablanca European market place killing nineteen people. This became the first signal of a violent transition to come. Shootings, armed attacks, a massacre in one small town ensued. French authorities deployed more troops and even the feared Foreign Legion. By 1955, it was no longer safe for us to live in the Medina and we moved to the Guéliz, the French quarter outside the traditional walls. Then one day Mihai, our son now 15 years-old, rushed home to say that a man had aimed a gun at him. Zézé and I knew then that it was time to leave.

Sailing alone on a Yugoslav freighter, the *S.S. Serbia*, our boys, Mihai and Dan born in England and thus equipped with British passports, left late in December. After a few months stay in New Jersey at their sister's American home, they crossed the United States by bus and reached San Francisco, California. There they were welcome by Phoebe Hearst Brown, who generously offered to look after them until we arrived. Hers was the first of several gestures of support that helped us through difficult times as money dwindled and future prospects grew dim.

Several weeks later, on January 20, 1956, after 43 years of rule and suffering from terminal cancer T'hami El Glaoui died. "The Last of the Lords of the Atlas," as Gavin Maxwell had named him, was gone and with him the passing of an era in Moroccan history. His family's power now lost to the ruling Sultan in the north, a rioting mob got hold of his body and scattered its remains.

Our own application for visas to the U.S. were denied for unexplained reasons. This was the McCarthy era and only much later did I find out that an FBI file had been created on me. With some irony in it was a critical piece of 'evidence,' a Christmas card I had hand-drawn, as I usually did every year, with a dove holding an olive branch in its beak. This was labeled as evidence of Communist sympathy given that doves and olive branches appeared on many leftist 'peace' banners. It took a year and the intercession of various people to unwind the accusation and finally get immigration visas.

We sailed to New York late in 1956.

❦

END

AFTERWORD

Coming to America was not easy. Homes had been lost to bombs and fire, families divided and wealth lost to Communist expropriation and then to revolution in Morocco. The family settled in Hartford, Connecticut, penniless. Were it not for the generosity of the Fleischmann family the transition would have been impossible. For my father starting anew at age 60 was hard. His early life training as an engineer helped find temporary employment spending weekdays in New York and later Hartford. To add to family income my mother worked as a department store clerk and then as an administrator in an insurance company. A decade later her mother, Getta Rădulescu, was allowed to emigrate from Romania.

Dimitri D. Dimancescu died in 1984.

Little could my father have conceived connections back to Romania or the sudden implosion of the Soviet Empire. Or even less that in its wake would come the demise of a tragic Communist era that brought enormous suffering to Romania.

As children we each found our way. For Sandra marriage and seven children ended badly though far luckier in a second marriage. Dimitri Jr. would graduate from Tufts University, marry and eventually build a career at a rapidly growing computer company in the Boston area; his two daughters live in Europe. My brother Mihai was admitted to Yale University and went on to medical studies in France, married and had two sons now living in the U.S. and Europe. His career took him on a long and successful neurosurgical practice. My own path drew me to Dartmouth College, the Fletcher School of Law and Diplomacy, and some years later to the Harvard Business School. This led to both entrepreneurial and consulting successes in the high-technology world. And of personal reward to my parents was my luck after College graduation in originating three National Geographic Magazine *supported expeditions. Two of them would take me to Romania[80] and a chance to meet aging relatives for the first time in 1964 and again in 1968. My marriage to Katherine was fortuitous, too, in her developing a love for all things Romanian as too with our son Nicholas.*

In 2005 I was designated Honorary Consul of Romania in Boston later amended to the title of Honorary Consul General. Family property was recovered included a portion of the family home in Bucharest after 13 years of court proceed-

---

[80] "Down the Danube by Canoe," *National Geographic Magazine,* July 1965 (1700 mile canoe trip from Germany to the Black Sea); and "Americans Afoot in Rumania," *National Geographic Magazine,* June 1969 (a 500 mile Carpathian Mountain hiking journey from the Ukrainian border to the Iron Gates)

ings. It was with some irony that the building was occupied by the feared Secret Police (Securitate) and then the post-Communist PSD Party and ex-President Ion Iliescu, a close associate of Nicolae Ceausescu, the Communist dictator.

Our daughter Katie became a historian and published writer delving into her American family's origins and heritage.* Our son, Nicholas, took a special liking to Romania and was, at his request, issued Romanian citizenship alongside his American one. At age 23, he founded a documentary film company** and directed two films on Romanian subjects: one about his grandfathers's WW-II experiences, and another describing the American bombing of the Ploiești oil wells in WW-II. He started a third describing the Roman invasion of Dacia by Emperor Trajan in 101-106AD. During the filming at Cioclovina Cave in the Carpathian Mountains, while filming atop a cliff during a thunderstorm, he slipped and fell to his death.

೨೦ಲ

The past is there for us to remember. Hence the value of 'memoirs' such as my father's and others. As our son Nicholas liked to say: "The past tells us who we have been and who we are."

Photo: Nicholas and Dan in 2009 on Mt. Cosna "Hill 789" trench-lines where Dimitri D. fought in WW-I.

* www.facebook.com/TheForgottenChapters/

** www.kogainon.com:
"HILL 789: The Last Stronghold"; "Knights of the Sky: Romania at War": "Decoding Dacia: Trajan's Invasion"

INDEX